VIRGINIA Real Estate PRACTICE & LAW

F.A. Dan Daniels, ABR,
Consulting Editor

Florence L. Daniels, GRI,
Consulting Editor

EIGHTH EDITION

Dearborn™
Real Estate Education

President: Mehul Patel
Executive Director of Product Development: Kate DeVivo
Associate Development Editor: Ewurama Ewusi-Mensah
Director of Production: Daniel Frey
Production Editor: Bill Guerriero
Production Artist: Virginia Byrne
Creative Director: Lucy Jenkins
Director of Product Management: Melissa Kleeman

Published by Dearborn™ Real Estate Education
30 South Wacker Drive
Chicago, Illinois 60606-7481
(312) 836-4400
www.dearbornRE.com

Printed in the United States of America

10 11 12 10 9 8 7 6 5 4 3

The Library of Congress has cataloged the 7th edition as follows:
Virginia real estate : practice & law / F.A. Dan Daniels, consulting editor.—7th ed.
p. cm.
Includes index.
ISBN 1-4195-0350-2
1. Vendors and purchasers—Virginia. 2. Real property—Virginia. I. Daniels, F.A. Dan. II. Dearborn Real Estate Education (Firm)
KFV2526.Z9V57 2005
346.75504'3—dc22

8th edition ISBN-13: 978-1-4277-6704-2
8th edition ISBN-10: 1-4277-6704-1

Contents

Preface

Although real estate activity in Virginia is subject to federal laws and regulations, it is controlled primarily by Virginia's laws, rules, and regulations and by state customs that prevail where no law covers a practice.

Virginia Real Estate: Practice & Law offers current real estate professionals a practical handbook of Virginia's real estate law and rules, along with the most current developments. Every effort has been made to ensure that the information contained in this book is both relevant and current. There are numerous references to Virginia statutes and the Real Estate Board's Rules and Regulations, so readers can look up the law themselves in most public and university libraries and online.

Virginia Real Estate: Practice & Law is a component of Dearborn™ Real Estate Education's Complete Learning System. It may be used effectively with other Dearborn principles books or software:

- *Modern Real Estate Practice*
- *Mastering Real Estate Principles*
- *Real Estate Fundamentals*
- *Virginia Real Estate Principles*

The conversion chart on page viii indicates which chapter or chapters in each of the national products corresponds with your Virginia-specific text. We hope the conversion chart will be helpful as you study for your real estate exam.

Each chapter in this book is followed by a quiz. These quizzes serve as both learning and teaching devices. As you finish each chapter, and before going on to the next, be sure that you can answer each question and that you understand all the material covered. There is a 70-question examination in Appendix A. An answer key for all questions is included in Appendix B.

ABOUT THE CONSULTING EDITORS

F.A. Dan Daniels, ABR, principal broker of Governmental Employees Realty Associates, Alexandria, Virginia, served as Consulting Co-Editor for *Virginia Real Estate: Practice & Law*, Eighth Edition. Mr. Daniels has been in the real estate business for over 15 years, working half that time with one of the predominant brokerages in his region before starting a small boutique agency in 1997. The vibrant growth of the real estate industry in Mr. Daniels's region along with his active participation in the largest REALTOR® association in Virginia has helped give Mr. Daniels a great perspective on the practice of real estate.

As an instructor, Dan brings a wealth of day-to-day experience into his classes as he trains licensees through continuing education courses in the areas of agency, contracts, brokerage start-ups, fair housing, ethics, antitrust, and legislative issues.

Florence L. Daniels, GRI, and Associate Broker of Governmental Employees Realty Associates (Alexandria, VA) served as Consulting Co-Editor for *Virginia Real Estate: Practice & Law*, Eighth Edition. Ms. Daniels has been in the real estate business for 18 years, starting first with two prominent brokerages in her region before cofounding a small boutique agency in 1997. In 2002, Ms. Daniels was appointed by the governor to the nine-member Virginia Real Estate Board for a four-year term. The Virginia Real Estate Board regulates approximately 68,000 licensees in Virginia. She was reappointed in 2006 to a second four-year term. She brings her knowledge of real estate regulations and statutes, plus her hands-on experience in regulation implementation, to this edition.

Ms. Daniels is also a licensed instructor, regularly teaching the various educational disciplines coincident to the maintenance of an active real estate license in the Commonwealth. She has also served as a member of the board of directors of the Northern Virginia Association of REALTORS®, and as an instructor, mediator, and chair and member of many key association committees, including the Professional Standards Committee, which oversees ethics complaints.

ACKNOWLEDGMENTS

Mr. Daniels would like to extend his gratitude to the reviewers. Creating a book that includes so many different areas of real estate practice requires a true team effort. The reviewers who took the time to thoroughly review the material and submit comments, questions, and suggestions have helped make this seventh edition as accurate and useful as possible.

Thanks especially to Vicki H. Breedlove, Long & Foster Institute of Real Estate; Lyn Broad, Associate Broker, Weichert REALTORS® and Senior Instructor, Weichert Real Estate School; Dee Hester, Associate Broker, Keller Williams Realty, Northern Virginia Association of REALTORS®; and JoAnne Johnson, Westgate Realty Group, Inc.

Thanks also to the Northern Virginia Association of REALTORS®, Inc. (NVAR), for providing the forms used in this book. The forms have been reprinted with permission from NVAR for educational purposes only. Any other use of these forms without the express written consent of NVAR is strictly prohibited.

Chapter Conversion Table

Virginia Real Estate: Practice & Law, 7th Edition		*Modern Real Estate Practice*	*Real Estate Fundamentals*	*Mastering Real Estate Principles*	*Virginia Real Estate Principles (Software)*	*Guide to Passing the PSI Real Estate Exam*
1.	Real Estate Brokerage and Agency	4, 5	7	13	4, 5	7, 14
2.	Seller and Buyer Agency Agreements	6	8	15	6	9
3.	Interests in Real Estate	7	3	7	7	3
4.	Forms of Real Estate Ownership	8	5	9	8	3
5.	Legal Descriptions	9	2	6	9	3
6.	Real Estate Taxes and Other Liens	10	3, 10	5, 25, 26	10	10
7.	Real Estate Contracts and Documentation	11	8	14	11	9
8.	Transfer of Title	12	4	10	10	10
9.	Title Records	13	6	11	13	10
10.	Virginia's Real Estate License Law	—	—	—	35	—
11.	Real Estate Financing Principles	14, 15	12, 13	Unit 7	14, 15	6, 14
12.	Leasing	16	9	8	16	13
13.	Fair Housing and Ethical Practices	20	15	17	20	11

Virginia Real Estate: Practice & Law also may be used with other tools from Dearborn™ Real Estate Education. The conversion chart indicates which chapter or chapters in each of the national products corresponds with your Virginia-specific text. We hope this conversion chart will be helpful to you as you study for your real estate exam.

CHAPTER 1

Real Estate Brokerage and Agency

The practice of real estate in the Commonwealth of Virginia is governed under statute by Title 54.1, Chapter 21 of the Code of Virginia. The Real Estate Board is Agency 135. The agency rules and regulations of the Real Estate Board can be found in Title 18 of the Virginia Administrative Code (VAC), Professional and Occupational Licensing. The Virginia General Assembly is solely responsible for creating and amending the Code of Virginia. As part of the Department of Professional and Occupational Regulation (DPOR), the Real Estate Board (REB) is charged with issuing regulations that further describe what will be expected of both salespersons and brokers. All regulations must be consistent with the Code of Virginia.

The most current issue of the Real Estate Board Rules and Regulations is available from the Department of Professional and Occupational Regulation, 9960 Mayland Drive, Suite 400, Richmond, VA 23233. All licensees, real estate brokers, and real estate salespersons are responsible for staying informed about licensing laws, regulations, and current changes.

References may be made throughout this text to either the Code of Virginia, Title 54.1 (Chapter 21, Professions and Occupations) [§54.1 et seq.] or to the VAC, Title 18 [18 VAC 135-10 et seq.] Title 18 comprises the rules and regulations of the REB. If you have questions about the laws or regulations governing the practice of real estate in Virginia, you may write or call the REB at (804) 367-8500. Information is also available on the Internet; see Code of Virginia and Virginia Administrative Code at the following Web address (scroll to 54.1, Chapter 21):

WEB LINK

http://leg1.state.va.us/cgi-bin/legp504.exe?000+cod+TOC (Code of Virginia)

www.dpor.virginia.gov/dporweb/reb_main.cfm (Virginia Real Estate Board)

BROKERAGE DEFINITIONS

In Virginia, a real estate **broker** is defined by statute as

> *any person or business entity, including, but not limited to, a partnership, association, corporation, or limited liability corporation, who, for compensation or valuable consideration (i) sells or offers for sale, buys or offers to buy, or negotiates the purchase or sale or exchange of real estate, including units or interest in condominiums, cooperative interest . . . or time shares in a time-share program . . . or (ii) who leases or offers to lease, or rents or offers for rent, any real estate or the improvements thereon for others. [§54.1-2100]*

In practice the word *broker* may refer to a firm, a sole proprietor who transacts real estate business, a managing broker for a branch office of a larger firm, or a person who holds a broker's license but practices under the supervision of a principal broker. It is important to note that the brokerage relationship is established between the *broker* (principal broker or sole proprietor) as the *agent* and the *client* as the *principal.* All supervising brokers, managing brokers, associate brokers, and salespersons are general agents of the principal broker. There can only be one principal broker of a brokerage.

Some other definitions you should be familiar with follow.

- **Firm**—any sole proprietorship (broker-owned or nonbroker-owned) partnership, association, limited liability company, or corporation, other than a sole proprietorship (principal-broker-owned) that is required by regulation to obtain a separate brokerage firm license.
- **Sole proprietor**—an individual, not a corporation, who is doing business under either his or her own name or under a legally registered fictitious name. A licensed broker who is a sole proprietor shall have the same responsibilities as a principal broker. A sole proprietor who is not licensed must designate a licensed broker to perform the duties of a principal broker.
- **Salesperson**—the statutory definition of a real estate salesperson is *any person, or business entity of not more than two persons unless related by blood or marriage, who for compensation or valuable consideration is employed either directly or indirectly by, or affiliated as an independent contractor with, a real estate broker, to sell or offer to sell, or to buy or offer to buy, or to negotiate the purchase, sale, or exchange of real estate, or to lease, rent or offer for rent, any real estate, or to negotiate leases thereof, or of the improvements thereon.* [§54.1-2101] Although a salesperson may generally perform the same functions as a broker, the salesperson must be employed by or affiliated with a licensed real estate broker. Brokers are expected to supervise all activities of the salespersons affiliated with their company and are responsible for the actions of every salesperson. Salespersons are considered to be general agents of the principal brokers they represent.

Brokers and salespersons can be further defined according to their specific roles within a brokerage firm.

- **Licensee**—any person, partnership, association, limited liability company, or corporation that holds a license issued by the REB to act as a real estate broker or salesperson.
- **Principal broker**—the individual broker designated by each firm to ensure compliance with Chapter 21 of Title 54.1 of the Code of Virginia, and to receive all communications and notices from the REB that may affect the firm and/or its licensees. In the case of a sole proprietorship, the licensed broker who is the sole proprietor has the responsibilities of the principal broker. The principal broker shall have responsibility for the activities of the firm and all of its licensees.
- **Supervising broker** (or *managing broker*)—an individual associate broker who shall be designated by the firm to supervise the activities of a branch office. The regulations do not require the physical presence of the supervising broker.
- **Associate broker**—any individual licensed as a broker who practices within a brokerage firm as a sales associate. An associate broker is required to meet the same educational, experience, and testing requirements as a principal broker but is subject to the same restrictions of brokerage activity as a salesperson.
- **Standard agent**—a licensee, either broker or salesperson, who acts for or represents a client in an agency relationship according to the statutory duties later described on page 6 under "Duties to a Client."
- **Independent contractor**—a licensee who acts for or represents a client according to a written contract (e.g., a Buyer Representation Agreement) between the licensee and the client instead of as a standard agent. This is a specific distinction pertaining to agency law and is not related to the definition of "independent contractor" as used for tax purposes by the Internal Revenue Service (IRS).
- **Designated agent** (or *designated representative)*—a licensee designated by the principal or supervising broker to represent one party to a transaction when the broker is also representing another party in the same transaction.
- **Dual agent** (or *dual representative)*—a licensee who has a brokerage relationship with both seller and buyer, or both landlord and tenant, in the same real estate transaction. Because the brokerage relationship is established between the broker and the client, the principal broker, or supervising broker, would always remain in a dual agent position in the transaction even though the broker may designate one salesperson to represent one party to the transaction and another salesperson to represent the other party to the transaction.
- **Common source information company**—any person or entity that compiles or provides information regarding real estate for sale or lease and other data, and includes but is not limited to a multiple-listing service (MLS). No broker or salesperson license is required.

WHO MUST HAVE A LICENSE

Any person or business entity that performs or advertises brokerage services must be licensed by the REB. Licenses are issued for individuals, partnerships, limited liability companies (LLCs), associations, corporations, and nonbroker-owned sole proprietorships. The license may be granted in a fictitious name, that is, a name other than that of the principal broker.

IN PRACTICE

J is a principal broker who wishes to operate and be known as ABC Realty. *J* must obtain a broker's license as a principal broker, and ABC Realty must obtain a separate firm license.

O is a salesperson whose name is difficult to say, and she wishes to be known by a pseudonym. *O* must obtain a license in her real name with a dba (doing business as) for the pseudonym endorsement.

Z is a salesperson who heads a team of licensees within a brokerage and wishes to advertise under the team name. *Z* must obtain a business entity license for the team.

Individual licenses are issued to the business entity or firm, principal brokers, associate brokers, and salespersons. (See Chapter 10 for licensing requirements.) Every principal broker shall have the following readily available to the public: the business entity or firm license, the managing broker's license, and a roster of every salesperson and broker assigned to the office. If a firm has more than one physical location (e.g., branch offices), then all actual licenses are to be readily available at the firm's main office, with the exception of the entity's branch office license, which shall be available at the branch office.

An individual with a broker's license may operate as a sole proprietor (sole proprietorship—broker-owned) without further licensure unless the sole proprietorship operates under a fictitious name, in which case a separate brokerage firm license is required.

Additional regulations for a firm license include the following:

1. Every member or officer who actively participates in brokerage business must hold a license as a broker.
2. Every employee or independent contractor who acts as a salesperson must hold a license as either salesperson or broker.
3. A salesperson and a broker may not be principals in a firm together. By law, all salespersons come under the *supervision* of a principal broker.

A separate branch office license must be issued for each branch office of a brokerage firm, including the name of the supervising broker. The branch office license and a roster of every salesperson and broker assigned to the branch office shall be available to the public in each branch office.

Note: The requirements for licenses stated herein pertain only to the practice of real estate in the Commonwealth of Virginia as governed by Title 54.1, Chapter 21 of the Code of Virginia and Title 18 of the VAC. Further licensing or authority to conduct a brokerage business at a specific physical location is usually required by local jurisdictions.

■ EXEMPTIONS

Not everyone who performs an act of real estate brokerage or related real estate activities is required to hold a Virginia real estate license. The following are a few examples of persons exempt from the state licensing requirement. These and other exemptions will be discussed in detail in Chapter 10.

- Individuals who are selling or renting their own property
- Persons selling or renting property owned by their employers
- Attorneys involved in real estate transactions in their normal role as attorneys
- Licensed auctioneers selling real estate at public auction

■ AGENCY

In 2006, in response to changing real estate industry business models, the Virginia General Assembly modified the Agency Statute by introducing and stating the duties of a limited services representative under §54.1-2138.1.

Under the new statute, a licensee may act as a limited service representative only pursuant to a written brokerage agreement. The limited service representative must disclose his or her status as a limited services representative and present in writing to the client a disclosure that compares the services that he or she *will* provide with the duties required of a standard agent, specifically listing the standard agency duties and services that they will *not* perform.

The concept of common law of agency as it relates to real estate brokerage no longer exists in Virginia. In 1995, the Virginia General Assembly expressly abrogated the common law of agency in real estate transactions. [§54.1-2144] In its place, the legislature enacted an agency statute that codifies the agency relationships among brokers, buyers, sellers, landlords, and tenants. [§§54.1-2130 through 54.1-2144] This is referred to as *standard* or *statutory agency*.

In addition to establishing new rules and standards for agency relationships in real estate transactions, the statute provides that neither compensation nor use of a common source information company, such as an MLS, creates a brokerage relationship. [§54.1-2140]

Definitions [§54.1-2130]

Virginia's agency statute provides the following definitions:

Agency is defined as any relationship in which a real estate licensee acts for or represents a person by such person's express authority in a real estate transaction.

The parties are free to enter into a brokerage relationship that establishes licensee responsibilities to the client other than those imposed by standard agency. In this situation the broker is an independent contractor. A written agreement, not the statute, governs the relationship. The lack of a specific written agreement would impose the duties of standard agency.

A **brokerage relationship** is a contractual relationship between client and broker in which the broker licensee has been engaged by the client to procure a seller, buyer, option, tenant, or landlord who is ready, willing, and able to sell, buy, option, exchange, or rent real estate. Note that although it is often the salesperson who initiates the brokerage relationship with the client, it is in fact the broker who has the brokerage relationship with the client. In this context, the "broker licensee" refers to the brokerage firm. For example: XYZ Realty as a nonbroker-owned sole proprietor may have hired Mary Smith to act as principal broker of the firm. The broker/client relationship is with XYZ Realty, not with Mary Smith.

The brokerage relationship is limited to a broker and a client. A **client** is a person who has entered into a brokerage relationship with a broker licensee; any other party to the transaction with whom the licensee does not have a brokerage relationship but for whom the licensee may perform routine services, referred to as *ministerial acts*, is a **customer. Ministerial acts** are routine acts that a licensee can perform for a person that do not involve discretion or the exercise of the licensee's own judgment.

The term *limited service representative* refers to a licensee who acts for or represents a client with respect to real property containing from one to four residential units, pursuant to a brokerage agreement that provides that the limited service representative will not provide one or more of the duties set forth in subdivision A 2 of §§54.1-2131, 54.1-2132, 54.1-2133, and 54.1-2134, inclusive.

Duties to a Client [§§54.1-2131 to 54.1-2134]

The Virginia agency statute establishes specific duties for a licensee who is in an agency relationship as a standard agent with a seller, buyer, landlord, or tenant. These statutory duties for a client require that licensees

1. perform according to the terms of the brokerage relationship;
2. promote the best interests of the client by
   — *seeking a sale (or lease) at the price and terms established in the brokerage relationship*, or at some other price and terms acceptable to the client (once the property is under contract, the licensee is not expected to continue to pursue additional offers unless he or she is required to do so under the brokerage agreement or sales contract);
   — *presenting all written offers and counteroffers* in a timely manner, even after the property is under contract;
   — *disclosing* to the client all material facts related to the property or concerning the transaction of which the licensee has actual knowledge;
   — *accounting* in a timely manner for all money and property received in which the client has or may have an interest;
3. maintain *confidentiality* of all personal and financial information received from the client during the brokerage relationship, and all information characterized as confidential by the client, unless the seller consents in writing to its release or unless the licensee is required by law to release the information—under Virginia law, such confidential information is to remain confidential forever;
4. exercise ordinary care; and
5. comply with all applicable laws, including fair housing statutes and regulations and all other statutes and regulations required by the state.

The traditional "fiduciary" responsibilities that were a part of the common law of agency are basically included in the new statutory duties but with far less implied liability.

Duties to a Customer

Customers, the parties with whom the licensee does *not* have a brokerage relationship, must be treated honestly and may not knowingly be given false information. In addition, they must be informed of any material adverse facts regarding the property's physical condition of which the licensee has actual knowledge. No legal action may be brought against a licensee for making such required disclosures:

> *A licensee will not be held liable for providing false information if the false information was provided to the licensee by the seller; and the licensee did not actually know that the information was false; or did not act in reckless disregard of the truth. [§54-2131B]*

A licensee having a brokerage relationship with a client is permitted to assist customers by performing ministerial acts. The performance of ministerial acts does not violate the licensee's brokerage relationship with the client. Similarly, the brokerage relationship is not violated if the licensee shows alternative properties to prospective buyers or tenants or represents other sellers (or landlords).

Additional Disclosure Required by Buyer's Agent

In the case of a residential transaction, a licensee must disclose to the seller the buyer's *intent to occupy* the property as a principal residence. [§54.1-2132B] This disclosure is often stated in the body of a purchase agreement.

Property Management

Licensees who are engaged to manage real estate are required by Virginia law to perform according to the management agreement, exercise ordinary care, disclose all material facts concerning the property of which the licensee has actual knowledge, maintain confidentiality of information, account for all money and property received, and comply with all relevant real estate and fair housing laws and regulations. The licensee is expected to perform his or her services in accordance with the property management agreement. Licensees are permitted to represent other owners in the management of real property and to represent the owner as seller or landlord under a brokerage agreement. [§54.1-2135] The broker is a general agent to the owner of the property under a Property Management Agreement.

Establishing the Brokerage Relationship [§54.1-2136]

Prior to entering into a brokerage relationship, the licensee is required to advise the prospective client of

- the type of brokerage relationship proposed by the broker;
- the broker's compensation; and
- whether the broker will share the compensation with a broker who may have a brokerage relationship with another party to the transaction.

Remember, compensation does not imply or create a brokerage relationship.

Although oral contracts are legal in Virginia, they are not enforceable, and it is highly recommended by legal counsel and the REB that all brokerage relationships be established in writing.

Commencement and Termination of Brokerage Relationship [§54.1-2137]

Under Virginia's agency statute, the brokerage relationship begins at the time the client engages a licensee. Ideally, the relationship terminates when the brokerage agreement's terms have been completely performed. However, the relationship may also be terminated by

- the expiration of the agreement;
- a mutual agreement to terminate;
- a default by any party;
- the licensee's withdrawal when a client refuses to consent to disclosed dual agency (Additional reference in §54.1-2139D); or
- the death of the only broker in a sole proprietorship.

All brokerage relationships must have a definite termination date. If no date is specified, the statute establishes a mandatory termination date of 90 days after the commencement of the brokerage relationship. [§54.1-2137B]

Once a brokerage relationship has terminated or expired, the licensee owes no further duties to the client. However, the licensee is nonetheless required to account for all monies and property relating to the brokerage relationship and must *preserve the confidentiality* of information.

Disclosure Requirements

Virginia agency law requires full disclosure of any existing brokerage relationships. It is essential that the party to the transaction who is not the client of the licensee and who is not represented by another licensee clearly understand that the licensee represents only his or her client. Although the licensee is required to treat a customer honestly and to disclose any material adverse facts about the physical condition of the property, the agent's primary responsibility is to protect and promote the best interest of his or her client.

At the time of the first substantive discussion about a specific property with an actual or prospective buyer, seller, landlord, or tenant who is not a client of the licensee and who is not represented by another licensee, a licensee is required to disclose any broker relationship he or she has with any other party to the transaction. The disclosure will be made in writing at the earliest practical time but no later than the time when specific real estate assistance is provided for sales transactions or at the time of a lease application or in the lease, whichever occurs first. Disclosure is not required for lease terms of less than two months.

The written disclosure must be in substantially the same form as that illustrated in Figure 1.1.

Note: The Disclosure of Brokerage Relationship is required for the person who is *not* the client of the agent and is *not* represented by another licensee. Signature of this disclosure *by a client* is not required because a brokerage relationship has been previously established by an Exclusive Right to Represent, a buyer agency agreement, an Exclusive Right to Sell, or a listing agreement. However, it is not uncommon for the agent to have both *clients and customers* sign a Disclosure of Brokerage Relationship for emphasis; some brokers require this of their agents to alleviate the possibility of not making the proper disclosure.

If the required disclosure is given in combination with other disclosures or information, the disclosure must be conspicuous, printed in bold lettering, all capitals,

FIGURE 1.1

Disclosure of Brokerage Relationship

DISCLOSURE OF BROKERAGE RELATIONSHIP

THIS IS NOT A CONTRACT; IT DOES NOT CREATE AN OBLIGATION

In connection with this transaction, whether purchase, sale, lease or option,
the client of the Broker/Firm is: *(check one)*

☐ Seller	☐ Buyer
☐ Lessor (Landlord)	☐ Lessee (Tenant)
☐ Optionor	☒ Optionee

The duties of real estate licensees in Virginia are set forth in Section 54.1-2130 et seq. of the Code of Virginia and in the regulations of the Virginia Real Estate Board. You should be aware that in addition to the information contained in this disclosure pertaining to brokerage relationships, there may be other information relative to the transaction which may be obtained from other sources. Each party should carefully read all documents to assure that the terms accurately express his or her understanding and intent. Licensees can counsel on real estate matters, but if legal or tax advice is desired, you should consult an attorney or a financial professional.

Date Name ____________________ Date Name ____________________

Date Name ____________________ Date Name ____________________

Brokerage Firm ____________________ Sales Associate ____________________

REALTOR

EQUAL HOUSING OPPORTUNITY

NVAR - 1207 - 10/00

Reprinted with permission from the Virginia Department of Professional and Occupational Regulation (DPOR) and Northern Virginia Association of Realtors®, Inc. (NVAR) for educational purposes only.

underlined, or within a separate box. [§54.1-2139B] If the licensee's relationship with any party to the transaction changes, all clients and customers involved in the transaction must be informed—in writing—of the change. Copies of all disclosures that are a part of an executed lease or a consummated transaction must be kept for three years.

Disclosed Dual Representation [§54.1-2139]

In Virginia, a licensee may represent both parties in the same real estate transaction—seller and buyer or landlord and tenant—only with the written consent of all clients in the transaction. The client's signature on the written disclosure form is presumptive evidence of the brokerage relationship. The disclosure must be substantially in the same form as that illustrated in Figure 1.2.

A dual representative does not terminate any brokerage relationship by making the required disclosures of dual representation. [§54.1-2139C] As mentioned previously, a licensee may withdraw from representing a client who refuses to consent to disclosed dual agency. The licensee may withdraw under such circumstances without liability and may continue to represent the other client. Further, the licensee may continue to represent in other transactions the client who refused dual representation. [§54.1-2139D]

FIGURE 1.2

Disclosure of Dual Representation

DISCLOSURE OF DUAL REPRESENTATION

The undersigned do hereby acknowledge disclosure that:

The licensee ....

(Name of Broker, Firm, or Salesperson as applicable)

represents more than one party in this real estate transaction as indicated below:

.... Seller(s) and Buyer(s)

.... Landlord(s) and Tenant(s).

The undersigned understands that the foregoing dual representative may not disclose to either client or such client's designated representative any information that has been given to the dual representative by the other client within the confidence and trust of the brokerage relationship except for that information which is otherwise required or permitted by Article 3 (§54.1-2130 et seq.) of Chapter 21 of Title 54.1 of the Code of Virginia to be disclosed. The undersigned by signing this notice do hereby acknowledge their informed consent to the disclosed dual representation by the licensee.

....	....
Date	Name (One Party)
....	....
Date	Name (One Party)
....	....
Date	Name (Other Party)
....	....
Date	Name (Other Party)

FIGURE 1.3

Disclosure of the Use of Designated Representatives

DISCLOSURE OF THE USE OF DESIGNATED REPRESENTATIVES

The undersigned do hereby acknowledge disclosure that:

The licensee ....
(Name of Broker and Firm)

represents more than one party in this real estate transaction as indicated below:

.... Seller(s) and Buyer(s)

.... Landlord(s) and Tenant(s).

The undersigned understands that the foregoing dual representative may not disclose to either client or such client's designated representative any information that has been given to the dual representative by the other client within the confidence and trust of the brokerage relationship except for that information which is otherwise required or permitted by Article 3 (§54.1-2130 et seq.) of Chapter 21 of Title 54.1 of the Code of Virginia to be disclosed. The undersigned by signing this notice do hereby acknowledge their informed consent to the disclosed dual representation by the licensee.

The principal or supervising broker has assigned

.... to act as Designated Representative (Licensee/Sales Associate) for the one party as indicated below:

.... Seller(s) or .... Buyer(s)

.... Landlord(s) or ....Tenant(s)

and

.... to act as Designated Representative (Licensee/Sales Associate) for the other party as indicated below:

.... Seller(s) or .... Buyer(s)

.... Landlord(s) or ....Tenant(s)

....
Date Name (One Party)

....
Date Name (One Party)

....
Date Name (Other Party)

....
Date Name (Other Party)

Designated Representation

A principal or supervising broker may assign different affiliated licensees as *designated representatives* to represent different clients in the same transaction. The appointment of designated representatives excludes other licensees in the firm from involvement in the transaction. *The use of designated representatives does not constitute dual representation if each designee represents only one client in a particular real estate transaction.* [§54.1-2139E] The designated representatives are pledged to maintain all confidential information received from their clients. Such information may be shared with the principal or supervising broker who remains in the position of a dual representative with equal responsibilities to both clients. The disclosure must be made in writing and must be similar to Figure 1.3.

IN PRACTICE

James is the principal broker of ABC Realty. Through the actions of his agent, Maggie, James has established a brokerage relationship with prospective buyer Sharon by having her sign an Exclusive Right to Represent agreement. Sharon decides to make an offer on a property that is listed with ABC Realty with Ben as listing agent. Broker James may now designate Maggie to be the "designated agent" for the buyer and Ben to be the "designated agent" for the seller. Both Maggie and Ben will be able to meet all of the statutory obligations of duties to their clients. James, as the principal broker, will remain in a "dual agency" position with equal responsibility to both clients.

If the buyer, Sharon, wished to purchase a property listed by ABC Realty with Maggie as listing agent, Maggie could then enter into a disclosed "dual agent" role where he would have statutory responsibilities to both clients. ABC Realty would have brokerage relationships with both the buyer, through the signing of an Exclusive Right to Represent agreement, and the seller, through the signing of a listing agreement.

Another alternative would be to withdraw from the buyer representation brokerage agreement with Sharon and continue to represent only the seller. Buyer Sharon would then be a "customer" instead of a "client." The statutory obligation would be to treat Sharon honestly. Maggie would also be able to perform "ministerial acts" for her, but his primary responsibility would be to the seller.

In all cases where "dual agency" or "designated agency" is practiced, the need for written consent of all parties to the transaction is a requirement of the statute.

Imputed Knowledge [§54.1-2142]

One aspect of the Virginia agency law that differs from the formerly used common law of agency with respect to real estate transactions is that there is no longer imputed liability on the part of either the client or the broker.

A client is not liable for misrepresentations made by a licensee, nor is a broker liable for misrepresentation on the part of another broker engaged to assist in a real estate transaction. In both cases, liability for another's actions would occur only if the client and/or broker knew, or should have known, of the misrepresentation or failed to take steps to correct it.

Knowledge or information between clients or brokers is not imputed. Each is responsible only for actual knowledge or information, although liability may still occur in a case of unlawful housing discriminatory practices.

NEW LEGISLATION AFFECTING SALESPERSONS

National Do-Not-Call Registry

Individuals who cold call must now comply with the provisions of the National Do-Not-Call Registry. There are certain exemptions to the new rule. A telemarketer may call the following:

- Consumers with whom the caller has an existing relationship (This applies to existing clients and customers and extends for up to 18 months after

the end of a transaction. If a consumer makes an inquiry, the telemarketer can call the person for up to three months after the inquiry.)
- Persons who have granted express written permission to call

In addition, the rules do not apply to

- Charities and tax-exempt nonprofit organizations
- Political campaigns
- Callers taking surveys or polls

On January 1, 2005, the FTC and FCC rules tightening the National Do-Not-Call Registry scrubbing requirement took effect. It is now mandatory to check a phone number against a version of the Registry that is no more than 31 days old before placing a telemarketing call.

It is important to check with your broker to stay updated on this law and its rules. Information is also available at

WEB LINK @

www.ftc.gov/donotcall/

The CAN-SPAM Act

The CAN-SPAM Act of 2003 (Controlling the Assault of Non-Solicited Pornography and Marketing) became effective January 1, 2004. It is designed to create a national standard to control the growing problem of deceptive or fraudulent commercial e-mail and outlines a series of practices that e-mail senders must follow. The law

- bans false or misleading header information;
- prohibits deceptive subject lines;
- requires that a sender's e-mail provide recipients an opt-out method—a clear and conspicuous mechanism allowing the recipient to ask not to receive future e-mail messages to that e-mail address; and
- requires that commercial e-mail be identified as an advertisement and include the sender's valid physical postal address.

CAN-SPAM information can be found at

WEB LINK @

www.ftc.gov/bcp/conline/pubs/buspubs/canspam.shtm

QUESTIONS

1. By Virginia statutory definition, a salesperson may perform all of the following functions *EXCEPT*
   a. offer a residence for sale.
   b. negotiate an exchange.
   c. serve as a managing broker.
   d. lease rental apartments.

2. An individual wants to sell her own house. Which of the following statements is *TRUE*?
   a. She does not need a real estate license to sell her own property.
   b. In Virginia, anyone who sells real property must have a real estate license.
   c. An individual may obtain a temporary real estate license in order to legally sell her own house.
   d. She may sell her house without a real estate license because she is an attorney.

3. Any individual holding a broker's license in Virginia who is NOT designated as the principal broker is
   a. a supervising broker.
   b. a managing broker.
   c. an associate broker.
   d. none of the above.

4. An "agency" relationship could *best* be described as one in which a licensee
   a. has a signed agreement establishing a brokerage relationship.
   b. has a separate independent contractor agreement with a buyer.
   c. performs ministerial acts for a seller.
   d. acts for or represents another person in a real estate transaction.

5. Routine services that do *not* create an agency relationship are referred to as
   a. transactional acts.
   b. routine brokerage.
   c. ministerial acts.
   d. customer service.

6. All of the following are specific duties owed to a seller or buyer client *EXCEPT* to
   a. perform to the terms of the contract.
   b. protect and promote the best interests of the client.
   c. always be obedient to the client's demands.
   d. maintain confidentiality forever.

7. *P* is a real estate licensee who has signed a brokerage agreement with *H*, who is looking for an apartment to rent. *P* does not charge a fee to prospective tenants; rather, *P* receives a commission from landlords. *P* tells a landlord that *H* could probably pay a somewhat higher rent than the landlord is asking. Which of the following statements is *TRUE*?
   a. *P* owes statutory agency duties to the landlords who pay the commission.
   b. *P*'s disclosure to the landlord was appropriate under these circumstances.
   c. *P*'s disclosure violated the statutory duties owed to *H*.
   d. Because *P* is not charging a fee to prospective tenants, *P* has violated Virginia's agency statute.

8. A brokerage relationship can be terminated by any of the following *EXCEPT*
   a. one party's unilaterally "firing" the other.
   b. expiration of the agreement.
   c. a default by either party.
   d. a licensee's withdrawal when the client refuses to consent to dual agency.

9. George is representing buyer Juanita in the purchase of a town house listed with Sam. George has a signed Exclusive-Right-to-Represent contract with Juanita. George will need to have a Disclosure of Brokerage Relationship form signed by
   a. Juanita.
   b. the sellers of the town house.
   c. both Juanita and the sellers of the town house.
   d. no one because the sellers have their own agent.

10. M and *T* are licensed salespersons who are both affiliated with ABC Realty. M has listed a house, and *T* has a likely buyer. What should the supervising broker do?
   a. Nothing because neither M nor *T* wishes to act as disclosed dual representatives.
   b. The broker's only legal option is to insist that either M or *T* sign a disclosed dual representation agreement with the buyers and sellers.
   c. The broker may assign M and *T* as designated representatives and provide a disclosure form to the sellers only. The broker will be a subagent.
   d. The broker may assign M and *T* as designated representatives and provide a disclosure form to both the sellers and the prospective buyers. The broker will be a dual agent.

11. Where must a roster of salespersons and brokers assigned to the branch office be located?
   a. In a glass case in the branch office lobby
   b. In a glass case in the main office lobby
   c. At the branch office on request by any member of the public
   d. All of the above

12. When a licensee acts as an independent contractor and NOT as a standard agent, what governs the relationship between the licensee and the client?
   a. The common law of agency
   b. A standard Virginia REB contractor agreement
   c. A written agreement and not the statute
   d. No agreement at all

13. Buyer Sally calls listing agent Robert relating the fact that she has a signed buyer agency agreement with licensee Jesse but would like Robert to show her his listing on 1234 Main Street because her agent Jesse is out of town. When must Robert make an agency disclosure to Sally?
   a. Immediately, on the phone
   b. When he shows Sally the listing
   c. After Sally signs a new buyer agency agreement with Robert
   d. None of the above

14. Seller Tim hires agent Jack, a licensee with QXR Realty, to list and market his home. Jack lists the property in the local MLS, stating that it is connected to the public sewer when it is in fact not so. Six months after the sale the septic system fails and the new owner wants to sue the seller for misrepresentation. Which of the following is *TRUE*?
   a. The new owner can collect the cost of the county connection fee to the public sewer line from the seller.
   b. The new owner can collect the cost of repair or replacement of the septic system from the county.
   c. The seller is not liable for misrepresentations made by a licensee.
   d. The entire sale will be undone.

15. Prospective buyer Pat calls licensee Kim and spends 20 minutes talking about her real estate needs. They agree to meet and go for a drive to look at communities but never discuss or visit any specific property. Kim drops Pat back at her home later that day. When should Kim have made disclosure?
   a. During the 20-minute conversation
   b. Before Pat got in Kim's car
   c. No disclosure was required
   d. After Pat signs a buyer agency agreement

CHAPTER 2

Seller and Buyer Agency Agreements

When licensees assist buyers, sellers, tenants, landlords, and property owners and some type of agreement is required to formalize an agency relationship, this agreement takes form in documents that are familiar in the real estate industry. The Listing Agreement is probably the most widely used instrument for representing a seller in the sale of a property. The Buyer Agency or Buyer Representation Agreement is technically a *listing agreement for buyers* and is now in wide use by licensees throughout the Commonwealth of Virginia and many other states. Many REALTOR® associations publish and print various *standard* forms for use by their members, but regardless of the form used, they all embody some basic common features. The following is an examination of the agreements that today's licensees use.

SELLER REPRESENTATION—SELLER AGENCY AGREEMENT(S)

Typically, a Listing Agreement (Exclusive Right to Represent Seller) would contain information such as the following:

- Assurances that the seller has not entered into a listing agreement with another broker
- Complete list of what items (chattels) convey with the property, including items of personal property
- The sales price
- Specific terms of the agreement
- Disclosure of any retainer or administration fees required by the agent or the agent's firm and whether these fees will be refunded to the seller at the conclusion of the transaction

- Statement of the broker's duties; because the document will establish a brokerage relationship, a recital of the statutory duties of a broker is appropriate (See §54.1-2131, Licensees Engaged by Sellers)
- Statement of any duties owed by the client
- Description of the purpose of the agreement
- Complete disclosure of how the broker will be paid
- Recital of disclosed dual representation statutory information (See Disclosed Dual Representation [§54.1-2139] in Chapter 1)
- Statement of applicability of federal, state, and local disclosures including, but not limited to,
  - lead-based paint
  - mold
  - Megan's Law
  - disclosure statements
  - POA or condominium inclusion
- Local disclaimer information; some local multiple-listing service (MLS) systems have regional disclosure information or information that sellers should know prior to entering into a sales agreement
- Fair housing statement
- Recital of any other provisions pertaining to the brokerage relationship
- Statement describing how the listing agreement may be terminated by either party

A typical listing agreement is shown in Figure 2.1.

TYPES OF LISTING (AGENCY) AGREEMENTS

The standard types of listings—open, exclusive-agency, and exclusive-right-to-sell—are all legal in Virginia. Many brokers will not accept open listings, however, because there is no guarantee of payment for time and money spent on the listings. Also, open listings may not be allowed by many MLS systems. All listing agreements must include a definite termination date. The owner must be furnished a copy of the listing at the time it is signed.

Virginia Real Estate Board (REB) regulations specifically prohibit net listings. [18 VAC 135-20-280(5)] A **net listing** is an agreement in which an owner specifies a particular dollar amount that he or she must net from the sale or rental of a property; the broker may keep any amount over the seller's net that is generated by the transaction. Under a net listing, it is difficult to balance the broker's responsibility to the principal with the broker's own interest in making a profit. Because this practice is not permitted in Virginia, brokers must inform prospective clients that their fee will be a percentage of the selling price, a **commission,** or a flat fee for services.

FOR EXAMPLE *O*, a homeowner, called *D*, a Richmond real estate broker, and told her that he wanted to sell his house. "I don't have time to be bothered with percentages and bargaining and offers and counteroffers," *O* explained. "I just need to walk out of this deal with $150,000 in my pocket. If you sell this place for more than that, you can keep the rest." Broker *D* knew that homes such as *O*'s were selling for

FIGURE 2.1

Listing Agreement—Exclusive Right to Sell

EXCLUSIVE RIGHT TO SELL LISTING AGREEMENT

This Exclusive Right to Sell Listing Agreement ("Agreement") is made on______________________,
by and between ____ ("Seller") and
________________________("Broker").
(Insert Firm Name)

1. APPOINTMENT OF BROKER. In consideration of the services provided by Broker and described in this Agreement, Seller hereby appoints Broker as Seller's sole and exclusive listing agent and grants Broker the exclusive right to sell the real property described as follows ("Property"):

2. PROPERTY.

Street Address ________________________________ Unit # ____________

City________________________________, Virginia Zip Code ____________

TAX Map/ID # ________________________________ Parking Space(s) # ____________

Legal Description: Lot(s) __________ Block/Square __________ Section ______ Phase ______

Subdivision or Condominium ________________________________ Storage Unit #____________

County/Municipality ____________ Deed Book/Liber # ______ Page/Folio # ____________

Historic District Designation ________________________________

3. PARTIES' CONTACT INFORMATION.

Seller

Mailing Address: ________________________________

City, State, and Zip Code: ________________________________

Phone: (H) __________ (W) __________ (Cell) __________ (Fax) __________

Email: ________________________________

SS# (optional) ________________________________

Broker

Mailing Address: ________________________________

City, State, and Zip Code: ________________________________

Telephone: ________________________________

Email: ____________________ Fax: ____________________

4. TERM OF AGREEMENT. This Agreement shall commence when signed by all parties and shall expire at 11:59 PM on ________________________________ ("Listing Period"). If a sales contract for the Property is ratified during the Listing Period which provides for a settlement date beyond the Listing Period, this Agreement shall be extended automatically until final disposition of the sales contract.

5. LISTING PRICE. Seller instructs the Broker to offer the Property for sale at a selling price of $______________________, or such other price as later agreed upon by Seller, which price includes the Broker's compensation. (Note: Broker does not guarantee that the Property will appraise or sell at

FIGURE 2.1 (CONTINUED)

Listing Agreement—Exclusive Right to Sell

the price stated hereunder, nor does Broker guarantee any net amount Seller might realize from the sale of the Property).

6. **CONVEYANCES.** The Property includes the following existing personal property and fixtures: any built-in heating and central air conditioning equipment, plumbing and lighting fixtures, storm windows, storm doors, screens, installed wall-to-wall carpeting, exhaust fans, window shades, blinds, window treatment hardware, smoke and heat detectors, TV antennas, exterior trees and shrubs. Unless otherwise agreed to in writing, all surface or wall mounted electronic components/devices DO NOT convey. If more than one of an item convey, the number of items is noted.

The items marked YES below re currently installed or offered:

Yes	No	#	Items	Yes	No	#	Items	Yes	No	#	Items
❑	❑	__	Alarm System	❑	❑	__	Freezer	❑	❑	__	Storage Shed
❑	❑	__	Attic Fan	❑	❑	__	Furnace Humidifier	❑	❑	__	Stove or Range
❑	❑	__	Built-in Microwave	❑	❑	__	Garage Door Opener	❑	❑	__	Sump Pump
❑	❑	__	Ceiling Fan	❑	❑	__	w/ remote	❑	❑	__	Trash Compactor
❑	❑	__	Central Vacuum	❑	❑	__	Gas Log	❑	❑	__	Wall Oven
❑	❑	__	Clothes Dryer	❑	❑	__	Hot Tub, Equip & Cover	❑	❑	__	Wastewater Ejector Pump
❑	❑	__	Clothes Washer	❑	❑	__	Intercom	❑	❑	__	Water Treat System
❑	❑	__	Cooktop	❑	❑	__	Playground Equip	❑	❑	__	Window A/C Unit
❑	❑	__	Dishwasher	❑	❑	__	Pool, Equip & Cover	❑	❑	__	Window Fan
❑	❑	__	Disposer	❑	❑	__	Refrigerator	❑	❑	__	Window Treatments
❑	❑	__	Electric Air Filter	❑	❑	__	w/ ice maker	❑	❑	__	Wood Stove
❑	❑	__	Fireplace Screen/Door	❑	❑	__	Satellite Dish				

OTHER ____

____

____

AS IS ITEMS

Seller does not warrant the condition or working order of the following items and/or systems:

____

____

LEASED ITEMS, SYSTEMS AND/OR SERVICE CONTRACTS

Any leased items, systems or service contracts (including, but not limited to, termite or pest control, home warranty, fuel tanks, water treatment systems, lawn contracts, security system monitoring, and satellite contracts) DO NOT CONVEY absent an express written agreement by Purchaser and Seller. The following is a list of the leased items within the Property: ______________________

____

____

7. HOMEOWNER WARRANTY

FIGURE 2.1 (CONTINUED)

Listing Agreement—Exclusive Right to Sell

Seller has the option to purchase a homeowner warranty, which can be in effect during the Listing Period and will transfer to the Buyer upon settlement. Seller should review the scope of coverage, exclusions and limitations.

Cost not to exceed $________________. Warranty provider to be ______________________________.

8. UTILITIES (Check all that apply)

Water Supply:	❑ Public	❑ Private Well	❑ Community Well	
Sewage Disposal:	❑ Public	❑ Septic # BR: _____		
Type of Septic System:	❑ Community	❑ Conventional	❑ Alternative	❑ Experimental

Seller represents that the septic system ❑ is **OR** ❑ is not operating under a waiver from the State Board of Health.

*Section 32.1-164:1 of the Code of Virginia requires Seller to disclose whether the onsite septic system serving the Property is operating under a waiver of repair and/or maintenance requirements imposed by the State Board of Health. If the septic system is operating pursuant to a waiver, then the Seller must provide the buyer with the "Disclosure Regarding Validity of Septic System Permit" prior to contract ratification. Such waiver is not transferable to the buyer.

Hot Water:	❑ Oil	❑ Gas	❑ Elec.	❑ Other ________	Number of Gallons________	
Air Conditioning:	❑ Oil	❑ Gas	❑ Elec.	❑ Heat Pump	❑ Other ________	❑ Zones ____
Heating:	❑ Oil	❑ Gas	❑ Elec.	❑ Heat Pump	❑ Other ________	❑ Zones ____

9. BROKER DUTIES.

The Broker shall perform, and Seller hereby authorizes Broker to perform, the following duties. In performing these duties, the Broker shall exercise ordinary care, comply with all applicable laws and regulations and treat all parties honestly.

A) Broker shall protect and promote the interests of Seller and shall provide Seller with services consistent with the standards of practice and competence that are reasonably expected of licensees engaged in the business of real estate brokerage.

B) Broker shall use reasonable efforts and act diligently to seek buyers for the Property at the price and terms stated herein or otherwise acceptable to the Seller, to negotiate on behalf of the Seller and to assist in the consummation of the sale of the Property.

C) Broker shall market the Property, at Broker's discretion, including without limitation, use of the Property address, description, interior and exterior photographs in appropriate advertising mediums, such as publications, mailings, brochures and internet sites; provided, however, Broker shall not be obligated to continue to market the Property after the Seller has accepted an offer.

D) Broker shall make a blanket unilateral offer of cooperation and compensation to other brokers in any multiple listing service ("MLS") that the Broker deems appropriate. Broker shall disseminate information regarding the Property, including the entry date, listing price(s), final price and all terms, and expired or withdrawn status, by printed form and/or electronic computer service, which may include the internet, during and after the expiration of this agreement.

Upon full ratification of this Agreement, Broker shall enter the listing information into the MLS database:

❑ Within 48 hours (excluding weekends and holidays); **OR**

❑ On or before: ______________________________

FIGURE 2.1 (CONTINUED)

Listing Agreement—Exclusive Right to Sell

E) Broker shall install "For Sale" signs on the Property, as permitted. Seller is responsible for clearly marking the location of underground utilities, equipment or other items that may be damaged by the placement of the sign.

F) Broker shall show the Property during reasonable hours to prospective buyers and shall accompany or accommodate, as needed, other real estate licensees, their prospective buyers, inspectors, appraisers, exterminators and other parties necessary for showings and inspections of the Property, to facilitate and/or consummate the sale of the Property. Broker shall install an electronic keybox on the Property to allow access and showings by real estate licensees who are authorized to use the electronic keybox system by area REALTOR® Associations.

G) Broker shall present all written offers or counteroffers to and from the Seller, in a timely manner, even if the Property is already subject to a ratified contract of sale, unless otherwise instructed by the Seller in writing.

H) Broker shall account, in a timely manner, for all money and property received in trust by Broker, in which the Seller has or may have an interest.

10. CONFIDENTIAL INFORMATION. Broker shall maintain the confidentiality of all personal and financial information and other matters identified as confidential by the client which were obtained by the Broker during the brokerage relationship, unless the client consents in writing to the release of such information or as otherwise provided by law. The obligation of Broker to preserve confidential information continues after termination of the brokerage relationship. Information concerning material defects about the Property is not considered confidential information.

11. TYPES OF REAL ESTATE REPRESENTATION - DISCLOSURE AND INFORMED CONSENT.

Seller Representation occurs by virtue of this Agreement with Seller's contract to use the Broker's services and may also include any cooperating brokers who act on behalf of the Seller as subagent of the Broker. (Note: Broker may assist a buyer or prospective buyer by performing ministerial acts that are not inconsistent with the Broker's duties as Seller's listing agent under this Agreement.)

Buyer Representation occurs when buyers contract to use the services of their own broker (known as a buyer representative) to act on their behalf.

Designated Representation occurs when a buyer and seller in one transaction are represented by different sales associate(s) affiliated with the same Broker. Each of these sales associates, known as a Designated Representative, represents fully the interests of a different client in the same transaction. Designated Representatives are not dual representatives if each represents only the buyer or only the seller in a specific real estate transaction. In the event of designated representatives, each representative shall be bound by client confidentiality requirements, set forth above. The Broker remains a dual representative.

❑ The Seller consents to designated representation **OR** ❑ The Seller does not consent to designated representation which means the Seller does not allow the Property to be shown to a buyer represented by this Broker through another Designated Representative associated with the firm. The Broker will notify other real estate licensees via the MLS whether the Seller consents or does not consent to Designated Representation.

Dual Representation occurs when the same Broker and the same sales associate(s) represent both the buyer and seller in one transaction. In the event of dual representation, the Broker shall be bound by confidentiality requirements for each client, as set forth above.

❑ The Seller consents to dual representation **OR** ❑ The Seller does not consent to dual representation, which means the Seller does not allow the Property to be shown to a buyer represented by this Broker through the same sales associate(s). The Broker will notify other real estate licensees via the MLS whether the Seller consents or does not consent to Dual Representation.

Non-Agency occurs when the real estate licensee does not represent either party and acts to facilitate the transaction by assisting the parties to reach an agreement, as an independent contractor and without being an advocate for the interest of either party. In the event of non-agency, the real estate licensee would not owe

FIGURE 2.1 (CONTINUED)

Listing Agreement—Exclusive Right to Sell

traditional fiduciary duties to the consumer, but would still owe the consumer duties imposed on all licensees by the Commonwealth of Virginia.

12. BROKER COMPENSATION.

A. Payment. The Seller shall pay the Broker in cash **total compensation** of ______________ (Compensation) if, during the term of this Agreement, anyone produces a buyer ready, willing and able to buy the Property.

The Compensation is also earned if within ______________ days after the expiration or termination of this Agreement, a contract is ratified with a ready, willing and able buyer to whom the Property had been shown during the term of this Agreement; provided, however, that the Compensation need not be paid if a contract is ratified on the Property while the Property is listed with another real estate company.

B. Selling Broker. The Broker shall offer a portion of the Compensation to the selling broker as indicated:

Sub-Agency Compensation: ____________________

Buyer Agency Compensation: ____________________

Non-Agency Compensation: ____________________

Note: Compensation may be shown by a percentage of the gross selling price, a definite dollar amount or "N" for no compensation.

The Broker's compensation and the sharing of compensation between brokers are not fixed, controlled, recommended or suggested by any multiple listing service or Association of REALTORS®.

C. Administrative Fee. In addition to the Compensation, an additional administrative fee of $ ________ will be collected from the Seller, payable to the Broker, at the time of settlement.

D. Retainer Fee. The Broker acknowledges receipt of a retainer fee in the amount of ______________ which ❑ shall, **OR** ❑ shall not be subtracted from the Compensation. The retainer is non-refundable and is earned when paid.

E. Early Termination. In the event Seller wishes to terminate this Agreement prior to the end of the Listing Period, without good cause, Seller shall pay Broker ______________________________ ("Early Termination Fee") before Broker's execution of a written release.

13. AUTHORIZATION TO DISCLOSE OTHER OFFERS. In response to inquiries from buyers or cooperating brokers, Broker may not disclose, without the Seller's approval, the existence of other written offers on the property.

Seller ❑ does **OR** ❑ does not authorize the Broker and sales associate to disclose such information to buyers or cooperating brokers.

If the Seller does give such authorization, the Seller acknowledges that the Broker and sales associate (s) must disclose whether the offers were obtained by the listing agent, another member of the listing Broker's firm, or by a cooperating broker.

14. COMPLIANCE WITH FAIR HOUSING LAWS. This Property shall be shown and made available without regard to race, color, religion, sex, handicap, familial status or national origin as well as all classes protected by the laws of the United States, the Commonwealth of Virginia and applicable local jurisdictions.

15. EMPLOYEE RELOCATION PROGRAM.

The Seller is participating in any type of employee relocation program ❑ Yes OR ❑ No.

If "Yes": (a) the program is named: ________________________, Contact #____________________ and

FIGURE 2.1 (CONTINUED)

Listing Agreement—Exclusive Right to Sell

(b) terms of the program are: ____

____

If "No" or the Seller has failed to list a specific employee relocation program, then the Broker shall have no obligation to cooperate with or compensate any undisclosed program.

16. CONDOMINIUM ASSOCIATION. The Seller represents that the Property ❒ is, **OR** ❒ is not located within a development which is a Condominium or Cooperative. Condominiums or Cooperatives being offered for sale are subject to the receipt by buyers of the required Disclosures, and the Seller is responsible for payment of appropriate fees and for providing these disclosure documents to prospective buyers as prescribed in the Condominium Act, Section 55-79.39 et seq., and the Cooperative Act, Section 55-424, et seq., of the Code of Virginia.

The Condominium or Cooperative dues are $ __________ per __________ (frequency of payment).

Special Assessment $ ______________ for ______________________________

Condominium or Cooperative Association Name: ______________________________

Management Company: ______________________________ Phone #: ______________

17. PROPERTY OWNER'S ASSOCIATION. The Seller represents that the Property ❒ is **OR** ❒ is not located within a development(s) which is subject to the Virginia Property Owners' Association Act, Sections 55-508 through 55-516 of the Code of Virginia. If the Property is within such a development, the Seller is responsible for payment of the appropriate fees and for providing these disclosure documents to the buyers.

The Property Owners Association dues are $ __________ per __________ (frequency of payment).

Special Assessment $ ______________ for ______________________________

Property Owners Association Name: ______________________________

Management Company: ______________________________ Phone #: ______________

18. PROPERTY CONDITION. The Seller acknowledges that the Broker has informed the Seller of the Seller's rights and obligations under the Virginia Residential Property Disclosure Act. This Property ❑is, **OR** ❑ is not exempt from the Act. If not exempt, the Seller has completed and provided to the Broker: ❑ a Residential Property Disclosure Statement where the Seller is making representations regarding the condition of the Property on which the buyer may rely, **OR** ❑ a Residential Property Disclaimer Statement where the Seller is making no representations regarding the condition of the Property and is selling the Property "as is", except as may be provided otherwise in the sales contract.

Seller acknowledges Broker is required to disclose to prospective buyers all material adverse facts pertaining to the physical condition of the Property actually known by the Broker. The Broker shall not, however, be obligated to discover latent defects in the Property or to advise on property condition matters outside the scope of the Broker's real estate license. Seller shall indemnify, save, and hold Broker harmless from all claims, complaints, disputes, litigation, judgments and attorney's fees arising from any incorrect information supplied by Seller or from Seller's failure to disclose any material adverse facts.

19. LEAD BASED PAINT DISCLOSURE. The Seller represents that the residential dwelling(s) at the Property ❑ were, **OR** ❑ were not constructed before 1978. If the dwelling(s) were constructed before 1978, the Seller is subject to Federal law concerning disclosure of the possible presence of lead-based paint at the Property, and the Seller acknowledges that the Broker has informed the Seller of the Seller's obligations under the law. If the dwelling(s) were constructed before 1978, unless exempt under 42 U.S.C. 4852d, the Seller has completed and provided to the Broker the form, "Sale: Disclosure And Acknowledgment Of Information On Lead-Based Paint And/Or Lead-Based Paint Hazards" or equivalent form.

FIGURE 2.1 (CONTINUED)

Listing Agreement—Exclusive Right to Sell

20. CURRENT LIENS. Seller represents to Broker that the below information is true and complete to the best of Seller's information, knowledge and belief:

A. The Property is security for a first mortgage or Deed of Trust loan held by (Lender Name): ______________________ Account # ______________________ with an approximate balance of $______________________. Lender Phone: ______________________
Address: ______________________

B. The Property is security for a second mortgage or Deed of Trust loan held by (Lender Name): ______________________ Account # ______________________ with an approximate balance of $______________________. Lender Phone: ______________________
Address: ______________________

C. The Property is security for a line of credit or home equity line of credit held by (Lender Name): ______________________ Account # ______________________ with an approximate balance of $______________________. Lender Phone: ______________________
Address: ______________________

Check where applicable:

D. ☐ The Property is not encumbered by any mortgage or Deed of Trust.

E. ☐ Seller is current on all payments for the loans identified in numbered items A, B, and C above.

F. ☐ Seller is not in default on any loan identified in numbered items A, B, and C, above; and has not received any notice(s) from the holder of any loan identified in numbered items A, B, and C above; or from any other lien holder of any kind, regarding a default under the loan; threatened foreclosure, notice of foreclosure; or the filing of foreclosure.

G. ☐ There are no liens secured against the Property for Federal, State or local income taxes; unpaid real property taxes; or unpaid condominium or homeowners' association fees.

H. ☐ There are no judgments against Seller (including each owner for jointly held property). Seller has no knowledge of any matter that might result in a judgment that may potentially affect the property.

I. ☐ Seller has not filed for bankruptcy protection under United States law and is not contemplating doing so during the term of the Listing Agreement.

During the term of the Listing Agreement, should any change occur with respect to answers A through I above, Seller shall immediately notify Broker and listing agent, in writing, of such change.

21. SELLER FINANCING. Seller agrees to offer seller financing by providing a ______________________ Deed of Trust loan in the amount of $______________________ with further terms to be negotiated.

22. CLOSING COSTS. Fees for the preparation of the deed of conveyance, that portion of the Settlement Agent's fee billed to the Seller, costs of releasing existing encumbrances, Seller's legal fees, Grantor's Tax, and any other proper charges assessed to Seller will be paid by Seller unless provided otherwise in the sales contract.

The "Seller's Estimated Cost of Settlement" form ☐ is, **OR** ☐ is not attached. These estimates are for informational purposes only and will change based upon the terms and conditions of the purchase offer.

FIGURE 2.1 (CONTINUED)

Listing Agreement—Exclusive Right to Sell

Sellers Proceeds: The Seller acknowledges that Seller's proceeds may not be available at the time of settlement. The receipt of proceeds may be subject to the **Virginia Wet Settlement Act**, and may be subject to other laws, rules and regulations (e.g. Virginia estate statutes and the **Foreign Investment Real Property Tax Act - FIRPTA**).

Sellers are advised to seek legal and/or financial advice concerning these matters.

23. **IRS/FIRPTA:** Section 1445 of the Internal Revenue Service (IRS) Code may require the settlement agent to report the gross sales price, Seller's federal tax identification number and other required information to the IRS. Seller will provide to the settlement agent such information upon request. In certain situations, the IRS requires a percentage (currently 10%) of the sales price to be withheld from Seller's proceeds if Seller is a foreign person for purposes of U.S. income taxation. A foreign person includes, but is not limited to, non-resident aliens, foreign corporations, foreign partnerships, foreign trusts or foreign estates.

Seller represents that Seller ☐ is **OR** ☐ is not, a foreign person for purposes of U.S. income taxation.

24. MISCELLANEOUS PROVISIONS.

A. Seller Representations and Warranties.

- Seller has capacity to convey insurable and marketable title to the Property.
- Seller is not a party to a listing agreement with another broker for the sale, exchange or lease of the Property.
- No person or entity has the right to purchase, lease or acquire the Property, by virtue of an option, right of first refusal or otherwise.
- The Seller ☐ is, **OR** ☐ is not a licensed (active/inactive) real estate agent/broker.
- Seller ☐ has **OR** ☐ has no knowledge of the existence, removal or abandonment of any underground storage tank on the property.

B. Access to the Property. Seller shall provide keys to Broker for access to the Property to facilitate the Broker's duties under this Agreement. In the event the Property is subject to a lease, the Seller shall provide Broker with the lease documents and shall use best efforts to obtain the full cooperation of the tenants, in connection with showings and inspections of the Property.

C. Seller Assumption of Risk. The Seller retains full responsibility for the property, including all utilities, maintenance, physical security and liability until title to the property is transferred to purchaser. Seller is advised to take all precautions for safekeeping of valuables and to maintain appropriate property and liability insurance through Seller's own insurance company.

Broker is not responsible for the security of the property or for inspecting the property on any periodic basis. If the property is or becomes vacant during the Listing Period, Seller must notify Seller's home owner's insurance company and request a "Vacancy Clause" to cover the property.

In consideration of the use of Brokers services and facilities and of the facilities of any Multiple Listing Service, the Seller and Seller's heirs and assigns hereby release the Broker, sales associates accompanying buyers or prospective buyers, any Multiple Listing Service and the Directors, Officers and employees thereof, including officials of any parent Association of REALTORS®, except for malfeasance on the part of such parties, from any liability to the Seller for vandalism, theft or damage of any nature whatsoever to the Property or its contents that occurs during the Listing Period. Seller waives any and all rights, claims and causes of actions against them and holds them harmless for any Property damage or personal injury arising from the use or access to the Property by any persons during the Listing Period.

FIGURE 2.1 (CONTINUED)

Listing Agreement—Exclusive Right to Sell

D. Appropriate Professional Advice. The Broker can counsel on real estate matters, but if the Seller desires legal advice, the Seller is advised to seek legal counsel. The Seller is advised further to seek appropriate professional advice concerning the condition of the Property or tax and insurance matters.

E. Subsequent Offers After Contract Acceptance. After a sales contract has been ratified on the Property, Broker recommends Seller obtain the advice of legal counsel prior to acceptance of any subsequent offer.

F. Governing Law. The laws of Virginia shall govern the validity, interpretation and enforcement of this Agreement.

G. Binding Agreement. This Agreement will be binding upon the parties, and each of their respective heirs, executors, administrators, successors and permitted assigns. The provisions hereof will survive the sale of the Property and will not be merged therein. This Agreement, unless amended in writing by the parties, contains the final and entire agreement and the parties will not be bound by any terms, conditions, oral statements, warranties or representations not herein contained.

25. ADDITIONAL TERMS: ____

____

____

____

______ Date ______________ Seller ______ Date ______________ Seller

______ Date ______________ Broker/Sales Manager ______________ Sales associate (Designated Listing Agent)

Sales associates Contact Information

Phone: (H) ____________ (W) ____________ (Cell) ____________ (Fax) ____________

Email: ______________________ Fax: ______________________

well over $200,000. On the other hand, *D* knew that net listings are illegal in Virginia. What should *D* do?

D should explain to *O* that net listings are illegal in Virginia and advise him of the range of values properties like his are bringing currently. *D* can negotiate a commission or fee for the services she will provide, sign a listing agreement with *O*, and proceed to market and sell *O*'s property.

LISTING FORMS/AGREEMENTS

Whereas there are no standard listing or buyer representation forms used throughout the entire Commonwealth, the Virginia Association of REALTORS® creates standard forms that are available in print and software versions and are used in many parts of the state. Additionally, several large associations such as NVAR (Northern Virginia Association of REALTORS®) have standard forms available for use in large regional, multijurisdictional areas. These are available in print, software, and via online subscription.

IN PRACTICE

In a listing form, the blanks are rarely optional. *All blanks should be filled in.* If an item does not apply in a particular transaction, the notation N/A, not applicable, should be used. Finding accurate information for each item may require additional research.

Some items on the listing forms may have to be entered as approximations, such as the mortgage balance—until a payoff statement is available from the lender—or the exact age of the dwelling. Accurate figures should be used wherever possible. Any changes involving financial responsibility, such as a price change, dates, or other major seller commitments, must be authorized in writing by the seller.

BUYER REPRESENTATION—BUYER AGENCY AGREEMENT(S)

A buyer's agent establishes a brokerage relationship with a client through a *buyer representation agreement.* (See Chapter 1.) A typical buyer's representation agreement used in Virginia is illustrated in Figure 2.2.

An Exclusive Right to Represent Buyer Agreement would typically contain information such as the following:

- Assurances that the buyer has not entered into a buyer representation agreement with another broker
- Information about other properties that the buyer may have been shown by other agents
- Specific terms of the agreement
- Disclosure of any retainer or administration fees required by the agent or the agent's firm and whether these fees will be refunded to the buyer at the conclusion of the transaction
- Statement of the broker's duties; because the document will establish a brokerage relationship, a recital of the statutory duties of a broker is appropriate (see §54.1-2132, Licensees Engaged by Buyers)
- Statement of any duties owed by the client

FIGURE 2.2

Buyer Representation Agreement

EXCLUSIVE RIGHT TO REPRESENT BUYER AGREEMENT

This Agreement is made on_________________________ between _________________________
_________________________ ("Buyer") and _________________________("Broker").
(Name of brokerage firm)

In consideration of services and facilities, the Broker is hereby granted the right to represent the Buyer in the acquisition of real property. (As used in this Agreement, "acquisition of real property" shall include any purchase, option, exchange or lease of property or an agreement to do so.)

1. **BUYER'S REPRESENTATIONS**. The Buyer represents that as of the commencement date of this Agreement, the Buyer is not a party to a buyer representation agreement with any other brokerage firm. The Buyer further represents that the Buyer has disclosed to the Sales Associate information about any properties that the Buyer has previously visited at any new homes communities or resale open houses, or that the Buyer has been shown by any other real estate sales associate(s) in any area where the Buyer seeks to acquire property under this Agreement.

2. **TERM**. This Agreement commences when signed and, subject to Paragraph 7, expires at ______ ❒ a.m. **OR** ❒ p.m. on _________________________.

3. **RETAINER FEE**. The Broker, _________________________(Name of brokerage firm), acknowledges receipt of a retainer fee in the amount of_______________, which ❒ shall **OR** ❒ shall not be subtracted from any compensation due the Broker under this Agreement. The retainer is non-refundable and is earned when paid.

4. **BROKER'S DUTIES**. The Broker and the Sales Associate shall

A) Promote the interests of the Buyer by:

1) performing the terms of this Agreement;
2) seeking property at a price and terms acceptable to the Buyer; however, Broker and Sales Associate shall not be obligated to seek other properties for the Buyer while the Buyer is a party to a contract to purchase property unless part of this brokerage agreement;
3) assisting in the drafting and negotiating of offers and counteroffers to and from the Buyer and Seller and in establishing strategies for accomplishing the Buyer's objectives;
4) providing reasonable assistance to the Buyer to satisfy the Buyer's contractual obligations and to facilitate the settlement of the purchase contract;
5) receiving and presenting in a timely manner all written offers or counteroffers to and from the Buyer and Seller, even when the Buyer is already a party to a contract to purchase property;
6) disclosing to the Buyer all material facts related to the property or concerning the transaction of which they have actual knowledge;
7) accounting in a timely manner for all money and property received in which the Buyer has or may have an interest.

B) Maintain the confidentiality of all personal and financial information and other matters identified as confidential by the Buyer, if that information is received from the Buyer during the brokerage relationship unless otherwise provided by law or the Buyer consents in writing to the release of the information. However, Sellers or Sellers' representatives may not treat the existence, terms, or conditions of offers as confidential unless confidentiality is required by law, regulation, or by any confidentiality agreement between the parties.

In satisfying these duties, the Broker shall exercise ordinary care, comply with all applicable laws and regulations, treat all prospective sellers honestly and not knowingly give them false information, and disclose whether or not the Buyer's intent is to occupy the property as a principal residence. In addition, the Broker may: show the same property to other buyers; represent other buyers on the same or different properties; represent Sellers relative to other properties; or provide assistance to a seller or prospective seller by performing ministerial acts that are not inconsistent with the Broker's duties under this Agreement.

FIGURE 2.2 (CONTINUED)

Buyer Representation Agreement

5. **BUYER'S DUTIES.** The Buyer shall: (a) work exclusively with the Broker during the term of this Agreement; (b) pay the Broker, directly or indirectly, the compensation set forth below; (c) comply with the reasonable requests of the Broker to supply any pertinent financial or personal data needed to fulfill the terms of this Agreement; (d) be available during the Broker's regular working hours to view properties.

6. **PURPOSE.** The Buyer is retaining the Broker to acquire the following type of property: ____________________ ____.

7. **COMPENSATION.** In consideration of the time and effort expended by the Broker on behalf of the Buyer, and in further consideration of the advice and counsel provided to the Buyer, the Buyer shall pay compensation ("Broker's Fee") to the Broker as described below. The Broker's Fee, less the Retainer Fee if so indicated in Paragraph 3 above, shall be earned, due and payable under any of these circumstances whether the transaction is consummated through the services of the Broker or otherwise:

A) If the Buyer enters into a contract to acquire real property during the term of this Agreement and goes to settlement on that contract any time thereafter; **OR**

B) If, within__________ days after expiration or termination of this Agreement, the Buyer enters into a contract to acquire real property that has been described to or shown to the Buyer by the Broker during the term of this Agreement, unless the Buyer has entered into a subsequent "Exclusive Right to Represent Buyer" agreement with another real estate broker; **OR**

C) If, having entered into an enforceable contract to acquire real property during the term of this Agreement, the Buyer defaults under the terms of that contract.

The Broker's Fee shall be ____________________________________. In addition to the Broker's compensation, an additional fee of _______________ will be collected from the Buyer payable to the Broker, at the time of settlement. If the seller or the seller's representative offers compensation to the Broker, then the Buyer authorizes the Broker to receive such compensation and the amount of such compensation shall be credited against the Buyer's obligation to pay the Broker's Fee. The Broker may retain any additional compensation offered by the seller or seller's representative, even if this causes the compensation paid to the Broker to exceed the fees specified above. In no case shall the compensation be less than the fees specified above.

Any obligation incurred under this Agreement on the part of the Buyer to pay the Broker's Fee shall survive the term of this Agreement.

8. The Buyer is participating in any type of employee relocation program ❒ Yes **OR** ❒ No.

If "Yes": (a) the program is named: ____, and
(b) terms of the program are: ____
____.

If "No" or the Buyer has failed to list a specific employee relocation program, then the Broker shall have no obligation to cooperate with or compensate any undisclosed program.

9. **DISCLOSED DUAL REPRESENTATION.** The Buyer acknowledges that in the normal course of business the Broker may represent sellers of properties in which the Buyer is interested. If the Buyer wishes to acquire any property listed with the Broker, then the Buyer will be represented in one of the two ways that are permitted under Virginia law in this situation. The written consent required from the parties in each case will be accomplished via execution of the appropriate disclosure form at the time of the contract offer.

Dual representation occurs when a buyer and seller in one transaction are represented by the same Broker and the same Sales Associate. When the parties agree to dual representation, the ability of the Broker and the Sales Associate to represent either party fully and exclusively is limited. The confidentiality of all clients shall be maintained as in Paragraph 4 above.

Designated representation occurs when a buyer and seller in one transaction are represented by different Sales Associates affiliated with the same Broker. Each of these Sales Associates, known as a Designated Representative, represents fully the interests of a different client in the same transaction. Designated Representatives are not dual representatives if each represents only the buyer or only the seller in a specific real estate transaction. Except for disclosure of confidential information to the Broker, each Designated Representative is bound by the confidentiality requirements in Paragraph 4 above. The Broker remains a dual representative.

CHECK ONE CHOICE IN EACH SECTION:

FIGURE 2.2 (CONTINUED)

Buyer Representation Agreement

Dual representation: The Buyer ❒ does **OR** ❒ does not consent to be shown and to consider acquiring properties listed with the Broker through the Sales Associate.
Designated representation: The Buyer ❒ does **OR** ❒ does not consent to be shown and to consider acquiring properties listed with the Broker through another Designated Representative associated with the firm.

10. **DISCLAIMER.** The buyer acknowledges that the Broker is being retained solely as a real estate agent and not as an attorney, tax advisor, lender, appraiser, surveyor, structural engineer, mold or air quality expert, home inspector or other professional service provider. The Buyer is advised to seek professional advice concerning the condition of the property or concerning legal and tax matters. The Buyer should exercise whatever due diligence the Buyer deems necessary with respect to information on any sexual offenders registered under Chapter 23 (§19.2-387 et. seq.) of Title 19.2. Such information may be obtained by contacting your local police department or the Department of State Police, Central Criminal Records Exchange, at (804)674-2000 or www.vsp.state.va.us.

11. **EQUAL OPPORTUNITY.** Properties shall be shown and made available to the Buyer without regard to race, color, religion, sex, handicap, familial status or national origin as well as all classes protected by the laws of the United States, the Commonwealth of Virginia and applicable local jurisdictions.

12. **OTHER PROVISIONS.** ____
____
____

13. **MISCELLANEOUS.** This Agreement, any exhibits and any addenda signed by the parties constitute the entire agreement between the parties and supersedes any other written or oral agreements between the parties. This Agreement can only be modified in writing when signed by both parties. In any action or proceeding involving a dispute between the Buyer, the seller and/or the Broker, arising out of this Agreement, or to collect the Broker's Fee, the prevailing party shall be entitled to receive from the other party reasonable attorney's fees to be determined by the court or arbitrator(s).

(NOTE: The Buyer should consult with the Sales Associate before visiting any resale or new homes or contacting any other REALTORS® representing sellers, to avoid the possibility of confusion over the brokerage relationship and misunderstandings about liability for compensation.)

	______________________ Brokerage Firm
______ Date ______________________ Buyers Signature (SEAL)	______________________ Address
______ Date ______________________ Buyers Signature (SEAL)	______________________ City, State, Zip Code

The Buyer ❒ does **OR** ❒ does not hold an active or inactive Virginia real estate license.

______________________ Address	______ Date ______________________ Broker/Sales Manager's Signature (SEAL)
______________________ City, State, Zip Code	______________________ Sales Associate's/Designated Representative's Printed Name
Phone: __________ Work __________ Home	Phone: __________ Work __________ Home
Fax: __________ Email: __________	Fax: __________ Email: __________

- Description of the purpose of the agreement
- Complete disclosure of how the broker will be paid
- Recital of disclosed dual representation statutory information (See Disclosed Dual Representation [§54.1-2139] in Chapter 1)
- Local disclaimer information; some local MLS systems have regional disclosure information on information that buyers should know prior to entering into a purchase agreement
- Fair housing statement
- Recital of any other provisions pertaining to the brokerage relationship
- Statement describing how the listing agreement may be terminated by either party

STATUTE OF FRAUDS

It should be noted that while an oral listing or buyer representation agreement may be legal in Virginia, such an agreement would not be enforceable.

VIRGINIA RESIDENTIAL PROPERTY DISCLOSURE ACT [§55-519 ET SEQ.]

In 2007, the General Assembly implemented a new law eliminating the old disclosure and disclaimer forms. The new form contains only disclosures mandated by General Assembly (see Figure 2.3).

With regard to transfers described in §55-517 of this chapter of the Virginia Code, the seller of the residential real property shall furnish to the purchaser a residential property disclosure statement in a form provided by the Real Estate Board stating that the seller makes the following representations as to the real property:

- The owner makes no representations or warranties as to the condition of the real property or any improvements thereon.
- The owner makes no representations with respect to any matters that may pertain to parcels adjacent to the subject parcel.
- The owner makes no representations to any matters that pertain to whether the provisions of any historic district ordinance affect the property.
- The owner makes no representations with respect to whether the property contains any resource protection areas established in an ordinance implementing the Chesapeake Bay Preservation Act (§10.1-2100 et seq.).
- The owner makes no representations with respect to information on any sexual offenders registered under Chapter 23 (§19.2-387 et seq.) of Title 19.2.
- The owner represents that there are no pending enforcement actions pursuant to the Uniform Statewide Building Code (§36-97 et seq.) that affect the safe, decent, sanitary living conditions of the property.

The seller is required to disclose only known adverse material defects. Failure of a seller to disclose known adverse material defects does not relieve the seller of responsibility.

FIGURE 2.3

Disclosure Statement

RESIDENTIAL PROPERTY DISCLOSURE STATEMENT

NOTICE TO SELLER AND PURCHASER

The Virginia Residential Property Disclosure Act (§55-517 et seq. of the Code of Virginia) requires the owner of certain residential real property, whenever the property is to be sold or leased with an option to buy, to furnish to the purchaser a RESIDENTIAL PROPERTY DISCLOSURE STATEMENT stating the owner makes the following representations as to the real property. Certain transfers of residential property are excluded from this requirement (see §55-518).

Property Address/
Legal Description: ______________________________

The undersigned owner(s) of the real property described above makes no representations or warranties as to the condition of the real property or any improvements thereon, and the purchaser(s) is advised to exercise whatever due diligence the purchaser(s) deems necessary including obtaining a certified home inspection, as defined in § 54.1-500, in accordance with the terms and conditions as may be contained in the real estate purchase contract, but in any event, prior to settlement on the parcel of residential real property.

The undersigned owner(s) makes no representations with respect to any matters that may pertain to parcels adjacent to the subject parcel, and the purchaser(s) is advised to exercise whatever due diligence the purchaser(s) deems necessary with respect to adjacent parcels in accordance with terms and conditions as may be contained in the real estate purchase contract, but in any event, prior to settlement on the parcel of residential real property.

The undersigned owner(s) makes no representations to any matters that pertain to whether the provisions of any historic district ordinance affect the property, and the purchaser(s) is advised to exercise whatever due diligence the purchaser deems necessary with respect to any historic district designated by the locality pursuant to § 15.2-2306, including review of any local ordinance creating such district or any official map adopted by the locality depicting historic districts, in accordance with terms and conditions as may be contained in the real estate purchase contract, but in any event, prior to settlement on the parcel of residential real property.

The undersigned owner(s) makes no representations with respect to whether the property contains any resource protection areas established in an ordinance implementing the Chesapeake Bay Preservation Act (§ 10.1-2100 et seq.) adopted by the locality where the property is located pursuant to § 10.1-2109, and the purchaser(s) is advised to exercise whatever due diligence the purchaser(s) deems necessary to determine whether the provisions of any such ordinance affect the property, including review of any official map adopted by the locality depicting resource protection areas, in accordance with terms and conditions as may be contained in the real estate purchase contract, but in any event, prior to settlement on the parcel of residential real property.

The undersigned owner(s) makes no representations with respect to information on any sexual offenders registered under Chapter 23 (§ 19.2-387 et seq.) of Title 19.2, and the purchaser(s) is advised to exercise whatever due diligence the purchaser(s) deems necessary with respect to such information, in accordance with terms and conditions as may be contained in the real estate purchase contract, but in any event, prior to settlement pursuant to that contract.

The undersigned owner(s) represents that there are no pending enforcement actions pursuant to the Uniform Statewide Building Code (§36-97 et seq.) that affect the safe, decent, and sanitary living conditions of the real property described above of which the owner has been notified in writing by the locality, nor any pending violation of the local zoning ordinance which the violator has not abated or remedied under the

FIGURE 2.3 (CONTINUED)

Disclosure Statement

zoning ordinance, within a time period set out in the written notice of violation from the locality or established by a court of competent jurisdiction, except as disclosed on this statement.

____

____

Additional Written Disclosure Requirements

Section 55-518.B. contains other disclosure requirements for transfers involving the first sale of a dwelling because the first sale of a dwelling is exempt from the disclosure requirements listed above. The builder of a new dwelling shall disclose in writing to the purchaser thereof all known material defects which would constitute a violation of any applicable building code.

In addition, for property that is located wholly or partially in any locality comprising Planning District 15, the builder or owner, if the builder is not the owner of the property, shall disclose in writing whether the builder or owner has any knowledge of (i) whether mining operations have previously been conducted on the property or (ii) the presence of abandoned mines, shafts, or pits, if any.

The disclosures required by this subsection shall be made by a builder or owner (i) when selling a completed dwelling, before acceptance of the purchase contract or (ii) when selling a dwelling before or during its construction, after issuance of a certificate of occupancy. Such disclosure shall not abrogate any warranty or any other contractual obligations the builder or owner may have to the purchaser. The disclosure required by this subsection may be made on this disclosure form. If no defects are known by the builder to exist, no written disclosure is required by this subsection.

Section 55-519.1 contains a disclosure requirement for properties located in any locality in which there is a military air installation.

Section 32.1-164.1:1 contains a disclosure requirement regarding the validity of septic system operating permits.

See also the Virginia Condominium Act (§55-79.39 et seq.), the Virginia Cooperative Act (§55-424 et seq.) and the Virginia Property Owners' Association Act (§55-508 et seq.).

The owner(s) acknowledge having carefully examined this statement and further acknowledge that they have been informed of their rights and obligations under the Virginia Residential Property Disclosure Act.

Owner	Date	Owner	Date

The purchaser(s) acknowledge receipt of a copy of this disclosure statement and further acknowledge that they have been informed of their rights and obligations under the Virginia Residential Property Disclosure Act.

Purchaser	Date	Purchaser	Date

DPOR 1/01/08

Time for Disclosure and Purchaser's Options

The disclosure is required *before* contract ratification by the seller and buyer. If the disclosure is received *after* contract ratification, the sole remedy for the purchaser is to terminate the contract by giving written notice to the seller. Once the disclosure is received by the buyer, notice to terminate must be given to the seller

- within three days if the notice is hand-carried;
- within five days of postmark, if the notice is mailed;
- prior to settlement;
- prior to occupancy if occupancy occurs before settlement; or
- prior to loan application where the loan application discloses that the right of contract terminations ends when the loan application is taken.

The purchaser may allow the contract to remain valid if he or she

- provides a notice of waiver of rights to terminate the contract or
- remains silent and does nothing.

If the purchaser elects to terminate the contract in accordance with the disclosure law, he or she may do so without any penalty. Any monies already paid by the purchaser, such as earnest money deposits, must be returned.

The purchaser will lose the right to terminate the contract if the termination right is not exercised

- at the time the purchaser makes a written application to obtain a mortgage loan, and the loan application contains a disclosure that the right to terminate shall end; or
- at settlement or occupancy, in the event of a sale; or
- at the time of occupancy in the event of lease with option to buy.

Builders of new homes must disclose only known material defects that would constitute a violation of local building codes. Builders are required to disclose defects before acceptance of an offer for purchase of an already completed house or after issuance of an occupancy permit if the offer is accepted before or during construction.

The issuance of the disclosure does not relieve the builder of any other new home warranties or contractual obligations. While the disclosure may be in any form, the builder may *not* satisfy the disclosure requirement by the use of a disclaimer statement.

Megan's Law

Disclosure forms must contain a notice advising purchasers that they should exercise whatever due diligence they deem necessary with respect to information on violent sexual offenders registered with the Commonwealth. The form is not required for new home sales, transfers involving trusts, foreclosures, or residential leases. However, it is advocated that new disclosure language be added to all contracts and agency agreements.

Exemptions

Certain transactions are exempt from the disclosure requirements. These include

- court-ordered transfers
  - to settle an estate;
  - pursuant to a writ of execution;
  - for foreclosures;

- — by a trustee in bankruptcy;
- — by condemnation through the right of eminent domain; and
- — by suit for specific performance.

- voluntary transfers of property
  - — between co-owners;
  - — between relatives;
  - — under a divorce settlement;
  - — to or from any government entity or public or quasi-public housing authority or agency;
  - — as the result of an owner's failure to pay federal, state, or local taxes; and
  - — involving the first sale of a new home.

Buyer's Recourse

If the buyer learns of defects that either were not disclosed or were misrepresented in the disclosure statement, the buyer is entitled to seek recourse. Any action brought under this act must be commenced within one year from the date the disclosure was delivered. If no disclosure was delivered, action must be commenced within one year of settlement, or within one year of occupancy in the event of lease with option to buy.

The owner is not liable for any error, inaccuracy, or omission of information in the disclosure form if the information was provided to the owner by a *reliable third party* such as a surveyor, engineer, appraiser, home inspector, or public authority. The owner is also not liable if he or she *reasonably believed the information to be correct* and there was no gross negligence involved.

Licensee Liability

Like the owner, a real estate licensee cannot be liable for misrepresentation if he or she relied on information provided by others. However, a licensee must disclose material adverse facts pertaining to the physical condition of the property that are actually known by the licensee. [§54.1-2131B, 18 VAC 135-20-300(2)]

■ **FOR EXAMPLE** *T,* a real estate salesperson, is hosting an open house during a rainstorm. While no one is being shown the property, *T* notices that there is a leak in the attic and water seepage in the basement. *T* must disclose that information to any prospective buyers, even if the owner knowingly falsified the disclosure statement or filed a disclaimer because he or she did not want to admit that anything was wrong. If *T* fails to inform a prospective buyer about the leaking and seepage, *T* may be found guilty of misrepresentation.

■ STIGMATIZED PROPERTY

Stigmatized property refers to any property that is made undesirable by some event or circumstance that had no actual effect on its physical structure, environment, or improvements. For instance, a house in which a homicide, felony, or suicide occurred may be "tainted" by that event and be difficult to sell. Buyers may hesitate to make an offer on a property that is reputed to be haunted or one in which the current or former occupant suffered from a communicable disease.

Disclosure of this type of information, which in Virginia has been determined to be immaterial, is *not* required. In fact, a licensee who represents a seller and discloses stigmatizing information to a buyer could be construed as having breached his or her responsibilities to the client if the buyer cancels the contract due to the disclosure. The failure to disclose this information does not subject either the owner or a licensee to disciplinary action by the courts or the REB. There is also no disciplinary action of a licensee who does disclose such information as long as the seller has approved of such disclosure. The only topic of disclosure that is specifically prohibited is any discussion of HIV or AIDS.

IN PRACTICE

If information is disclosed regarding persons infected with HIV, a licensee could be in violation of fair housing laws and the federal privacy act.

Similarly, a broker who enlists an assistant broker in providing brokerage services to a client is not liable for that broker's misrepresentations unless he or she knew or should have known about them and failed to take reasonable corrective steps. A broker is not liable for the negligence, gross negligence, or intentional acts of an assisting broker or the assisting broker's licensee.

Both clients and licensees are fully liable for their own misrepresentations, negligence, gross negligence, or intentional acts in connection with a real estate transaction.

QUESTIONS

1. When a broker and seller enter into an exclusive-right-to-sell listing, which of the following is required?
   a. Net amount seller receives at closing
   b. Definite termination date
   c. Extension or protective clause
   d. Statement of the exact acreage or square footage of the parcel or lot

2. A seller offers you a listing agreement that contains the following clause: "Seller must receive the amount of $60,000 from the sale of this property. Seller agrees that the selling agent will receive, as his or her total compensation, any proceeds that remain beyond that amount after satisfaction of seller's mortgage loan and any closing costs incurred by seller." Based on these facts, you
   a. must decline this listing agreement because the clause violates REB regulations.
   b. must decline this listing agreement because it is not the standard form used in Virginia.
   c. may accept this listing agreement because the clause is standard in an open listing.
   d. may accept this listing agreement, because it specifically limits the amount of your compensation.

3. Which of the following would be the correct way to enter the termination date on a listing form?
   a. 90 days from today
   b. July 1, 2008
   c. Until property is sold
   d. Until seller decides to cancel

4. Issuing a real property disclosure statement
   a. relieves a builder of further liability for property condition.
   b. does not relieve the builder of new home warranties or contractual obligations.
   c. relieves a builder of new home warranties but not any contractual obligations.
   d. relieves a builder of contractual obligations but not any new home warranties.

5. In Virginia, all of the following must be disclosed *EXCEPT*
   a. material property defect known to seller.
   b. recent death on the property.
   c. broker's discovery of faulty wiring in basement.
   d. recent damage from leaky roof.

6. Which of the following circumstances is expressly forbidden to be disclosed to a prospective buyer?
   a. A triple murder occurred on the property.
   b. The seller's husband committed suicide on the property.
   c. An occupant of the property recently died of AIDS.
   d. Two ghosts have frequently been seen in the attic.

7. The responsibility for obtaining information regarding released sexual offenders in a community rests with the
   a. seller.
   b. buyer.
   c. listing broker.
   d. selling broker.

8. All of the following are exempt from the Residential Property Disclosure Act *EXCEPT*
   a. a foreclosure sale.
   b. a sale by an uncle to his niece.
   c. conveyance of a primary residence from one former spouse to another under a divorce settlement agreement.
   d. a sale by a real estate licensee of a two-unit residential property.

9. A real estate broker representing the seller knows that the property has a cracked foundation and that its former owner committed suicide in the kitchen. The broker must disclose
   a. both facts.
   b. the suicide, but not the foundation.
   c. the cracked foundation, but disclosing the suicide could constitute a breach of duty to the client.
   d. neither fact.

10. A seller of residential real property must disclose

a. known adverse material defects of the property.
b. property defects that would be revealed by a reasonably diligent property inspection.
c. no property defects.
d. known or suspected property defects.

CHAPTER 3

Interests in Real Estate

■ EMINENT DOMAIN

In Virginia, the power of eminent domain is provided by the state constitution and statutes. Virginia law provides that easements, ingress and egress rights, flowage rights, and all similar rights and uses constitute "property." As a result, just *compensation must be paid* if they are taken or damaged by the Commonwealth through the power of **eminent domain,** sometimes referred to as a *taking*. This process is called *condemnation*.

Just compensation means the fair market value of the property at the time of the taking. Payment of just compensation is a prerequisite to passing of title to the property. In addition, the Commonwealth must have made a genuine but ineffectual effort to purchase the property directly before beginning condemnation proceedings.

If the parties do not agree on what constitutes just compensation for the land, commissioners are appointed to hold a hearing and determine the amount. Virginia's Condemnation Act provides for a two-stage proceeding. First, the court determines the fair market value of the land taken and the damage, if any, to the remaining land. Second, if payment occurs, the court determines the rights and claims of all persons entitled to compensation.

Disclosures

Real estate licensees are required to disclose to all interested parties that a condemnation is planned for a parcel or an entire area. If a seller is aware that a governmental authority has made an offer to acquire the property and that condemnation proceedings are contemplated, prospective buyers should be made aware of this information. Because condemnation can affect the value of both the condemned property and neighboring properties, it is an important consideration for buyers and sellers alike.

■ **FOR EXAMPLE** *O*'s property was condemned for street construction. This had an adverse impact on the value of *O*'s remaining property. However, the value of adjacent parcels increased as a result of the improved access provided by the street.

■ ESTATES IN LAND

Virginia recognizes all the major estates in land, such as fee simple and life estates; defeasible and determinable estates; and remainders, reversions, and the possibility of reverter.

■ DESCENT AND DISTRIBUTION IN MARITAL ESTATES

In 1991, the Virginia legislature abolished the concepts of dower and curtesy. The Augmented Estate and Elective Share Act [§64.1-16.1] defines to whom a deceased person's property is distributed if he or she dies **intestate,** that is, without having executed a valid will. Commonly referred to as the *law of descent and distribution*, this statute is similar to the old dower and curtesy statutes because it establishes the rights of ownership to property by a surviving spouse and others.

The statute defines **property** or **estate** as including

- insurance policies,
- retirement benefits (exclusive of Social Security),
- annuities,
- pension plans and deferred compensation arrangements, and
- employee benefit plans.

Intestate Distributions

This whole discussion of descent and distribution is a simplified overview of this complex law. (See the Code of Virginia, Table of Contents, Title 64.1 Wills and Decedent's Estates on the following Web site for more detailed information.)

WEB LINK @

http://leg1.state.va.us/cgi-bin/legp504.exe?000+cod+TOC

The term **intestate** indicates that a person has died without executing a will. The act defines the rights of natural children, adopted children, children by previous marriages, illegitimate children, children of surrogates, and children born by in vitro fertilization. Real estate licensees are cautioned that their involvement in real estate transactions involving part of an estate can open the door to complications that may arise from claims by the heirs.

If a person dies **testate,** that is, having executed a valid will, but fails to specifically devise or bequeath all of his or her property, the undistributed property is treated as if the person died intestate.

When a person dies intestate, distribution is made first to the surviving spouse. If there are children or their descendents, two-thirds of the estate passes to the children with the remaining third to the surviving spouse. If there is no surviving spouse or children, the estate is distributed in accordance with the Virginia Code rules of descent and distribution. (See Virginia Code Ann. §64.1-1.)

■ **FOR EXAMPLE** *D* died without having made a valid will. *D*'s estate, valued at $785,950, was distributed among *D*'s surviving spouse and *D*'s children (*X*, *Y*, and *Z*) as follows:

D's surviving spouse: $261,983.33 = ⅓ of $785,950

Children (*X*, *Y*, and *Z*): $174,655.55 each = ⅔ divided by 3 (*X*, *Y*, and *Z*)

If *D* had left a valid will disposing of $500,000 of the estate, the remaining $285,950 would be distributed to *D*'s spouse and children as follows:

D's surviving spouse: $95,316.67 = ⅓ of $285,950

Children (*X*, *Y*, and *Z*): $63,544.44 each = ⅔ of $285,950 divided by 3 (*X*, *Y*, and *Z*)

Although a surviving spouse could be named in a will to receive certain property and to be further entitled to receive a share of the surplus, it is possible for the spouse to renounce the will and claim an *elective share* of the augmented estate.

Augmented Estate

An augmented estate consists of the property, both real and personal, owned by the deceased at the time of death. This is *added to the value* of property transferred during the marriage to third parties without the consent of the surviving spouse, if it can be established that the deceased did not receive adequate and full consideration for the property transferred. The value of the augmented estate is the value that remains after the payment of funeral expenses, the cost of the estate administrator, and personal debts of the decedent.

Other items that *could be excluded from* the augmented estate include

- property owned by the surviving spouse;
- property owned by the decedent and another, with right of survivorship;
- property conveyed during the marriage with the consent of the surviving spouse;
- property acquired by the decedent in severalty, as a gift, by will or intestate succession from someone other than the surviving spouse; and
- property transferred prior to January 1, 1991, if such transfer was irrevocable as of that date.

If a claim for an elective share is made, the surviving spouse receives one-third of the estate if there are children. If there are no children or descendants of children, the surviving spouse is entitled to one-half of the estate. [§64.1 1-16]

A surviving spouse has the right to possess and occupy the principal family residence during the period of time that the estate matters are being settled, although the residence may be a part of the augmented estate of the deceased.

Abandonment

If a husband or wife willfully deserts or abandons his or her spouse until the death of the deserted spouse, the deserting spouse is barred from all interest of the other by intestate succession, elective share, exempt property, family allowance, and homestead allowance.

HOMESTEAD EXEMPTION

Under Virginia's homestead exemption, a householder is entitled to hold a certain amount of real or personal property exempt from unsecured debts. The total value of the property may not exceed $5,000, plus $500 for each dependent.

Only a householder or head of a family may have the benefit of the homestead exemption. A husband and wife living together may both be deemed householders if each contributes to maintaining the household.

The exemption does not apply against

- claims for the purchase price of the homestead property,
- mechanics' liens, and
- claims for taxes.

The claim to homestead must be made by deed in the case of real property or by an inventory under oath for personal property. The owner of the homestead may sell or encumber the homestead property.

The key words in the homestead exemption are *unsecured debts*. For instance, a credit card balance is an unsecured debt. On the other hand, because a mortgage or a deed of trust is secured by real property, it has priority over the homestead exemption. The property may be sold at foreclosure to satisfy a secured debt.

In addition to the homestead estate, the householder is entitled to hold certain other items of real and personal property exempt from sale for the satisfaction of a debt, such as a family bible, wedding and engagement rings, and a burial plot.

In certain circumstances, other items such as personal clothing, household furnishings, photographs, health aids, and occupational tools also may be declared exempt.

IN PRACTICE

A real estate agent may be unaware that a homestead deed has been filed. The exemption is usually revealed in a title search conducted by an attorney or title examiner. The agent should be aware that the filing could indicate financial difficulties or even pending bankruptcy, or that judgments may be recorded.

EASEMENTS

Creating an Easement

Simply put, an **easement** is a right to use someone else's land. The most common easement is a utility company's right to access and use a landowner's land (property) for the purposes of delivering the utility either to the landowner or other landowners.

An easement may be acquired by express grant or may be created by covenant or agreement. In Virginia, the owner of a dominant tenement may convey the land without the easement. Where the easement is not an **easement by necessity,** that is, not necessary for access to the property, and the appurtenance is expressly excluded by the grant, it will not convey. When a grantor conveys land by a deed

TABLE 3.1

Easement by Prescription versus Adverse Possession

Criteria	Easement by Prescription	Adverse Possession (see Chapter 8)
Use of the property	Use of the property occurs with the knowledge and acquiescence of the landowner	Use of the property is hostile and without the true owner's permission
Prescriptive period	20 years	15 years
Tacking allowed?	Tacking is permitted	Tacking is NOT permitted

that describes the property as bounded by a road or street that the grantor owns, the grantor is implying that a right-of-way exists. The grantee acquires the benefit of the easement automatically.

If the width of a right-of-way is not specified in the grant, it is limited to the width as it existed at the time of the grant. If an easement has a definite location, it may be changed with the express or implied consent of the interested parties. The change may also be implied by the parties' actions.

If the grantor reserves an easement in the property conveyed, the reservation must be expressly stated.

Easement by Prescription

An **easement by prescription** is somewhat similar to the acquisition of property by adverse possession and the two terms are often confused. An easement by prescription differs from adverse possession in significant ways, as shown in Figure 3.1.

In an action to establish an easement by prescription in Virginia, the court must find that use of the property was

- adverse,
- under a claim of right,
- exclusive,
- continuous,
- uninterrupted, and
- with the knowledge and acquiescence of the landowner.

In Virginia, the prescriptive period is 20 years. **Tacking**—combining successive periods of continuous uninterrupted use by different parties—is permitted in Virginia.

When an easement is terminated, no document needs to be recorded in the clerk's office of the county where the land is located.

QUESTIONS

1. Which of the following does *NOT* constitute the exercise of eminent domain by the process of condemnation?
   a. A county taking a farmer's cropland for a highway
   b. The state taking from a private woodland for the construction of a roadside visitor center
   c. A county zoning ordinance change
   d. Port Authority of Hampton Roads taking riparian rights for a pier

2. For condemnation purposes, *just compensation* means
   a. fair market value at the time of the taking.
   b. fair market value at the time of purchase by the current owner.
   c. fair market value less court costs and attorneys' fees.
   d. a statutory percentage of fair market value.

3. What must happen before a condemnation suit is initiated?
   a. The owner and the government must agree.
   b. A genuine but ineffective effort to purchase must be made.
   c. The owner must have the property appraised.
   d. A statement of alternative solutions to the taking must be supplied to the owner by the condemning authority.

4. What is the status of dower and curtesy rights in Virginia?
   a. Dower and curtesy rights have been abolished.
   b. Dower is a fee simple estate; curtesy is a life estate.
   c. Dower and curtesy are identical rights in fee simple.
   d. Dower and curtesy have been combined by statute into one right.

5. *J* dies intestate. This means that she
   a. died penniless.
   b. left a will leaving everything to her dog.
   c. died without executing a will.
   d. died in a different state from her legal residence.

6. All of the following items could be *excluded* from G's augmented estate *EXCEPT* a
   a. condominium owned by G's wife S.
   b. small farm willed to G by his grandmother.
   c. beach property sold with S's consent.
   d. 52-foot sailboat purchased during the marriage.

7. *P* is a single parent of three young children. *P*'s house is worth $275,000. What is the total maximum value of *P*'s homestead exemption?
   a. $5,000
   b. $6,500
   c. $70,000
   d. $75,000

8. Which of the following statements concerning the homestead exemption is *CORRECT*?
   a. Exemption is automatic; every homeowner has one.
   b. The homeowner's filing for homestead exemption indicates financial difficulties.
   c. The homestead exemption is protection against claims for taxes, mechanics' liens, and deeds of trust against the property.
   d. The family bible, wedding rings, and burial plots are in addition to the $5,000 exemption.

9. All of the following are true of an easement by necessity *EXCEPT*
   a. it must be an appurtenant easement.
   b. both the dominant and the servient estates must have at some time in the past been owned by the same person.
   c. the only reasonable means of access is over the servient estate.
   d. inconvenience is a basis for the easement.

10. G has a ten-foot easement through *H*'s forested lot for the purpose of walking to the bank of Otter River. G widens the path to 14 feet to accommodate his truck so he can launch his boat. *H* is furious. Which of the following is *true* in this situation?

a. G's original use was a right; *H* can do nothing.

b. The new use is hostile, and if not stopped within 20 years, it could become an easement by prescription.

c. The additional four feet is a reasonable extension of the original easement and must be granted.

d. If G uses the extension for ten years, the original easement is his through adverse possession.

CHAPTER 4

Forms of Real Estate Ownership

CO-OWNERSHIP

Joint Tenancy

Virginia's **joint tenancy** is similar to that of most other states, insofar as the four unities of time, title, interest, and possession must be present. However, Virginia's interpretation of *unity of interest* is that one joint tenant cannot be a tenant for life and another for years. Similarly, one tenant cannot be a tenant in fee and another a tenant for life. Joint tenancy is always created by an act of the parties, never by descent or operation of law.

The doctrine of *automatic survivorship* has been abolished in Virginia. The legislature intended to place joint tenants in the same situation as tenants in common as far as augmented estates were concerned. If the deed *expressly* creates a joint tenancy with right of survivorship, as at common law, then on the death of a joint tenant the entire estate continues in the surviving tenant or tenants. The surviving spouse of the deceased joint tenant has no liability, and the deceased's creditors have no claim against the enlarged interests of the surviving tenants. Property owners who wish to have a property pass at their death to particular persons frequently create a joint tenancy as a substitute for a will.

A tenant in common or a joint tenant who commits waste may be liable to the other cotenant(s) for damages. By statute, a joint tenant or a tenant in common may demand an accounting from a cotenant who receives more than his or her fair share of rents and profits from the property. Similarly, joint tenants or tenants in common who improve a common property at their own expense are entitled to file a partition suit to divide and sell the property to obtain compensation for the improvements. However, if one tenant makes improvements without the consent of the other, the amount of compensation is limited to the amount by which the value of the common property has been enhanced.

Tenancy in Common

In Virginia, **tenancy in common** may be created by

- an *express limitation* to two or more persons to hold land as tenants in common;
- a *grant* of part interest in one's land to another;
- a *devise* or *grant* of land to two or more persons to be divided between them;
- a *breakup* of estates in joint tenancy; and
- the *dissolving* of a tenancy by the entirety as a result of the divorce or mutual agreement of the parties.

A tenant in common may convey his or her undivided interest; however, a contract by one tenant in common relating to the whole estate is voidable by any cotenant who did not join in the contract.

A deceased cotenant's interest, in passing through his or her will or to his or her heirs, is subject to the statute of Wills and Decedents Estates, which protects the rights of the surviving spouse. (See "Augmented Estate" in Chapter 3.) Tenancy in common carries no right of survivorship, and the interest of the deceased does not automatically pass to a surviving cotenant.

Tenancy by the Entirety

Tenancy by the entirety is a special type of joint tenancy created between husband and wife. There is no right to partition or to convey a half interest. The tenancy is indestructible except by mutual agreement or divorce, in which case the tenancy by the entirety is converted into a tenancy in common.

Property held by husband and wife as tenants by the entirety is legally an asset of both parties. If one spouse contracts to convey the property, he or she cannot do so alone. The conveying spouse would be answerable to the would-be purchaser for the inability to perform.

IN PRACTICE

If a married woman has retained her maiden name, the deed should grant to, for example, "John Doe and Mary Jones, husband and wife, as tenants by the entirety," *not* to "Mary Doe, also known as Mary Jones."

Neither spouse alone may encumber the property. Any debts that could become liens on the property must be entered into jointly by both parties.

Community Property

There are no community property laws in Virginia.

LAND TRUST

Land trusts are permitted in Virginia. A **land trust** is a trust in which the assets consist of real estate. While the deed to a trustee may appear to confer full powers to deal with the real property and complete legal and equitable title to the trust property, the trustee's powers are in fact restricted by a trust agreement mentioned in the deed. The agreement typically gives the beneficiary full powers of management and control. However, even the beneficiary cannot deal with the property as if no trust existed. Land trusts generally continue for a definite term.

TENANCY IN PARTNERSHIP

A partnership may own real property, but each individual partner's interest is considered personal property. A partner is co-owner with the other partners of real property as a *tenant in partnership*.

Tenancy in partnership has the following features:

- A partner (subject to the partnership agreement) has an equal right with the other partners to possess the property for partnership purposes but may not possess it for any other purpose without the other partners' consent.
- A partner's right in a property is not assignable unless all the partners assign their rights in the same property.
- A partner's right in the property is not subject to creditors, except for a claim against the partnership itself. When partnership property is attached for a partnership debt, no rights can be claimed under homestead exemption laws by any partner or by the representative of a deceased partner.
- On the death of a partner, his or her interest in partnership property passes to the surviving partners. If the decedent was the last surviving partner, his or her right in the property vests in his or her legal representative. The surviving partner, or legal representative, has no right to possess the property for anything other than a partnership purpose.
- A partner can transfer property on behalf of all the partners if acting within the scope of the firm's business and purposes. Partners may transfer partnership property among themselves, provided all partners consent.

IN PRACTICE

Whenever a real estate licensee represents a buyer who is purchasing partnership-owned property, the licensee should have an attorney review the partnership agreement to ensure that a general partner with power to bind all other general partners executes conveyance. It is desirable to have a written resolution of the partnership authorizing the sale.

CORPORATIONS

A corporation may acquire and convey real property in its corporate name. A contract entered into by a corporation under an assumed name may be enforced by either party. If an instrument bears both a corporate seal and the signatures of the responsible corporate officers, it is presumed to be a corporate instrument, even if it lacks the required number of signatures or the corporate name.

IN PRACTICE

Anyone who purchases real estate from a corporation should require a written corporate resolution that duly authorizes the sale of property by the corporation.

PUBLIC OFFERING STATEMENTS

Some forms of ownership involve the use of a Public Offering Statement (POS). The sale of a cooperative, a condominium, or a time-share uses the POS to fully and accurately disclose the characteristics of the project. Additionally, the Virginia Property Owners Association Act may require the use of the POS.

COOPERATIVE OWNERSHIP

Cooperative ownership is governed by the Virginia Real Estate Cooperative Act. [§§55-424 through 55-506] The Real Estate Board (REB) is charged with administrative responsibility for the Virginia Cooperative Act. A **cooperative** is "real estate owned by an association, each of the members of which is entitled, by virtue of his [or her] ownership interest in the association, to exclusive possession of a unit."

Cooperative possession is evidenced by a proprietary lease. A cooperative has common elements and *limited* common elements; it is created by a *declaration of cooperative*, filed in the clerk's office of the circuit court in the district in which the real estate is located.

When an individual purchases a cooperative unit, he or she is purchasing shares in the corporation (considered personal property) and signing a proprietary lease that allows for use of that particular unit.

The cooperative association may adopt and amend bylaws, rules, and regulations; adopt and amend budgets; hire and discharge management agents; regulate the use, maintenance, and repair of common elements; impose charges; and exercise other powers conferred by the declaration and bylaws.

Unless otherwise provided by the cooperative declaration, the association is responsible for the common elements and the proprietary lessee is responsible for the individual unit. The association has a lien on the cooperative interest for unpaid assessments. Nonpayment of assessment may be cause for eviction and resale of the cooperative interest.

Sale of a Cooperative Interest

Before the contract for the resale of a cooperative interest is executed or before conveyance, the purchaser must be given, among other things, a proprietary lease, a copy of the declaration and bylaws, a copy of the rules and regulations of the association, and a certificate containing the following statements:

- Disclosure of the effect of any right of first refusal or other restraint on transferability
- The amount of the monthly common expense assessment, as well as any unpaid expense currently due or payable from the sale and from the lessee
- Any other fees payable by proprietary lessees
- Any capital expenditures anticipated by the association for the current and next two succeeding fiscal years
- The amount of reserves for capital expenditures designated for specific projects
- The most recent regularly prepared balance sheet and income/expense statement, if any, of the association
- The current operating budget of the association and other pertinent information
- Unsatisfied judgments and pending suits
- Insurance coverage
- Health or building code violations against the unit or common elements

- Remaining term of any leasehold estate and provisions for extensions or renewal, if any
- Disclosure that the Public Offering Statement (POS), if one was prepared, is available for inspection
- Deductibility of any real estate taxes and interest
- Restrictions in the declaration that may affect the amount received by the proprietary lease holder on sale, condemnation, or loss, to the unit or cooperative upon termination of the cooperative
- Certification that the association has filed the required reports to the REB

Alternately, the documents can be provided *after the ratification* of a contract when the contract is made contingent on the receipt of such documents and when it provides for the statutory rescission period to the purchaser.

In the case of an initial sale of the cooperative, the purchaser must be given a POS. The POS must be provided before conveyance and not later than the date of the contract. If this does not occur, the seller has a financial liability. [§55-483]

IN PRACTICE

In the sale of a cooperative interest, it is the seller's obligation to provide a buyer with the required information. The real estate licensee, however, may facilitate the transfer of information from the seller to the buyer as a service to the client.

Buyer's Right to Rescind

In Virginia, purchasers of a cooperative interest have certain rights to rescind the contract. There are two types of rescission rights: initial sale rescission and resale rescission. In an **initial sale**, the first time the cooperative interest is sold after the cooperative is established, the buyer has the right to rescind within ten days following ratification of the contract or after receiving the public offering statement, whichever is later. When a cooperative unit is *resold*, that is, by an owner to a buyer, the purchase contract is voidable by the purchaser until the certificate has been provided and for five days thereafter or until conveyance, whichever occurs first. [§55-484]

CONDOMINIUM OWNERSHIP

The REB is charged with the administrative responsibility for the Virginia Condominium Act. [§§55-79.39 through 55-79.103]

A condominium can be a multiunit structure, an attached single-family dwelling such as a town home, or a detached single-family dwelling. Even commercial properties may be condominiums. It is important to recognize that a **condominium** is a form of ownership and *not* a type of property or structure. The owner of property may convert his or her property to condominium status. The owner is referred to as the *declarant* because he or she must *declare* his or her intent to have the property considered a condominium.

The declarant must provide declaration instruments to the REB that include the following:

- Name of the condominium (the name must include the word *condominium*)
- Legal description of the property
- Plats and/or plans that identify each unit

- An exact description of the horizontal and vertical boundaries of each unit
- Designation and description of common elements and limited common elements
- Exact allocation of the undivided ownership interest in the common elements
- If the property is being converted from rental property, the name of each current lessee and the date his or her lease expires
- Any easements that exist or that will be created
- An exact description of any proposed alterations to any existing units or common elements

In addition, the declarant must submit a copy of the *bylaws* under which the condominium will operate. The bylaws shall be specific regarding such issues as

- the form of self-governance for the unit owners;
- whether there are to be trustees, a board of directors, or other officers;
- their exact duties and the means by which they are to be appointed or elected;
- the extent to which the governing or executive body may delegate responsibilities to a management agent;
- the accounting and management records that will be maintained;
- a schedule of meetings of all owners and of the executive body;
- statutory requirements for meeting notices (21 days); and
- the rules and regulations that will apply to all owners.

Condominium Public Offering Statement

The declarant must also provide a POS. The POS includes all declaration documentation and bylaws, as well as

- the name of the declarant;
- a narrative description of the condominium, including the number of units and future plans for the addition of more units;
- copies of the bylaws and any current management contracts, including a statement of the relationship between the declarant and the contractor(s);
- a statement of the overall status of any construction or improvements;
- any encumbrances, liens, or easements that affect the title;
- the terms and conditions of any financing offered to purchasers; and
- a statement of warranties, a statement of the declarant's obligation to complete planned improvements, and a statement identifying the common elements and any user fees.

Initial Sale of a Condominium Unit

At the *initial sale* of a condominium unit, the purchaser receives a copy of the POS along with the sales contract. The first purchaser of a condominium unit has the right to rescind a ratified contract, without penalty, within ten days, for any reason. The ten-day period begins with the date of contract ratification or on receipt of the POS, whichever is later. The right to rescind cannot be waived.

At closing, the purchaser acquires a fee simple interest in the individual unit and an *undivided percentage interest* in the common elements as a tenant in common with the other unit owners. At this time, the purchaser assumes responsibility for the individual unit purchased.

The declarant remains responsible for all unsold units and for the overall management and maintenance of the condominium development until 75 percent of the units are sold. At that point, responsibility for maintenance and management of the property shifts to the owners' association. The declarant becomes a member of the association as owner of the remaining units.

Voting Rights

Each unit owner has an assigned ownership interest and voting rights in the governance of the condominium. This interest is usually in proportion to the size of each individual unit and the amenities of the unit. The exact percentage of ownership interest is established in the declaration.

Bylaw Changes

The Condominium Act states that two-thirds of the total voting interest is required to change the bylaws.

Termination

Once a property has been declared a condominium, its status can be changed by abandoning or dissolving it; 80 percent of the voting interest must approve the termination of a condominium's status.

Statutory Lien Rights

The unit owners' association has a statutory lien on every unit for unpaid assessments levied against the unit. This lien is secondary to real estate tax liens and other liens recorded prior to the filing of the original condominium declaration.

Resale of a Condominium Unit

All unit owners have the right to resell their individual units. In the event of an intended resale, the seller must obtain certain documents from the unit owners' association. These documents are collectively called the *resale certificate*.

The unit owners' association shall furnish the resale certificate upon the written notice request of any unit owner within 14 days of the receipt of such request. Payment of actual costs of preparing the resale certificate may be required of the unit owner requesting it as a prerequisite to its issuance, but the total fee shall not exceed $0.10 per page in copying costs or a total of $100, including and not in addition to, any fee charged pursuant to subsection H of §55-79.84 (Lien for assessments) and §55-79.85 (Restraints on alienation), for all costs incurred in preparing the resale certificate.

However, the unit owners' association may

1. upon mutual agreement with the seller, collect for actual costs incurred, in addition to any fee charged pursuant to this subsection,
   - a rush fee, not to exceed $25, for furnishing the resale certificate within three business days from the actual receipt of the request;
   - the actual cost of any mailing or delivery requested by the seller pursuant to this subsection; and
   - any actual cost incurred at the request and with the consent of the purchaser; and
2. collect a reasonable fee for preparing the resale certificate, not to exceed $325, if the amount of the fee
   - reflects actual cost;
   - is established in the contract between the unit owners' association and any managing agent; and
   - is disclosed on the unit owners' association Web site or the Web site of its managing agent.

Neither the unit owners' association nor its management agent, if any, shall require cash or certified funds unless the unit owner is delinquent in any payments due to the unit owners' association in excess of 30 days, or if a check of the unit owner made payable to the unit owners' association was returned for insufficient funds within the last six months.

New legislation allows buyers to electronically deliver notice of cancellation under the POA and Condominium Acts.

The resale certificate shall be current as of the date specified on the resale certificate. This means that the seller may obtain the certificate in advance of any purchase contract and have it immediately available for the purchaser. The buyer's rights to receive the certificate and to cancel the contract are waived if the right is not exercised prior to settlement.

Right to Rescind

The purchaser also has a statutory right to request an update of the certificate prior to settlement. If there are one or more material changes to the certificate, the contract may be voided by the purchaser.

The certificate must be provided to the purchaser. The purchaser may cancel the contract under the following conditions:

- Within three days after the date of the contract if the certificate was provided to the purchaser on or before the date that the purchaser signs the contract
- Within three days after receiving the certificate if hand-delivered
- Within six days of the postmark date if the certificate is mailed

The buyer also has the right to void the contract if the certificate does not include the following disclosures:

- The unit is located in a community subject to the Condominium Act
- Seller is required to provide the buyer with a resale certificate from the owner's association
- Buyer may cancel the contract within three days after receiving the resale certificate (six days from date of postmark if sent by U.S. mail)
- Buyer has the right to request an update of the resale certificate
- The right to receive the resale certificate and the right to cancel the contract are waived if not exercised before settlement

Condominium Disclosure Packet

The documents required in the resale certificate include the following statements:

- Unpaid assessments against the unit
- Any assessments in addition to the regular assessment for both the current and succeeding fiscal years
- Assessments currently imposed by the association relative to the unit and common elements
- Identification of other entities for which the unit owner may be liable
- Status of reserve and replacement funds
- The most recent budget and financial reports of the association
- Any unpaid judgments or pending suits to which the association is a party
- Specific details of the association's insurance coverage

- Declaration that any improvements made to the individual unit or to the limited common elements comply with the condominium instruments
- Current copy of the bylaws and rules and regulations
- Whether the condominium is located within a development subject to the Property Owners' Association Act (POA Act)
- A copy of the notice to the current unit owner of any current or pending rule of architectural violation
- Certification that the association has filed the appropriate reports to the REB
- Any occupancy limitations

TIME-SHARE OWNERSHIP

Following are two types of **time-share ownership** recognized by the Virginia Time-Share Act [§55-360 et seq.]:

1. *Time-share estate* means a right to occupy a unit, or any of several units, during five or more separated time periods over a period of at least five years. The time-share estate includes renewal options, coupled with either a freehold interest or an estate for years, that is, a lease, in all or part of a time-share project.
2. *Time-share use* means a right to occupy a time-share unit or any of several time-share units, during five or more separated time periods over a period of at least five years, including renewal options, *not coupled with* a freehold estate or an estate for years in a time-share project. Time-share use does not mean a right subject to a first-come, first-served, space-available basis such as exists in a country club, motel, or health spa.

The REB is charged with the administrative responsibility for the Time-Share Act.

Creation of a Time-Share

The developer of a time-share project must file and record with the REB a time-share *project instrument* that defines the project being created. This process establishes a time-share association in accordance with the Virginia Nonstock Corporations Act. [§13.1-801]

A time-share association must be set up before any time-share estates may be sold. The project must be named, and the name must include the words *time-share*, *time-share interest*, *interval ownership*, *vacation ownership*, or other terms recognized in the industry.

Some of the items that are to be included in the project instrument include

- the name of the time-share project;
- the complete address and legal description of the project;
- a description of the property;
- identification of the time periods;
- identification of the time-shares and the method by which additional time-shares may be created;
- the method used to allocate common expenses and voting rights assigned to each time-share;

- restrictions on use, occupancy, alteration, or alienation;
- the method by which the managing entity will provide maintenance of the time-share, if maintenance is to be provided; and
- provisions for amending the time-share instrument.

Time-Share Public Offering Statement

The POS filed for a time-share project is similar to the POS filed for a condominium. The developer may not convey any interest or advertise the property until the POS has been approved. If the time-share is being converted from another type of ownership, additional information is required regarding repairs made during the preceding three years and the physical condition of the structure. The purpose and value of reserve funds must be disclosed.

If the property to be converted is currently leased, tenants must be given 90 days' notice of the intent to convert the property to a time-share project. The tenants then have 60 days in which to contract with the developer to purchase the unit currently occupied if that unit is to be part of the overall project. Tenants on month-to-month leases must be given 120 days' notice to vacate.

Right to Rescind

The purchaser of a time-share interest at the project's *initial sale* has seven calendar days from execution of contract in which to cancel the contract without penalty. The developer is required to deliver the POS to the purchaser *prior* to the execution of the contract. The cancellation period commences on the date of contract ratification. If the seventh day falls on a Sunday or legal holiday, the right to cancel will expire on the day following the Sunday or legal holiday. The purchaser's right of cancellation cannot be waived, which must be identified in the contract.

Further, if there are material changes to the POS prior to settlement and after the initial time of contracting to purchase, the developer must provide the purchaser with the amended statement. The purchaser's right of cancellation is reinstated.

Deposits

Money received by the developer as earnest money deposits or down payments must be placed in an escrow account established by the developer and held there through the rescission period. The developer also must post a surety bond with the REB in the amount of $25,000 or the amount of the deposits received, whichever is greater. If any purchaser exercises the statutory right of rescission, the developer has 45 days in which to refund all monies paid by the purchaser.

Advertisements

Advertisements used for the marketing of time-share interests that offer gifts or prizes must clearly disclose the retail value of the gift or prize offered. The ad must also disclose the terms and conditions under which the gift is offered, the odds of actually winning a prize, and the number of gifts or prizes to be awarded. The ad must include the offer's expiration date and a statement that the offer is made for the purpose of soliciting the purchase of a time-share estate.

Transfer of Control

The developer remains in control of the project until 90 percent of the time-share estate has been sold or when all amenities and facilities have been completed, whichever is later. This is referred to as the *developer control period*. The developer control period may not exceed ten years after the sale of the first time-share interest. At the conclusion of the developer control period, the time-share owners' association assumes control and responsibility for the management and maintenance of the project. The developer must transfer control of the project to the owners' association without charging any fee. The owners' association may appoint or elect a managing agent for the project.

The owners' association has a statutory lien on every time-share estate in the project for unpaid regular and special assessments.

Beginning in the second year of owners' association management of the time-share project, the association must file an annual report with all owners. The report includes financial statements of the association, a list of officers and/or directors, and projected assessments for the coming year. The bylaws of the association may be changed by a vote of the owners. Should the owners decide to terminate the time-share project, approval by 51 percent of the voting interest of the association is required.

Resale of Time-Share

A *resale* of a time-share interest by any person other than the developer is subject to rules similar to those governing the resale of a condominium. The seller must obtain a *Certificate of Resale* from the owners' association. The certificate contains a copy of the time-share instruments; current financial statements; current bylaws; current rules and regulations of the association; fees and assessments; a disclosure of any liens that may be pending on the time-share for nonpayment of fees; and a statement of pending litigation against the developer, owners' association, or managing entity relative to the time-share project. The association may charge up to $50 for the certificate of resale.

The buyer in a time-share resale has the right to rescind the contract within five days following receipt of the certificate of resale or actual transfer, whichever occurs first. This right is without penalty and may be for any reason. Once the contract has closed, however, all rights of rescission are waived.

Statute of Limitations

Any action for misrepresentation of information in the project instruments, the POS, or any contract must be initiated within two years of the date of the contract.

VIRGINIA PROPERTY OWNERS' ASSOCIATION ACT

The Virginia POA Act [§55, Chapter 26] sets forth requirements for the formation and operation of the property owners' association. Each association subject to the act is governed by covenants, deed restrictions, POSs, bylaws, and other restrictions designed to manage, regulate, and control the specific development, community, subdivision, or neighborhood and their common areas, if any. The specifics of the various governing documents vary among associations.

The REB is charged with the administrative responsibility for the Virginia POA Act.

An association may be either self-managed or an independent management company may be employed to manage the affairs of the association. The act allows for a board of directors that may consist of property owners, developer representatives, and even representation from the independent management company, if used. Actions of the board, meetings, records, budgets, reports, and other association functions are governed by the act and the specific association documents. The board has the power to establish, adopt, and enforce rules with respect to the use of common areas and/or other areas of responsibility as established in the original declaration. A majority of votes from a quorum of the property members is usually required to repeal or amend rules and regulations. Violations of rules and regulations by the member property owner may result in the member being suspended from use of the common area facilities.

Property owners may be assessed routine fees, as allowed by the association documents, for the maintenance and upkeep of the association and common areas. Special assessments may be levied by the association. These special assessments usually require a majority vote of the property owners in accordance with the association's bylaws. Failure of a property owner to pay the authorized assessments entitles the association to place a lien on the property. [§55-516]

Exemptions

Condominiums, cooperatives, time-shares, and campgrounds are exempt from the act. However, if one of these types of ownership is located within an area that has been declared to be under the POA Act, the property is subject to both sets of regulations.

Disclosure Requirements

Because each association may impose certain restrictions and fees on the member property owners, potential purchasers must receive sufficient information prior to settlement about the association in order to make an informed decision to continue with the purchase. Therefore, any party who sells property subject to the act must include a statement *in the sales contract* to the effect that

- the property is located in a development that is subject to the POA Act;
- the act requires that the seller obtain a disclosure packet from the POA and provide that packet to the buyer;
- the buyer may cancel the contract within three days after receiving the packet or being advised that the packet will not be provided;
- the buyer has the right to request an update of the packet; and
- the rights to cancel the contract are waived if those rights are not exercised prior to closing.

If the contract does not contain these disclosures, the sole remedy for the buyer is to rescind the contract prior to closing. [§55-511]

POA Disclosure Packet

The information in the POA disclosure packet must be current as of the date of the packet. This allows the property owner to have a packet available for the buyer at the time of contract.

The association is required to make the packet available within 14 days after an owner/member, or an owner/member's authorized agent, files a written request. The association may charge a fee reflecting the actual cost for preparation of the packet but shall not exceed ten cents per page for copying or a total of $100 for all costs incurred. [§55-512C] The association's failure to deliver the packet in a timely manner waives any claim for delinquent assessments or fines. The maximum liability to the association for failing to provide the packet in a timely manner is actual damages, not to exceed $500. [§55-512E]

Contents of the POA Disclosure Packet

Each disclosure packet must include the name of the association plus the name and address of the registered agent, if incorporated. The packet must also include

- a statement of all assessments, fees, or charges currently imposed plus any planned expenditure that would result in additional assessment;
- a copy of the current budget plus statement of income and expenses or financial condition for the past year;
- any pending suit or unpaid judgment;
- a statement of what insurance coverage is provided for lot owners and what is expected of each individual lot owner;
- plans for any alteration of lot or uses of common areas;
- any restrictions on the placement of For Sale signs or flags;
- a copy of the current declaration, articles of incorporation and bylaws, and all rules and regulations or architectural guidelines adopted by the association;
- any current or pending violation of rules by the current owner; and
- certification that required reports have been filed with the REB.

An informational form prepared by the REB must accompany all POA disclosure packets. The purpose of this form is to describe the special circumstances and the relationship between lot owners and the association in order to educate the prospective purchasers and foster a better understanding between the property owners and the association.

Purchaser's Right to Request Update

The purchaser may submit a copy of the contract to the association with a request for updating of the disclosure packet. The association must respond within ten days and has the right to charge the purchaser a fee for preparation of the new packet that reflects the actual cost but not to exceed $50. [§55-512B] The purpose of this request for update of the packet is to both assure the buyer that there have been no changes and to identify the specifics of any material changes. If there have been any material changes, the buyer has no recourse for cancellation of the contract unless that right had previously been agreed on in the purchase contract.

IN PRACTICE

When purchasing a property bound by a POA, it is wise to include terms in the contract allowing the purchaser to request an update and to be able to void the contract if an update to a previously provided POA packet is not forthcoming within a specified period of time.

Purchaser's Right to Rescind

The purchaser has the right to cancel the contract

- within three days after the date of the contract, if the packet or notice that the packet is unavailable was provided before signing of the contract; *or*
- within three days after receiving the packet or notice that the packet is not available (if hand-delivered); or
- within six days after the postmark date of either the packet or the notice that packet is not available was sent by U.S. mail.

The purchaser may also cancel the contract any time prior to settlement if not notified that the disclosure packet will not be available nor the packet delivered.

If the purchaser elects to rescind, the notice of rescission must be hand-delivered or sent by U.S. mail, return receipt requested, to the owner. Rescission is without penalty, and the purchaser is entitled to a full refund of any earnest money given. Any rights to rescind the contract must be exercised prior to closing.

A complete discussion of interests in real estate in Virginia may be found in the Code of Virginia, Title 55—Property and Conveyances; see the table of contents, Title 55, at the following Web address.

WEB LINK

@

http://leg1.state.va.us/cgi-bin/legp504.exe?000+cod+TOC

QUESTIONS

1. *B*, *J*, and *E* own a parcel of property as tenants in common. *E* sells the entire parcel to *D*. Which of the following is *TRUE* of this situation?
   a. *D* is now a tenant in common with *B* and *J*.
   b. *D* owns the parcel in severalty.
   c. *B* or *J* can void the contract, but *E* is bound.
   d. The contract is void; no one is bound and nothing conveys.
2. How is a joint tenancy created in Virginia?
   a. By an act of the parties
   b. By operation of law
   c. By dissolution of a tenancy in common
   d. By all of the above
3. G and B own real property as joint tenants with right of survivorship. G dies owing money to creditors. Which of the following is *CORRECT?*
   a. B owns the property in severalty and is liable to the creditors.
   b. B owns the property and is not liable to the creditors.
   c. B owns the property except for a share owned by the creditors that represents the debts' percentage of the property value.
   d. G's wife owns the property interest held by her husband and is liable for the debts incurred by her husband.
4. B and M own land as tenants by the entirety. B signs a contract to sell his share of the property to *J*. Based on these facts, all of the following are *TRUE, EXCEPT*
   a. B cannot sell his half-interest.
   b. While the contract appears valid, B cannot perform under the contract.
   c. *J* could hold B answerable for his inability to perform under the contract.
   d. M is now the sole owner of the land.
5. Which of the following is *TRUE* regarding Virginia's community property laws?
   a. Since 2001, the Virginia statute is patterned after California's.
   b. Virginia recognizes only some community property provisions.
   c. Augmented estates are the same as community property provisions.
   d. Virginia is not a community property state.
6. M and H are partners in a successful accounting practice. They are in the process of purchasing a small office condominium for their practice. They would *NOT* be able to take title as
   a. tenants by the entirety.
   b. tenants in common.
   c. joint tenants.
   d. tenants in partnership.
7. Which of the following is necessary for a corporation to convey property by deed?
   a. Corporate seal
   b. Corporate seal and signatures of corporate officers
   c. Corporate name and required number of signatures
   d. Notarization
8. When a person wants to create a condominium, which of the following statements is *CORRECT?*
   a. The structures on the property being declared a condominium must be at least two stories.
   b. A condominium regime can only be created on unimproved land.
   c. The word *condominium* must appear in the name of the property.
   d. A condominium regime can be created only for residential use.

9. Contracts for the *initial* purchase of a condominium may be rescinded without penalty how many days after the later of contract ratification or receipt of the POS?

   a. Five days
   b. Ten days
   c. 14 days
   d. 21 days

10. If a condominium unit owner fails to pay the owners' association's assessment against his or her unit, the owners' association may

    a. place a lien against the unit.
    b. garnish the owner's wages.
    c. do nothing; as a stockholder, the unit owner has priority.
    d. revoke the unit owner's privileges and rights.

11. Some of the owners of the Riverview Condominium have decided they would like to dissolve the condominium status of the property. What vote will be necessary to do this?

    a. Majority of owners
    b. 75 percent
    c. 80 percent
    d. Cannot be done

12. *B* has a ratified contract to purchase a two-bedroom condominium unit from *T*. *B* is now suffering from "buyer's remorse" and wishes to back out of the contract. She has not yet received the condominium documents. After hand-delivery of the documents, she will have how many days to cancel the contract?

    a. Three days
    b. Five days
    c. Seven days
    d. Ten days

13. *H* is the owner of a time-share unit, which he bought several years ago from the developer. On March 2, *H* accepts an offer from *J* to buy the unit. On March 4, *H* hand-delivers the certificate of resale to *J*. On April 12, *H* transfers ownership of the unit to *J*. If *J* should decide to rescind the contract, what is the latest date when *J* may do so without incurring a penalty?

    a. March 7
    b. March 9
    c. March 15
    d. April 17

14. When the owner's interest in a time-share includes either a freehold interest or an estate for years, it is what type?

    a. Time-share use
    b. Time-share estate
    c. Time-share fee
    d. Time-share demise

15. *H* recently visited a brand-new time-share project on the Eastern Shore. If she decides to make an offer on the property, how long will she have to cancel the contract without penalty?

    a. None; *H* is bound to the contract
    b. Three days after ratification of contract
    c. Seven days after ratification of contract
    d. Ten days after ratification of contract

16. What is the statute of limitations on any action for misrepresentation of information as it applies to time-shares?

    a. Seven years
    b. Two years
    c. One year
    d. No limitation

17. M has decided she no longer wishes to purchase the town house which she currently has under contract. The town house is covered by the POA Act. M can cancel her contract

    a. whenever she wishes.
    b. within ten days after ratification of contract.
    c. within three days after receiving the POA disclosure packet.
    d. within 14 days after receiving the property disclosure packet.

18. *S* is six months behind in his POA fees. The association has the right to

   a. confiscate *S*'s property.
   b. place a lien on the property.
   c. sue S for punitive damages.
   d. change the locks on *S*'s house.

19. Both the Condominium Act and the Property Owner Association Act have a set limit on the amount that may be charged for preparation of the required document packet of

   a. $50.
   b. up to $325.
   c. actual cost of copying.
   d. any amount they choose.

20. The REB is charged with the administration of all the following *EXCEPT* the

   a. Property Owners' Association Act.
   b. Virginia Condominium Act.
   c. Virginia Time-Share Act.
   d. Virginia Residential Property Disclosure Act.

21. Which of the following *CANNOT* be true about a condominium?

   a. The dwelling can be a town house.
   b. The dwelling can be a single-family home.
   c. The unit owner obtains a fee simple interest in an individual unit and the common elements of the condominium.
   d. A unit owner may sell his or her unit on the open market and retain any profit from the sale.

22. *J* signs an agreement to purchase a condominium unit on April 1. On April 10, *J* receives the condominium documents and immediately requests an update to the condominium documents. On April 20, settlement day, the update has still not arrived. *J* can do which of the following?

   a. Rescind the contract and not settle and be in default
   b. Settle, wait for the documents, and rescind the contract after settlement
   c. Waive the condominium documents and proceed with settlement
   d. Request a postponement of the settlement pending receipt and acceptance of the update

23. Kito is about to submit a contract to purchase a single-family home in the Greenfall (PUD) subdivision in which homes have recently sold in record times. Kito's agent suggests some ways to make his offer more competitive with the other offers that are sure to come in. Which concession can Kito *NOT* make?

   a. Home inspection
   b. Appraisal
   c. Financing
   d. POA documents

24. Mohammed ratified a contract to purchase a single-family home located in the Forester subdivision (a PUD). The ratified contract does not contain a provision for the update of the POA documents, and the house has been on the market for three months. He receives the documents but waits four days to request an update so he can accept them. Which of the following is *TRUE*?

   a. The time for rescission of the contract has passed.
   b. He can rescind the contract with no penalty.
   c. He can demand an update under his statutory right.
   d. Mohammed's buyer agent exercised ordinary care.

25. A couple engaged to be married is planning to purchase a home prior to the wedding. They can take title in all of the following ways *EXCEPT* as

   a. tenants in common.
   b. joint tenants with survivorship.
   c. tenants by the entirety.
   d. joint tenancy.

CHAPTER 5

Legal Descriptions

DESCRIBING REAL ESTATE

The most common method of describing real estate in Virginia is a combination of the metes-and-bounds and lot-and-block methods.

Licensees should use great care in describing property. Both the real estate plat map and county or city tax records, as well as at least one deed by which the land was conveyed in the past, may be checked to verify that the proper legal description is being used. The description should enable the parties—or a court—to determine exactly what land the parties intended to convey. **Parol evidence,** that is, evidence of facts and circumstances not included in the deed or contract, is admissible in a court proceeding if the facts were well known in the community at the time the deed was made.

When two parties agree to form a contract, they attempt to write down all of the specific terms of the agreement (drafting the contract). Occasionally, however, one party later feels that all the terms of the agreement were not included in the written document and wishes to introduce evidence of prior oral agreements to alter the terms of the existing contract.

IN PRACTICE

A sales contract is mute as to the disposition of a dual-axle 24-foot camping trailer that is currently on blocks and tied down to the ground behind the house at the rear corner of the property. The wheels have also been removed and there is a cement patio in front of the camping trailer. In showing the property, the seller remarks that they rarely use the trailer anymore but they keep it tied down for insurance purposes when it's not actually in use on road trips. Lacking any exclusion of conveyance in the contract, the purchaser assumes that it now conveys with the sale.

In recent years, courts have been increasingly willing to admit parol evidence varying the terms of a written agreement. The modern approach is to interpret a formal document's language in light of all relevant circumstances, including the prior dealings between the parties and usages of the trade.

METHODS OF DESCRIPTION

The description of land by any of the following methods is legally sufficient, if the county or city and state are included:

- By courses and distances with an identifiable starting point **(metes-and-bounds method)**
- As bounded by natural or artificial objects or by the land of named persons **(monuments method)**
- By reference to a recorded map, plat, survey, deed, or other writing **(lot-and-block method)**
- By number or code on a recorded subdivision **(subdivision method)**
- By geodetic survey of townships, ranges, meridians, and so forth **(rectangular government survey method)**
- By house number and named street, where there is an established system of numbering (in many cases, this is not considered to be an adequate legal description because house numbers and even street names are frequently subject to change)
- By any name by which the land is generally known and identifiable
- As occupied or acquired by a named person at a definite time
- As being all the land of the grantor in a designated way or acquired in a specific way

FOR EXAMPLE This is a common property description:
All those certain lots, pieces, or parcels of land, situated in the city of Norfolk, Virginia, known, numbered, and designated on the Plat of Estabrook Corporation, made by S.W. Armistead, C.E., February, 1920, and recorded in the clerk's office of the Circuit Court of the City of Chesapeake, Virginia, in Map Book 17, page 4, as Lots No. 35 and 36, located on the North side of Amherst Street in Block "E" in said Subdivision known as Estabrook, and appurtenances thereunto belonging said lots being 25 x 100 feet each.

A shortened form is frequently used in listing agreements and sales contracts:
Lots 35 and 36, Block E, Plat of Estabrook, Norfolk, Virginia 23513, also known and described as 36 Amherst Street.

The following would also be an acceptable description:
All that land known as Warrens Crossing, as purchased by Nicholas Lilly on June 17, 1984, and bounded on the north by Richmond Hwy., on the south by Muddy Run, on the east by the farm belonging to John Evans, and on the south by the Redly Estate owned by Elizabeth Davies.

False Descriptions

A false description does not invalidate the deed if, after rejecting the false description, enough information remains to permit reliable identification of the land to be conveyed. A complete description can be found in the deed that conveyed the property to the seller. The identical description should be used to convey the land to the buyer.

Settlement of Disputes

Disputed boundaries between two adjoining lands may be settled by express agreement. Virginia law provides for a court proceeding to establish boundaries.

In conflicts concerning true boundaries, Virginia law gives preference to methods of description in the following order:

1. Natural monuments or landmarks
2. Artificial monuments and established lines
3. Adjacent boundaries or lines of adjoining tracts
4. Calls for courses and distances
5. Designation of quantity, such as "approximately 3.5 acres"

This preference will not be applied where it would frustrate the intent of the parties.

In disputes among purchasers of a lot shown on a plat, the metes-and-bounds established accurate survey and corresponding calls of courses and distances noted on the plat will supersede errors in the plat and will control dimensions and configuration of the lots.

SURVEYING AND SURVEYS

To engage in the practice of land surveying in Virginia, a person must hold a valid surveyor's license, unless exempted by the statute. Lenders are not allowed to require that a particular surveyor perform the survey in connection with making a loan to purchase real property. Surveys are recorded in the clerk's office of the circuit court where the land is located.

Four Types of Surveys

Following are four types of surveys commonly used in Virginia:

1. A **subdivision plat** is a map of each parcel of land. The plat shows subdivided lots, streets, and similar features. The plat is generally created from a tract of land to subdivide it. The subdivided lots may or may not be "staked on the ground" once the plat has been created.
2. A **boundary survey**, as opposed to a subdivision plat, shows the boundary or perimeter of the parcel as taken from and applied to the ground. Corner stakes or other physical landmarks appear.
3. A **house location survey** is a boundary survey with the location of the house shown.
4. A **physical** or **as-built survey** is a house location survey with all other physical features of the subject property shown, including water courses, utility lines, fence lines, outbuildings, and similar features.

A recently recorded survey of a subject property may reveal matters not shown in the record.

The attorney is primarily the person obligated to examine the survey. The following conditions suggest that potential problems may exist and should be brought to the attention of an attorney:

- Property boundaries that do not conform with the recorded plat

- Structural encroachments by the property onto neighboring properties, or by neighboring structures onto the subject property
- Fences that are not on the boundary line
- Party walls
- Riparian rights of others in streams, lakes, and other bodies of water
- Utilities that service other properties
- Old roadways
- Cemeteries
- Violation of setback, side, or rear building lines
- Property that may be landlocked

Any defect shown on the survey should be reported and corrective action taken where necessary.

Plat Maps

In areas of Virginia where recorded plat maps are used in lieu of individual surveys, the appropriate lot must be identified and lot dimensions must be legibly shown. Necessary endorsements to the title insurance policy must be issued pertaining to easements, deed restrictions, and property identification. The closing lawyer is responsible for obtaining the endorsements.

Subdivision Plat

In Virginia, a subdivision plat must contain all the necessary approvals of county or city officials. In addition, the dedications or consents of all owners, trustees, and other similar parties must be properly recorded. The law provides that the mere recordation of a plat transfers the streets, alleys, and other areas set aside for public use to the county or municipality in fee simple.

QUESTIONS

1. All of the following are satisfactory legal descriptions in Virginia, *EXCEPT*
   a. Lot 7, Block D, Plat of Red Valley, Martin County, Virginia.
   b. the entire 77.5 acres purchased by Edna Kelly on June 20, 1991, and known as Seaside Neck, Roanoke.
   c. 727 Olean Drive, Fletcherton, Virginia.
   d. proceeding 120 feet due west of the intersection of the east line of J Street and the north line of 11th Street to a point; thence north 10 degrees 31 minutes west 100 feet.

2. A deed contains the following description: *Lots 7 and 8, Block F, Section 3, Plat of Greydon, otherwise known as 14 Havers Drive, Venus, Virginia.* In fact, Block F has only six lots, and the street address is Lot 5. Is this deed valid?
   a. No; a false element in a description invalidates the deed.
   b. No; because the lot description is faulty, a new deed is needed.
   c. Yes, if the buyer knows which property is meant.
   d. Yes; enough correct information remains to permit identification.

3. *J* and *B* bought neighboring lots in a subdivision. The representation of the lots on the plat shows that *B*'s land reaches to a creek and *J*'s land falls just short of the creek. At the closing, a survey of the lots shows *J* with access to the creek and leaves *B* without access. Who prevails regarding access to the creek?
   a. *B*, because the original plat representation governs.
   b. *B*, because otherwise the developer is guilty of misrepresentation.
   c. *J*, because the survey supersedes errors in the plat.
   d. A new survey must be drawn giving both buyers creek access.

4. A lender wishes to use the services of only licensed surveyors and says he will *NOT* accept the surveys of unlicensed or nonexempt surveyors. Is this practice legal?
   a. Yes; a lender may use the services of either licensed or exempt surveyors, but the lender cannot require that a particular surveyor conduct the survey.
   b. Yes, as long as the surveyor holds a valid license.
   c. No; surveyors are selected by the clerk's office.
   d. Yes; the lender can require that a particular surveyor conduct the survey.

5. The survey for 1234 Grand Avenue shows the location of the house, the garage, the fence, utility lines, and the children's playhouse in the backyard. This is most likely which type of survey?
   a. Subdivision plat
   b. Boundary survey
   c. House location survey
   d. As-built survey

CHAPTER 6

Real Estate Taxes and Other Liens

TAX LIENS

Uniform Taxation

In Virginia, real estate taxes are levied according to the proportion designated by tax laws. The Virginia Constitution requires that taxation be uniform. Uniform taxation requires that both the tax rate and the mode of assessing the taxable value must be uniformly applied to similar properties, that is, all property of the same class must be taxed alike.

However, the principle of uniformity does not prevent differences in taxation or the classification for taxation purposes of properties according to use in a business, trade, or occupation.

Exemptions from Taxation

Burial grounds and cemetery lots owned by a cemetery company or by lot owners and used exclusively for burial purposes are exempt from taxation.

The Virginia Constitution exempts property owned and exclusively occupied or used by religious organizations for worship purposes or ministerial residences. The exemption applies to both real and personal property.

Property owned by public libraries or nonprofit educational institutions is exempt, as long as it is primarily used for literary, scientific, or educational purposes.

In addition, property used by its owner for religious, charitable, patriotic, historical, benevolent, cultural, or public park and playground purposes is also exempt.

The controlling factor in determining whether private property is exempt from taxation is the use of the property. Public property, however, may be exempted from taxation without regard to its use.

Assessment

Taxes run with the land. The buyer of a property is responsible for paying real estate taxes for the current tax year from the date of purchase until the end of the year. In Virginia, the buyer is said to own the property on the date of closing or settlement. Taxes should be prorated between the vendee (buyer) and vendor (seller) as of the date of the sale. Any delinquent taxes should be paid by the vendor at closing. Penalties and interest on delinquent taxes are established by statute.

IN PRACTICE

Unpaid taxes are a lien on real property. The settlement agent must verify that prior years' taxes have been paid and ascertain the status of the current year's taxes. Any other information should be obtained from city or county tax offices.

Taxes are generally not payable in advance of the due date. However, each city and county has its own particular manner of assessing taxes and setting the due date. Real estate licensees should be aware of four phases of taxes:

1. Past-due taxes
2. Taxes currently due and payable
3. Taxes not yet due
4. Prepaid taxes

The taxes for the first two phases will be collected from the seller's proceeds and paid to the proper authority by the settlement attorney. In the third and fourth phases, there are no taxes to be paid at the time a sale is closed. The closer will prorate the taxes between buyer and seller.

In phase three, the seller will be charged with the portion of the taxes that represents the number of days he or she occupied the property. The buyer will be credited with the same amount.

In phase four, where the taxes have been prepaid, the seller will receive a credit for the amount of taxes already paid for the period of time that he or she will not be occupying the property. The buyer will be charged with the same amount.

Estimating Taxes

Sometimes, past-year taxes cannot be used to estimate current taxes. On occasion a licensee may desire to prepare either a seller or buyer an illustration (through the use of a "Net Sheet") of the costs associated with the transaction. If this occurs, the licensee should obtain tax information directly from the tax assessor's office or from the owner's records.

New Construction

In the case of new construction, the taxes on the land are prorated based on taxes for the past year. The licensee should alert the purchaser that the taxes for the previous year are artificially low because they are based on the value of the land only and not the improvement (new home) recently constructed on it. Taxes on the new improvements are estimated using the purchase price multiplied by the county or city assessment rate. Taxes are estimated from the date the certificate of occupancy is issued, or a partial assessment may be levied against new construction not yet completed. Any additional tax bills should be presented to the settlement agent for proper disposition and prorating of additional taxes to be paid. The settlement agent can address the finalization of tax costs at closing.

Leases

As a general rule, the landlord under any ordinary lease is responsible for the taxes on the property; however, this does not apply to a perpetual leaseholder who is, in effect, the owner of the property and is entitled to its use forever. In such a case, the burden of taxation is placed on the lessee. In the case of net leases, the tenant is usually responsible for payment of the taxes.

Tax Liens

Delinquent real property taxes are both a personal debt and a lien against the property. A tax lien on real property has priority over all other liens except court costs. Thus, a tax lien overrides a vendor's lien, even though the vendor's lien may have been first. A tax lien is also prior to the landlord's lien for rent. The Virginia statutes give real estate taxes priority over a deed of trust in the distribution of proceeds under a foreclosure sale. The foreclosing trustee must satisfy all outstanding deficiencies before distributing the remaining proceeds to other creditors. If the statute's requirements are not complied with, delinquent taxes remain a debt against the purchaser at the sale.

A lien in favor of the United States for unpaid taxes, interest, and penalties may arise against all real and personal property belonging to a taxpayer. The lien is perfected under Virginia law by filing a notice of tax lien in the circuit court for the jurisdiction in which the taxpayer resides. The tax lien remains in effect until the taxes are paid.

When taxes on real estate in a county, city, or town are delinquent on December 31 following the third anniversary of the date on which the taxes became due, the real estate may be sold to collect the tax.

■ **FOR EXAMPLE** *G*'s property tax was due on June 10, 2002. *G* failed to pay. If the tax is still delinquent on December 31, 2005, *G*'s property may be sold for taxes on January 1, 2006.

At least 30 days before taking any action to sell the property, the tax-collecting officer must send a notice to the last known address of the property owner. Notice of the sale must be published in a newspaper of general circulation in the area 30 to 60 days prior to the commencement of the sale proceedings.

The sale proceedings are initiated by filing a suit in the circuit court of the county or city where the real estate is located. Owners of real estate, or their heirs, successors, and assigns, have the right to redeem the real estate *prior to the sale date* by paying all taxes, penalties, and interest due, plus costs, including the cost of publication and a reasonable attorney's fee set by the court. The former owner of any real estate sold for delinquent real estate taxes is entitled to any receipts from the sale in excess of the taxes, penalties, interest, and costs.

Special Assessments

There is a distinction between special assessments and general tax levies for purposes of funding government services and operations. **Special assessments** are taxes levied against specific benefited properties to pay for limited local improvements. They are founded on the theory of benefits brought about by improvements to adjacent properties. This public improvement enhances the value of a specific property—a sidewalk, for instance, or a repaved alley. A special assessment is distinguished from an improvement that benefits the entire community, such as a park.

The statute specifically provides that notice must be given to abutting landowners of the contemplated improvements before the ordinance authorizing the improvements is put into effect. This gives the landowner an opportunity to be heard concerning the adoption or rejection of such an ordinance. The statute provides for special assessments relating to sewers, street paving, and other local public improvements.

The only properties subject to special assessments are those of abutting landowners. Local improvements may be ordered by a town or city council (with costs to be defrayed by special assessment) following receipt of a petition from not less than three-fourths of the landowners who will be affected by the assessment. However, the council may issue such an improvement order without a petition.

The amount of special assessment for a local improvement constitutes a lien on the property benefited by the improvement, enforceable by a suit in court. Property owners have the right to appear before the municipal authorities and protest both the authorization of the improvements and the assessments. For a complete discussion of real estate taxes, see Code of Virginia, Table of Contents, Title 58.1—Taxation, at the following Web site:

WEB LINK @

http://leg1.state.va.us/cgi-bin/legp504.exe?000+cod+TOC

LIENS OTHER THAN TAXES

Mechanics' Liens

Anyone who performs labor or furnishes material with a value of $50 or more for the construction, removal, repair, or improvement of any structure has a right of lien on both the land and the building. The object of the law is to give laborers and materialmen the security of a lien on the property to the extent that they have added to its value.

The Virginia Mechanics' Lien Disclosure Act, Code of Virginia, Title 43, Chapter 1, requires that the seller of property disclose in the sales contract a warning that an effective mechanic's lien may be filed against the real property even after settlement.

The act's purpose is to protect contractors, brokers, purchasers, title agents, and insurers from builders or owners who contracted for improvements, sold the property, and never paid the contractor. The act requires that each residential sales contract include the following:

> NOTICE *Virginia law §43.1 et seq. permits persons who have performed labor or furnished materials for the construction, removal, repair, or improvement of any building or structure to file a lien against the property. This lien may be filed at any time after the work is commenced or the material is furnished, but not later than the*

> *earlier of (1) 90 days from the last day of the month in which the lienor last performed work or furnished materials, or (2) 90 days from the time the construction, removal, repair, or improvement is terminated.*
>
> *An effective lien for work performed, prior to the date of settlement, may be filed after settlement. Legal counsel should be consulted.*

While inclusion of the statement is mandatory, failure to include it will not void the contract.

A general contractor or a subcontractor may perfect a mechanic's lien by filing a memorandum of mechanic's lien and an affidavit with the clerk of court in the jurisdiction in which the property or structure is located. The filing must be within 90 days of the last day of the month in which the contractor last performed labor or furnished materials. However, under no circumstances may filing occur later than 90 days from the time the building is completed or the work otherwise terminated.

Written notice must be given to the owner of the property. The notice memorandum generally contains

- the name of the owner of the property;
- the name of the claimant;
- the amount of the claim;
- the time when the amount is due and/or payable; and
- a brief description of the property.

A mechanic's lien is enforced by a suit filed within six months of recording the memorandum of lien or 60 days from the completion or termination of work on the structure, whichever is later. If the person who ordered the work owns less than the fee simple estate in the land, only his or her actual interest is subject to the lien.

When a buyer constructs a building or structure, or undertakes repairs to an existing building or structure before the transaction has closed, the owner's interest will be subject to any mechanic's lien if the owner knows about the activity.

When a lien, such as a deed of trust, is created on land before work is begun or materials furnished, the deed of trust is a first lien on the land and a second lien on the building or structure. A deed of trust that is recorded before the work began is entitled to priority to the extent of the estimated value of the property *without improvements for which the lien is claimed.*

Typically, the seller must execute an affidavit at closing that declares no work has been performed or any materials furnished within 120 days before the date of closing. This declaration ensures that no mechanic can file a lien on the property after closing for labor performed or materials furnished prior to closing. Nonetheless, a buyer should be advised to obtain additional assurances that no mechanic's lien can be filed.

Closing agents are charged with the responsibility to advise buyers of possible mechanic's lien filings and must inform buyers about title insurance protection.

A lien waiver should be demanded for new construction stating that all amounts have been paid for labor performed and materials furnished in connection with the construction. The waiver should be executed by the general contractor and all subcontractors. However, no waiver is required if affirmative mechanic's lien coverage is provided by a title insurance company.

Judgments

Every money judgment rendered in Virginia by any court, or by confession of judgment, constitutes a lien on any real estate the judgment debtor owns or may own in the future. The lien is effective from the date the judgment is docketed, that is, indexed by the clerk of court. It is prudent to docket the judgment in the city or county in which the debtor's property is located. If the debtor currently has no property, it is wise to docket the judgment wherever property is located that may become the debtor's in the future (for instance, property owned by family members).

A writ of execution may be issued and the judgment enforced within 20 years from the date the judgment was rendered. A judgment may be extended beyond its 20-year life by a motion made in the circuit court, following notice to the judgment debtor and redocketing of the judgment.

If the real estate is conveyed to a grantee for value subject to a judgment lien, the judgment creditor must bring the suit to enforce the judgment lien within ten years from the date the grantee's deed was recorded.

If the judgment is for recovery of specific real property, a *writ of possession* is needed. If the judgment debtor owns real estate outside Virginia, the debtor may be required to convey it to a sheriff.

Within 30 days of the satisfaction, that is, payment of a judgment, a judgment creditor must release the judgment wherever it is docketed. Failure to do so within ten days of demand by the judgment debtor makes the creditor subject to a fine.

Estate and Inheritance Tax Liens

A lien arises on all property, real and personal, of every decedent who has a taxable estate located in the Commonwealth of Virginia if the decedent's estate fails to pay the tax imposed by the Virginia Estate Tax Act.

In the case of a nonresident decedent who has a taxable estate in Virginia, the lien arises automatically at the time of the nonresident's death. In the case of a resident decedent, the liens attach to the real estate only when a memorandum is filed by the department of taxation in the clerk's office of the county or city where such real estate is located. Once it attaches, the lien is enforceable for ten years from the date of the decedent's death.

In Virginia, the tax imposed is a *succession tax* rather than an estate tax: It is a tax on the right to succeed to the property or an interest in it, not the right to transmit it. The tax is not levied on the property of which an estate is composed but on the shifting of economic benefits and the privilege of receiving such benefits.

Attachments

The mere issuance of an attachment creates no lien on the real estate. To create a lien, it is necessary for the officer to show that levy (actual attachment or seizure) was made.

Lis Pendens

A **lis pendens,** or pending suit, does not bind or affect a subsequent purchaser of real estate unless a memorandum is properly recorded giving notice of the suit. The memorandum of notice states the title of the suit, its general object, and the court in which it is pending. The notice declares the amount of the claim, describes the property, and names the person whose estate is intended to be affected.

If the lis pendens is not docketed as provided by the statutes, a purchaser without notice of the pending suit takes good title, with no lien on the land by virtue of the pending suit.

Vendor's Lien

In Virginia, if any person conveys any real estate and the purchase money remains unpaid at the time of the conveyance, the vendor will not have a lien for the unpaid purchase money unless the lien is expressly reserved on the face of the deed. The object of this statute is to make the lien a matter of record, putting all persons who deal with the property on notice of all liens and encumbrances. The extent of the vendor's lien does not depend on the extent of the vendor's interest in the land conveyed but on the contract of the parties as gathered from the deed itself.

Landlord's Lien

The Virginia statutes give a landlord a right of lien. It exists independently of the right to hold property for payment of rent. When the landlord's lien for rent is obtained, it relates back to the very beginning of the tenancy and takes precedence over any lien that any other person has obtained or created against goods (personal property) on the leased premises since the tenancy began. A lien legally attaches to all property on the premises when it is asserted or on the premises within 30 days prior to attachment of lien. The landlord can seize the tenant's goods only to the extent necessary to satisfy the rent justly believed to be due.

Commercial Broker's Lien

A commercial real estate broker has a lien on the rent paid by the tenant in the amount of the compensation (commission) agreed on by the owner and the broker.

QUESTIONS

1. Which of the following is *true* of uniform real estate taxation in Virginia?
   a. Tax rates and assessments must be uniformly applied to similar properties.
   b. All properties pay the same amount of tax.
   c. Only the tax rate needs to be uniform.
   d. Uniformity is a common-law principle.
2. B's house is near the end of a block; right beside her house on the corner lot is Tasty Bakery. How must these properties be treated for real estate tax purposes?
   a. There can be no difference between them.
   b. They will be classified differently, according to use.
   c. A sliding value scale may be applied to businesses but not to residences, which are strictly ad valorem.
   d. Because the bakery abuts a residential zone, it must be treated as a residence.
3. All of the following types of real property are exempt from real property taxation *EXCEPT*
   a. burial grounds.
   b. government-owned land.
   c. land owned by nonprofit educational institutions.
   d. land owned by handicapped persons.
4. Which of the following statements is *TRUE* regarding taxes on new construction?
   a. Taxes are estimated using the purchase price multiplied by the state assessment rate.
   b. Taxes are estimated from the date of the certificate of occupancy.
   c. Improvements are not assessed as part of the previously existing property.
   d. The statutory appreciation rate is applied to new construction to estimate the current year's fair market value.
5. In Virginia, who owns a property (for real estate tax purposes) on the date of sale?
   a. The buyer owns it.
   b. The seller owns it.
   c. It is divided evenly, with each party paying half of the tax for that day.
   d. This item must be negotiated.
6. Which of the following liens would have *FIRST* priority?
   a. Deed of trust
   b. Mechanic's lien
   c. Property tax lien
   d. Landlord's lien for rent
7. *J* is relieved to learn that her home will soon be served by a city sewer line. How will this improvement most likely be paid for?
   a. General real estate tax
   b. Municipal bonds
   c. Special assessment
   d. State road-use tax
8. How long after the work was done may a mechanic wait before filing a mechanic's lien?
   a. No more than 30 days
   b. No more than 60 days
   c. No more than 90 days
   d. No more than six months
9. How soon after filing the lien must the mechanic enforce it by filing suit?
   a. Within three months
   b. Within six months
   c. Within nine months
   d. Within one year
10. Within what period of time must a creditor on a judgment enforce the judgment once it is rendered?
    a. Within six months
    b. Within one year
    c. Within five years
    d. Within 20 years

CHAPTER 7

Real Estate Contracts and Documentation

■ THE CONTRACT

The Code of Virginia allows real estate licensees—brokers and salespersons—to prepare written contracts for the sale, purchase, option, exchange, or rental of real estate as long as the contract is incidental to a specific real estate transaction and there is no additional charge for preparing the contract. [§54.1-2101.1] In some states, brokers and salespersons are not authorized to prepare contracts. In Virginia, the operative word is *incidental.* For example: While a licensee assists a buyer in a variety of functions, such as locating property, arranging financing, selecting a settlement agent, and so on, the preparation of the sales contract is incidental to the variety of services provided. In the situation of a seller who hires the licensee, the licensee performs a variety of services such as marketing the property, advertising, showing the property to buyers, and so on. As in the case of the buyer example, the preparation of the sales contract is incidental to the transaction. In a situation where either a buyer or seller contacts a licensee to merely prepare a sales contract for a fee, the licensee may be guilty of practicing law without a license because the preparation of the contract was not incidental to the transaction.

The actual contract used for the purchase and sale of real property may take any form. The only requirement is that it be in enough detail to clearly state the agreement between the parties.

Typically, a sales contract would contain information covering the list below:

- Real Property
  - Personal property, fixtures, and utilities
  - Equipment, maintenance, and condition

- Price and Financing
  - Deposit
  - Down payment
  - Loan application, approval, and appraisal
- Inspections
  - Access to property
  - Well and septic system inspection
  - Termite and wood-destroying pest inspection
  - Repairs
- Damage or Loss
- Title and Settlement
  - Conveyances, deed(s) of trust
  - Possession date
  - Settlement
  - Fees: broker's, attorney's, adjustments
- Disclosures and Notices

Local real estate associations often have standard sales contract forms to be used by their members. As business practices change and regulations increase, contract documentation and forms change to meet these new requirements; at one time a sales contract was one page! An example of a regional sales contract and its addendums, the NVAR Regional Contract, is contained in Appendix E. Contact a local real estate association or real estate school for information on how to obtain up-to-date contract forms.

It is customary for real estate licensees to assist buyers and sellers with the preparation of the contract by filling in the blanks on the form. *As with all legal matters, real estate brokers and salespersons should refrain from trying to explain the legal technicalities.* Improper or misunderstood explanations could subject the licensee to legal action later.

IN PRACTICE

As with the listing agreement form, all blanks should be filled in. If the item does not apply, the notation N/A (not applicable) should be inserted. Licensees should be careful if striking out whole paragraphs or sections of a contract because important beneficial language often can be inadvertently deleted. Licensees should use a proper addendum of clauses or amendments or a standard clause from an addendum of clauses to alter terms specifically spelled out in the contract.

Though the word *contract* may imply the use of a single document, in actual practice the average real estate contract for a given *transaction* is a series of documents, the most important of which is the actual sales agreement between the seller and the purchaser. Other documents and forms are typically added to the basic sales contract forms to meet compliance with federal, state, and local requirements for the sale and transfer of property. It is not uncommon for these pages of the transaction "contract" to exceed the number of pages in the standard sales contract (form). For instance, Virginia has a Property Disclosure Law, which requires that a disclosure be made as a part of the "contract." This disclosure is contained on a separate set of forms and is included with the "contract." The Environmental Protection Agency (EPA) requires a disclosure on all properties constructed prior to 1978 when lead-based paint was available for sale. This disclosure, too, is contained on a separate set of forms and is included with the "contract."

TABLE 7.1

Contract Form

Standard Form	# of Pages
Agency Disclosure: An appropriate disclosure for the type of agency used in the transaction is included.	1
Sales Contract: Contains the basics of the sales transaction between the purchaser and the seller.	10
Jurisdictional Addendum: Some contracts, such as the Regional Contract used by NVAR, require the use of a regional addendum for the appropriate jurisdiction.	5
Contingencies and Clauses Addendum: Special contingencies (e.g., home inspections, radon inspection, third-party approval, or postoccupancy agreements) and optional standard paragraph clauses are far too numerous to include in the standard sales contract.	3
Property Disclosure: Virginia Residential Property Disclosure	1–2
Lead-Based Paint Disclosure: Required by EPA if the property was constructed prior to 1978.	1
FHA Home Inspection Notice: If FHA financing is used, a notice of information on a home inspection is required.	1
Approximate Total Pages (minimum)	24

When new construction is involved, the entire contract package is typically provided by the builder, although some associations have published New Homes Sales Contracts. In a transaction that involves the sale of land, a contract specifically designated for that purpose should be used.

While it would be impractical to include every scenario in which a particular form would be required, Table 7.1 provides an indication of how certain forms might be included in a total contract package.

IN PRACTICE

A contingency to a contract must be satisfied, removed, or approved before the parties can move forward with the other terms of the contract. For example: a home inspection contingency typically permits the purchaser to inspect the property with the aid of a certified or licensed professional. The contract is then said to be *contingent* on a mutual resolution between the purchaser and the seller of the outcome of the inspection. If a mutual resolution cannot be reached, typically the contract dies (becomes void). For a contingency to be effectual, it must contain an expiration date and/or time plus a list or description of option(s) available to the parties. **Definition: contingency** *n* **1:** possibility, **2:** probability

■ STATUTORY CONTINGENCIES

Once a contract is prepared for presentation to the seller, certain conditions of the purchase can appear in the form of contingencies to contract on ratification. Typical contingencies include a home inspection or a well and septic system inspection. These contingencies, while important, are generated by the wishes of the purchaser or as a requirement of the lender. There are other contingencies, however, that are generated by statute. If a property is a condominium or is in a subdivision bound by a property owners' association (POA), the seller must provide the purchaser with an opportunity to review the condominium resale packet or POA disclosure packet regarding the referenced property. This requirement of the law automatically creates a contingency to the contract and must be afforded to the purchaser exclusive of any other terms or conditions of the contract. The contracts (form) prepared by real estate associations for use by their members includes "trigger" language for these types of contingencies.

Request for Property Owners' Association Disclosure Packet

The Virginia POA Act requires that the seller request and furnish the disclosure packet regarding the referenced property. By the provisions of Virginia Code Section 55-512 this packet must be delivered to the seller within 14 days of the request. Payment accompanies the request.

Request for Condominium Disclosure

The Virginia Condominium Act requires that the seller request the condominium resale packet regarding the referenced property and furnish it to the buyer. By the provisions of Virginia Code Section 55-79.97 this packet must be delivered within 14 days of the request. Payment may accompany the request, or in certain circumstances the fee will then be assessed against the unit and paid at settlement rather than in advance.

Disclosure of Lead-Based Paint and/or Lead-Based Paint Hazards

The ingestion of lead into the human body is a known neurological hazard. Prior to January 1, 1978, the sale of lead-based paint was common throughout the United States. Even though the sale of this paint is now banned, the potential for it being found still exists in properties constructed prior to the cut-off date.

Federal law requires the disclosure of lead-based paint and/or lead-based paint hazards for properties constructed prior to January 1, 1978. (See Figure 7.1.)

STATUTORY INCLUSIONS

Federal and state laws require that certain disclosures be made during the course of a real estate transaction. Although disclosures were covered in Chapter 1, the information is reiterated here because it is in the actual assembly of a sales contract that these documents again come into play. The average sales contract will contain the required statutory disclosures as proof that they were actually made to the parties to the contract, as required by law. Additionally, many firms and brokers require stricter standards than those required by laws of the state. These practices by some firms and brokers help to ensure maximum compliance with state regulations.

Disclosure of Brokerage Relationship

According to Virginia Real Estate Board regulations, a disclosure of brokerage relationship must be made to nonrepresented buyers on the first substantive discussion about a specific property. Good real estate practice dictates this be done prior to showing any property to a nonrepresented buyer.

Disclosed Dual Representation [§54.1-2139] In Virginia, a licensee may represent both parties in the same real estate transaction—seller and buyer or landlord and tenant—only with the written consent of all clients in the transaction. The client's signature on the written disclosure form is presumptive evidence of the brokerage relationship. The disclosure must be substantially in the same form as shown in Chapter 1, Figure 1.2.

A dual representative does not terminate any brokerage relationship by making the required disclosures of dual representation. [§54.1-2139C] As mentioned previously, a licensee may withdraw from representing a client who refuses to consent to disclosed dual agency. The licensee may continue to represent in other transactions the client who refused dual representation. [§54.1-2139D]

Designated Representation A principal or supervising broker may assign different affiliated licensees as *designated representatives* to represent different clients in the same transaction. The appointment of designated representatives excludes other licensees in the firm from involvement in the transaction. *The use of designated representatives does not constitute dual representation if each designee represents only one client in a particular real estate transaction.* [§54.1-2139E] The designated representatives are pledged to maintain all confidential information received from their clients. Such information may be shared with the principal or supervising broker, who remains in the position of a dual representative with equal responsibilities to both clients. The disclosure must be made in writing and must be similar to the form shown in Chapter 1, Figure 1.3.

Limited Services Representation [§54.1-2138.1]

A licensee may act as a limited service representative only pursuant to a written brokerage agreement. The limited service representative must disclose his or her status as a limited services representative and present in writing to the client a disclosure that compares the services he or she *will* provide with the duties required of a standard agent specifically listing the standard agency duties and services that he or she will *not* perform.

■ RESIDENTIAL PROPERTY DISCLOSURE DOCUMENTATION

The Virginia Residential Property Disclosure Act requires that the owner of residential real property consisting of not less than one nor more than four dwelling units, whenever the property is to be sold or leased with an option to buy, furnish to the purchaser a Residential Property Disclosure Statement. This requirement is effective whether or not the transaction is with the assistance of a licensed real estate broker or salesperson. Certain transfers of residential property are excluded from this requirement.

The disclosure statement provides that no warranties or representations are made by the seller as to the following items:

- Property condition
- Adjacent properties
- Historic ordinances
- Resource protection areas
- Information on registered sexual offenders
- Location in a dam break inundation zone

The seller does represent, however, that there are no pending building code enforcement actions involving the property. There must also be disclosure of

- location in a locality in which there is a military air installation, and

FIGURE 7.1

Lead-Based Paint Disclosure Form

SALE: DISCLOSURE AND ACKNOWLEDGMENT OF INFORMATION ON LEAD-BASED PAINT AND/OR LEAD-BASED PAINT HAZARDS

Lead Warning Statement

Every purchaser of any interest in residential real property on which a residential dwelling was built prior to 1978 is notified that such property may present exposure to lead from lead-based paint that may place young children at risk of developing lead poisoning. Lead poisoning in young children may produce permanent neurological damage, including learning disabilities, reduced intelligence quotient, behavioral problems, and impaired memory. Lead poisoning also poses a particular risk to pregnant women. The seller of any interest in residential real property is required to provide the buyer with any information on lead-based paint hazards from risk assessments or inspections in the seller's possession and notify the buyer of any known lead-based paint hazards. A risk assessment or inspection for possible lead-based paint hazards is recommended prior to purchase.

Seller's Disclosure (initial)

___/___ (a) Presence of lead-based paint and/or lead-based paint hazard (check one below):

☐ Known lead-based paint and/or lead-based paint hazards are present in the housing (explain):

____

____

☐ Seller has no knowledge of lead-based paint and/or lead-based paint hazards in the housing.

___/___ (b) Records and Reports available to the seller (check one below):

☐ Seller has provided the purchaser with all available records and reports pertaining to lead-based paint and/or lead-based paint hazards in the housing (list documents below):

____

____

☐ Seller has no reports or records pertaining to lead-based paint and/or lead-based paint hazards in the housing.

Purchaser's Acknowledgment (initial)

___/___ (c) Purchaser has received and had an opportunity to review copies of all information listed above.

___/___ (d) Purchaser has received the pamphlet "Protect Your Family From Lead in Your Home".

___/___ (e) Purchaser has (check one below):

☐ Received a 10-day opportunity (or mutually agreed upon period) to conduct a risk assessment or inspection for the presence of lead-based paint or lead-based paint hazards; or

☐ Waived the opportunity to conduct a risk assessment or inspection for the presence of lead-based paint and/or lead-based paint hazards.

Sales Associates' Acknowledgments (initial)

___/___ (f) Listing and Selling Sales Associates are aware of their duty to ensure compliance with 42 U.S.C. 4852d. These Associates have informed the Seller of the Sellers' obligations under this law as evidenced by Seller and Purchaser having completed this form.

Certification of Accuracy

The undersigned have reviewed the information above and certify that to the best of their knowledge the information they have provided is true and accurate.

SELLER: **PURCHASER:**

Date ___/______________(SEAL) Signature — Date ___/______________(SEAL) Signature

Date ___/______________(SEAL) Signature — Date ___/______________(SEAL) Signature

Date ___/______________(SEAL) Signature of Listing Associate — Date ___/______________(SEAL) Signature of Selling Associate

For the sale of the Property at:______________________________

NVAR - 1034 - 9/96

- availability of septic system operating permits.

On the first sale of a newly constructed dwelling the builder or owner must disclose all known material defects that would constitute a violation of any applicable building code. The builder or owner must also disclose property location in Planning District 15.

The old disclosure/disclaimer forms are no longer in use and do not comply with the law as of January 2008.

STATUTE OF FRAUDS

The English law passed in 1667 known as the Statute of Frauds requires that the transfer of real estate be in writing. Virginia contract law prevents the enforcement of an oral contract or promise. [§11.1] The statute does not invalidate oral contracts; rather, it addresses the contract's enforceability. The statute bars any action concerning a contract for the sale of real estate or for a lease on real property for *more than one year* unless the document is in writing. Although an oral lease for a term of more than one year is unenforceable and the parties cannot be compelled to perform, they are nonetheless free to make and comply with such an agreement. Further discussion of the Statute of Frauds may be found in the Code of Virginia, Title 8.2A-201 (Commercial Code).

CONTRACT PROCEDURES

Use of a standard form does not excuse the licensee from pointing out to both parties that the contract is a legally binding document and that legal advice should be sought if either party has legal questions. The parties may make the agreement contingent on review and approval by an attorney.

Power of Attorney

Sometimes, a party cannot be present at the closing and must be represented by an attorney-in-fact acting under a power of attorney. In Virginia, the power of attorney must specify the transaction and the parties involved; a general power of attorney will not suffice. The power of attorney must be notarized and recorded with the deed.

It is not a good business practice and perhaps may even be a conflict of interest for licensees to perform as attorneys-in-fact for their seller or buyer clients. It is best to suggest that the client engage a licensed attorney to serve as an attorney-in-fact. Additionally, if a buyer is using a power of attorney, the buyer should be counseled to consult with the lender and the settlement company to ensure that the power of attorney document will be acceptable for loan purposes.

IN PRACTICE

Many military notaries are from outside Virginia and may not comply with the requirements of the Virginia Code. Most settlement companies use their *own* form of power of attorney; always check with them first.

Spousal Consent

If property is owned in severalty *and the owner is married*, the seller's spouse should join in the contract so that no claims can be made later. If one or the other spouse does not sign, the courts will not order specific performance on the contract unless the buyer is willing to accept a deed that remains subject to the spousal interest. The buyer may still sue the seller for breach of contract because the seller could not convey the property with a clear title.

The capacity in which each signer executes the contract should be clearly stated. The contract should indicate whether the signer is an individual, a married couple, a partnership, a corporation, a limited liability company, or any other legal entity.

Title

The buyer under a real estate sales contract expects to receive marketable title to the property from the seller. "Marketable title" and "insurable title" are not necessarily the same because a title insurance policy may list exceptions against which it does not insure.

Equitable Title

When the buyer and seller have ratified, that is, signed, the sales contract, the buyer's interest is called **equitable title.** A buyer's equitable title gives the buyer an insurable interest in the property. While Virginia law places the risk of damage to the property during this period on the buyer, most sales contracts in Virginia provide that the seller bears the risk of loss. Licensees should ensure that this point is addressed in the contract.

WARRANTIES

As discussed in previous chapters, the principle of *caveat emptor*, "let the buyer beware," is still the law in Virginia regarding previously owned homes.

Buyers and sellers should ensure that the sales contract is sufficiently complete in order to provide for the identification and resolution of deficient items for which they may have concern should the need(s) arise. These actions should include, but are not limited to, property inspection contingencies, a lead-based paint inspection, other environmental inspections or reviews, exterior insulation finishing system inspections (EIFS), wood-destroying pests and moisture inspections, mold inspection, appropriate property reviews through the appraisal process, well and septic inspections, final walk-through inspections, and a number of other possible inspections as the situation dictates. Many real estate jurisdictions have local consumer disclosure forms that alert the buyer to issues that may be pertinent to the locale, such as a Megan's Law disclosure. If in doubt, buyers should insist on a study period (contingency) in the sales contract to provide sufficient time to investigate various issues.

Existing Homes

In most areas, the seller will warrant that the heating, plumbing, electrical, and air-conditioning systems are in normal working order at the time of settlement. The buyer usually has the opportunity for a walk-through inspection prior to settlement to verify that no material changes have occurred since the signing of the sales contract (such as storm damage, vandalism, or the removal of fixtures). If there have been any changes, the seller is required to inform the buyer of them, regardless of whether a walk-through is to be performed. It is a buyer's responsibility to determine what conditions beyond the property's boundaries may affect its value.

New Construction

For new homes, the builder normally supplies a detailed warranty, primarily to limit his or her liability, which includes either a five-year or ten-year warranty against foundation defects. At the time of closing, there is an implied warranty that the dwelling and its fixtures (to the seller's best actual knowledge) are free from structural defects and constructed in a professional manner. A **structural defect** is a flaw that reduces the stability or safety of the structure below accepted standards or that restricts the normal use of the structure. The implied warranties continue for one year after the date of transfer of title or the buyer's taking possession, whichever occurs first.

QUESTIONS

1. The buyer and seller agree to the sale of Blackacre for $100,000. No written contract is signed, but the seller accepts payment in full from the buyer and delivers the deed. Which of the following statements is *TRUE*?
   a. The sale is without legal effect; the seller continues to own Blackacre.
   b. The sale violates the Statute of Frauds' maximum amount for oral contracts.
   c. The sale is enforceable in a court of law under the Statute of Frauds, due to the parties' compliance.
   d. The sale is unenforceable under the Statute of Frauds, but the parties are free to comply with its terms.

2. Which of the following statements with regard to a power of attorney is *FALSE*?
   a. A general power of attorney may be used in a real estate transaction.
   b. A party that cannot attend the closing on a property may designate an attorney-in-fact.
   c. A power of attorney must be notarized.
   d. A power of attorney must be recorded with the deed.

3. Two weeks after a buyer and seller signed a sales contract on a house, the house burned to the ground. If the contract is silent on the issue, which party is liable?
   a. The buyer only, under his or her equitable title interest
   b. The buyer and seller share the risk of loss equally
   c. The seller, because he or she continues to possess title to the property
   d. The seller, under the implied condition of good faith

4. *D* built a house with the intention of selling it. During construction, the foundation cracked and *D* was forced to build the bearing walls of a lighter material to keep the entire structure from collapsing. *D*'s engineer told him that a strong wind would probably blow the house down. Nonetheless, the cracked foundation and structural shortcuts were easily covered over, and *D* sold the house to a first-time homebuyer without mentioning the defects. Two weeks after closing, the house collapsed in a thunderstorm. Is *D* liable?
   a. No, under *caveat emptor*
   b. No, because the buyer never asked about specific defects
   c. Yes, due to the implied warranty against structural defects
   d. Yes, due to the failure to have the property inspected

5. *P* owns a vacation cabin in the Blue Ridge Mountains. *K* stops by *P*'s house and asks to rent the cabin from May through September for $900 per month. *P* agrees. If *K* fails to make the rent payments, is the contract enforceable?
   a. No; an oral contract for the sale or lease of real estate is not enforceable.
   b. No; contracts for more than $2,000 must be in writing to be enforceable.
   c. Yes; the Statute of Frauds applies only to the sale of real property.
   d. Yes; an oral lease for a term of less than one year is enforceable.

6. In a situation where either a buyer or seller contacts a licensee to merely prepare a sales contract for a fee, the licensee may
   a. be guilty of practicing law without a license.
   b. write the contract as long as the licensee does not charge a fee.
   c. write the contract as long as the fee does not exceed $300.
   d. not discuss a fee if the licensee wants to write the contract.

7. An actual contract used for the purchase and sale of real property
   a. must be on a form approved by the Real Estate Board.
   b. must be drafted by an attorney licensed to practice in the Commonwealth of Virginia.
   c. may take any form.
   d. does not need enough detail to clearly state the agreement between the parties.

8. A sales contract would contain all of the following *EXCEPT* the
   a. type of sewage system.
   b. amount of the down payment.
   c. ages of the parties to the contract.
   d. possession date.

9. How many days after a request for the POA disclosure packet regarding a referenced property must the packet be delivered to the purchaser?
   a. 15 days
   b. 14 days
   c. No specified amount of time for the delivery of the disclosure packet to the purchaser
   d. Two weeks to the seller and two weeks from the seller to the purchaser

10. When requesting the disclosure packet, payment
   a. may accompany the request.
   b. is due when the packet is delivered to the seller.
   c. is due when the packet is delivered to the purchaser.
   d. is due on the third day after the request is made.

CHAPTER 8

Transfer of Title

REQUIREMENTS FOR A VALID CONVEYANCE

In Virginia, the requirements for a valid deed are as follows:

- Grantor who has the legal capacity to execute the deed
- Grantee
- Consideration
- Granting clause
- Accurate legal description of the property
- Any relevant exceptions or reservations
- Signature of the grantor, sometimes with acknowledgment
- Delivery and acceptance of the deed

Grantor

In Virginia, the same person may be the grantor and grantee in a deed. For example: G can convey the deed to his farm to himself and his grandson M.

Grantee

The grantee named to receive a deed to real property should be legally competent to receive the property. The grantee's full name should be used in preparing the deed. A deed to a nonexistent person is a valid conveyance to the intended but misnamed grantee if the intended grantee exists and the intention of the parties can be determined.

Competence

The grantor is presumed to have been competent at the time a deed was executed. The test of legal capacity is the party's mental ability to understand the nature and consequences of the transaction at the time it is entered into. The burden of proving incompetence is on the party who attacks the validity of the deed.

In Virginia, a conveyance of land by a minor is a valid transfer of title, unless it is repudiated by the minor after he or she attains majority. Repudiation may occur even though the grantee has already conveyed the property to another purchaser without notice that a minor was the grantor in the previous transaction.

Habendum Clause

The *habendum clause,* "to have and to hold," is rarely used in Virginia.

Power of Attorney

If a seller or buyer is unable to attend the closing, there are two options:

1. Prepare all papers to be signed in advance of the closing *or*
2. Use a power of attorney (See also Chapter 7, Power of Attorney)

A power of attorney must be signed by the seller with the same formalities as a deed. Although a power of attorney can be general or specific, *a specific power of attorney is required to convey real property in Virginia.* In reviewing a power of attorney, the licensee should have a lawyer verify that it specifically authorizes performance of all necessary acts and that the attorney-in-fact performs in accordance with the authority granted in the power of attorney.

Affidavits and other sworn statements cannot be signed by the attorney-in-fact. These must be signed by the principal prior to the closing. The deed or other instrument to be signed must indicate that it is being signed by an attorney-in-fact. Normally, this is accomplished by a recital in the body of the instrument or under the signature line.

If an institutional lender is making a new loan, the lender's permission should be obtained for a borrower to execute a power of attorney. The lender may not allow the use of an attorney-in-fact, especially if the loan is subject to truth-in-lending requirements.

A power of attorney must be recorded, and the recording fees are charged to the party using the attorney-in-fact. If the power of attorney is not recorded, it is as though the deed were unsigned by the party being represented by the attorney-in-fact.

TRANSFER TAXES AND FEES

In Virginia, the tax on the transfer of property is levied on the seller and the purchaser individually. The seller pays a *grantor tax* and the purchaser pays a *recordation tax.* In some adjoining jurisdictions, the transaction is taxed as a whole and the tax liability is shared in some formula agreed on by the seller and the purchaser.

Recordation Tax

With certain exceptions, all deeds are subject to state and city or county recordation tax. The state tax is currently \$0.25 per \$100 (or fraction of \$100) of the consideration paid or the value of the property, whichever is greater. A more direct mathematical representation would be 0.0025 × the sales price. The county or city may charge up to one-third of that amount, which in the case of Fairfax County, for example, would be an additional 0.0008 × the sales price. County/city tax rates may differ.

These taxes are usually paid by the buyer and collected at closing. Payment of these taxes is a prerequisite to having the deed recorded.

IN PRACTICE

The state recordation tax is $0.25 per $100 or $0.0025 per $1,000. If the sales price of a home is $475,000, then the state recordation tax would be $475,000 × 0.0025 = $1,187.50. For Fairfax County, the recordation tax would be $475,000 × 0.0008 = $380.

Recording fees are subject to change. Licensees should always be aware of the most current tax rates and fees.

Grantor Tax

In addition to the recordation taxes, all deeds are subject to a grantor's tax of $0.50 per $500 (or a fraction of $500) of the purchase price or the value of the grantor's equity in the property being transferred, in the case of assumption. (In many areas of Virginia, the rate is quoted as $1.00 per $1,000.) The grantor's tax is paid by the seller and is collected at closing and paid to the clerk of the county where the deed is recorded.

In 2007, the Virginia General Assembly passed a law authorizing local tax levying entities (regional transportation authorities) around the state. In northern Virginia, the Regional Transportation Authority [entity] voted to increase the Grantors Tax effective January 2008 by $0.40 (40 cents) per $100 of value, making the overall rate of the Grantors Tax in the region equivalent to $5 per $1,000 of value. In 2008, the Virginia Supreme Court overturned the General Assembly's action.

MATH CONCEPTS

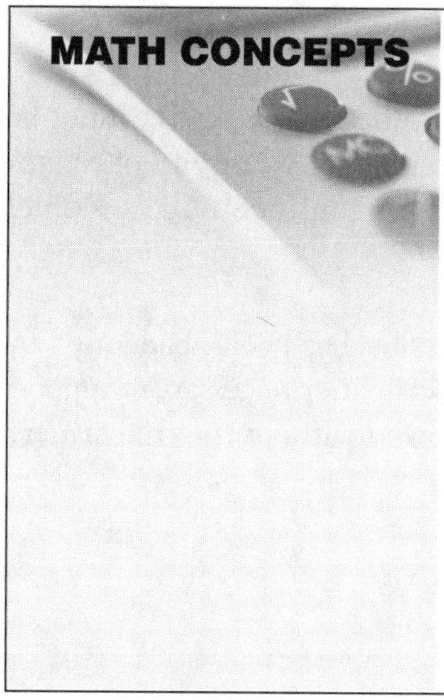

CALCULATING VIRGINIA TRANSFER TAXES

B purchases *S's* home for $675,600 in Fairfax County. The state recordation tax rate is $0.25 and the Fairfax County tax rate is $0.08.

1. STATE AND CITY RECORDATION TAX

$675,600 ÷ 100 = 6,756 "recordation tax units"

B will pay $1,689.00 in state recordation taxes (6,756 × $0.25 = $1,689.00) and $540.48 in county or city recordation tax (6,756 × $0.08 = $540.48)

2. GRANTOR TAX

$675,600 ÷ 500 = 1,351.2 "grantor tax units"

Round up to 1,352 "grantor tax units"

Sue's grantor tax is 1,352 "grantor tax units" × $2.50 = $3,380

A quick and easy calculation of the Grantor Tax based on $5 per $1,000 of value would actually be $2 lower; $675,600 ÷ 1,000 × $5 = 3,378.00. This figure will suffice for purposes of estimation

Tax on Deeds of Trust and Mortgages

Unless exempted, deeds of trust and mortgages are taxed on a sliding scale, according to the amount of the obligation (that is, the debt) that the instrument secures. If the amount is not ascertainable, the tax is based on the fair market value of the property, including the value of any improvements as of the date of the deed. Deeds of trust are also subject to city or county recordation taxes, clerk's fees, and any plat recordation fees.

Deeds of trust that secure both construction loans and permanent loans are normally subject to tax on deeds of trust.

Transfer and Clerk Fees

For each document admitted to record, the clerk of court collects a transfer fee that is generally paid by the buyer. In addition to the transfer fee, the clerk of court collects a clerk fee for recording plats, powers of attorney, certificates of satisfaction, and release of judgments. The amount of the fee is usually based on the number of pages that must be recorded.

The buyer generally pays the fees to record the "new" items, and the seller pays for the release of the "old" items. The payment of fees is usually negotiated between the parties.

■ ADVERSE POSSESSION

Establishing *title* to land by **adverse possession** is somewhat similar to an easement by prescription, which is described earlier in Chapter 3, "Interests in Real Estate."

To establish title to land by adverse possession in Virginia, it is necessary to show actual, hostile, exclusive, visible, and continuous possession of property for the statutory period of 15 years. The possession by the defendant must be actual and continuous; that is, more than just a sporadic taking of timber or occasional camping is required. The adverse possession must be exclusive to constitute an ouster of the true owner.

When several persons enter upon land in succession, these possessions cannot be "tacked" to preserve the essential continuity unless there is a "privity of estate" between them. In other words, the intent to establish a continuous succession of adverse possessors must be proven.

Adverse possession cannot be claimed if the possession has been abandoned by the claimant during the required time period. The occupancy necessary to support a claim of title of adverse possession must be hostile and without the true owner's permission.

■ TRANSFER OF A DECEASED PERSON'S PROPERTY

When any person with title to real estate that may be inherited dies **testate,** that is, having executed a legal will, the real estate will pass according to the terms of the instrument.

In Virginia, circuit courts serve as probate courts. Normally there is a probate section in the clerk's office where wills, lists of heirs, affidavits, and other documents related to probate are located. As with other documents, a "will index" is located in the circuit courts.

IN PRACTICE

When a licensee lists a property that is part of a decedent's estate, he or she should establish that the rate of commission to be paid has been approved by the court handling the probate.

Until probate, the **will** is only the legal declaration of a person's intended disposition. A will may be revoked at any time after execution, while a deed cannot be revoked after it has been delivered to the grantee. The rule of construction in determining whether an instrument is a will or a contract is that if it passes a *present interest*, it is a deed or contract; but if its rights or interests do not convey until the death of the maker, it is a testamentary paper, or will.

Validity

A testator can have only one last will and testament. A will may be set aside for fraud, undue influence, force, or coercion.

No person of unsound mind or under the age of 18 years is capable of making a valid will. Virginia law requires only testamentary capacity at the time the will is made; the testator's subsequent capacity is not relevant.

Neither the testator's poor health nor impaired intellect is sufficient, standing alone, to render a will invalid.

No will is valid unless it is in writing. A valid will must be signed by the testator or by some other person in the testator's presence and by his or her direction in such a way as to make it clear that the name is intended as his or her signature. A will is also valid that is wholly in the testator's handwriting (a **holographic will**) if the testator signs the will and acknowledges it in the presence of at least two competent witnesses who are both present at the same time. These witnesses also must sign the will in the presence of the testator. The testamentary intent must appear on the face of the paper itself. Virginia law is silent on the subject of oral **(unwritten)** or deathbed **(nuncupative)** wills.

IN PRACTICE

When representing the purchaser of property from a decedent's estate or in taking a listing of estate property, it is wise for a real estate licensee to request a certified copy of the will and determine whether the executor under the will has the power of sale. Where the executor does not have the power of sale, or in dealing with an intestate's property, all the heirs and their spouses must execute a deed as grantors conveying the property to the grantee.

QUESTIONS

1. Which of the following would most likely invalidate a deed?
   a. Grantee's name misspelled
   b. Property description consisting of street address, city, and state
   c. Failure of all grantors to sign
   d. Failure of all grantees to sign
2. An heir was to have inherited real property under his uncle's will. However, the uncle sold the property shortly before he died. The heir now wants to have the sale rescinded on grounds of the uncle's incompetence. Will the heir win?
   a. Yes; any such pleading by a close relative will prevail in court.
   b. Yes; the grantor would have had to prove competence in court during his or her lifetime.
   c. No; a deed can be invalidated due to incompetence only during the grantor's lifetime.
   d. No; a person is presumed competent unless a court has ruled otherwise.
3. Kendra, a minor, inherited the Blackacre estate and immediately sold it to William, who believed that Kendra was 23 years old. William then sold the property to Herb. Two years later, Kendra repudiated the sale of Blackacre. Which of the following is *TRUE*?
   a. Kendra's repudiation is without effect because William no longer owns the property.
   b. Kendra's original sale of Blackacre was voidable by Kendra, and she may recover the property from Herb.
   c. Because William believed that Kendra was not a minor, the sale cannot be invalidated.
   d. A minor cannot repudiate the sale of real property in Virginia.
4. Which of the following statements is *TRUE* with regard to using a power of attorney for a real estate transaction?
   a. Either a general or a specific power of attorney may be used.
   b. Both the seller and the purchaser must sign the power of attorney.
   c. Affidavits and other sworn statements may be signed by the attorney-in-fact.
   d. The lender's permission should be obtained for a borrower to execute a power of attorney.
5. The seller in a transaction was called out of town on business the day before the closing. Any affidavits or sworn statements the seller is required to deliver at the closing must be signed by the
   a. seller.
   b. seller's attorney-in-fact.
   c. buyer's attorney-in-fact.
   d. seller's real estate agent.
6. A property sold for $675,600. The state and county recordation tax rates are $0.25 and $0.08 respectively. The grantors tax is $5 per thousand or 0.5 percent. Which of the following is a correct statement of the recordation and grantor taxes to be paid?
   a. Seller will pay $2,229.48; buyer will pay $2,229.48.
   b. Buyer will pay $2,229.48; seller will pay $3,378.
   c. Buyer will pay $3,380; seller will pay $2,230
   d. Seller will pay $2,804.74; buyer will pay $2,804.74.
7. The seller would be expected to pay which of the following?
   a. Recordation tax for recording of the deed
   b. Recordation tax for recording of the deed of trust
   c. Grantor tax of $0.50 per $500 of purchase price
   d. Transfer fee for each document admitted to record

8. All of the following are entitled to prevail on a claim of title by adverse possession, *EXCEPT* a person who

a. has been in possession of the property for 19 years.
b. held the property for five years after "inheriting" it from a parent, who was in adverse possession for ten years.
c. has been entering an orchard and taking apples every October since 1972.
d. has erected a stall on and has been using a neighbor's property to sell produce for 20 years without permission.

9. M's great-aunt S has died and left M her lakeside cabin in her will. M will receive title to the property

a. as soon as the will is read.
b. after the will has gone through probate.
c. as soon as she arranges for a closing.
d. exactly one year from the day Aunt S died.

10. *K* was very ill, and she wrote a will in her own handwriting, leaving all her property to *L*. Three witnesses heard *K* say, "This is my will." The witnesses watched *K* 's friend sign *K* 's name to the document, because *K* was too exhausted to do it herself. "That's as good as my signature," *K* said weakly. The witnesses signed the will. What is the status of this document?

a. The will is invalid because Virginia does not recognize holographic wills.
b. The will is valid.
c. The will is invalid, because *K* did not sign it herself.
d. The will is valid, but cannot be enforced because it is a nuncupative will.

CHAPTER 9

Title Records

■ SETTLEMENT AGENT

Either as part of the purchase agreement or immediately subsequent to ratification, a settlement agent is selected by either the buyer or the seller and is subject to the agreement of both parties to the sales contract.

Consumer Real Estate Settlement Protection Act (CRESPA) [§6.1-2.19 et seq.]

This act requires that persons who perform escrow, closing, or settlement services comply with consumer protection safeguards with respect to licensing, financial responsibility, and the handling of settlement funds.

CRESPA provides specific language that is to be included in all contracts for the purchase of real estate containing not more than four residential dwelling units.

All contracts involving the purchase of real estate containing not more than four residential dwelling units shall include in boldface, ten-point type the following concepts:

- Purchaser's right to select the settlement agent
- Settlement agent's role and limitations
  - — Document collection
  - — Disbursement of funds
  - — Fulfillment of lender instructions
  - — Recordation

Settlement agents *cannot*

- practice law or
- provide legal advice unless they are practicing in Virginia.

A settlement agent who is an attorney practicing in Virginia may be retained by a party to the transaction for the purpose of providing legal services to that party.

The specific language to be used in all such contracts follows:

> CHOICE OF SETTLEMENT AGENT: *You have the right to select a settlement agent to handle the closing of this transaction. The settlement agent's role in closing your transaction involves the coordination of numerous administrative and clerical functions relating to the collection of documents and the collection and disbursement of funds required to carry out the terms of the contract between the parties. If part of the purchase price is financed, your lender will instruct the settlement agent as to the signing and recording of loan documents and the disbursement of loan proceeds. No settlement agent can provide legal advice to any party to the transaction except a settlement agent who is engaged in the private practice of law in Virginia and who has been retained or engaged by a party to the transaction for the purpose of providing legal services to that party.*

A person licensed under Chapter 21 [§54.1-2100 et seq.] of Title 54.1, or such licensee's employees or independent contractors, may perform escrow, closing, or settlement services, as defined by CRESPA, to facilitate the settlement of a transaction in which the licensee is involved so long as the licensee, the licensee's employees, or independent contractors are not named as the settlement agent on the settlement statement and the licensee is otherwise not prohibited from performing such services by law or regulation.

The **settlement agent** will usually be either an attorney or a title company and must be registered with the Virginia State Bar, carry errors and omissions or malpractice insurance at a minimum of $250,000, and maintain a surety bond of not less than $100,000.

In addition to the surety bond, a settlement agent is required to carry a blanket fidelity bond or employee dishonesty insurance policy covering persons employed by the settlement agent and providing a minimum of $100,000 in coverage. When the settlement agent has no employees except the owners, partners, shareholders, or members, the settlement agent may apply to the appropriate licensing authority for a waiver of this fidelity bond or employee dishonesty requirement.

No interest may be earned on funds deposited in connection with any escrow, settlement, or closing. The settlement agent is provided a copy of the purchase agreement by either the buyer or seller. See the Code of Virginia, Title 6.1-2.19, at the following Web address:

WEB LINK @

http://leg1.state.va.us/cgi-bin/legp504.exe?000+cod+TOC

The escrow, closing, or settlement services include placing orders for title insurance, receiving and issuing receipts for money received from the parties, ordering loan checks and payoffs, ordering surveys and inspections, preparing settlement statements, determining that all closing documents conform to the parties' contract requirements, setting the closing appointment, following up with the parties to ensure that the transaction progresses to closing, ascertaining that the lender's instructions have been satisfied, conducting a closing conference at which the documents are executed, receiving and disbursing funds, completing form documents and instruments selected by and in accordance with instructions of the parties to the transaction, handling or arranging for the recording of documents, sending recorded documents to the lender, sending the recorded deed and the title policy to the buyer, and reporting federal income tax information for the real estate sale to the Internal Revenue Service. [§6.1-2.20] For further information about the Internal Revenue Service, visit the following Web site:

WEB LINK @

http://www.irs.gov/

TITLE EXAMINATION

An important function of the settlement agent is to obtain a title examination. The seller should be asked to provide the settlement agent with any information specific to the title condition of the property, such as any unrealized deeds, existing title insurance policies, and any known unrecorded deed, lien, or encumbrance information. The seller is required to have marketable title at the time of settlement and must be given a reasonable time to correct any title defects found before settlement. If title defects are found, the seller should be formally notified and then take whatever actions are necessary to correct the defects.

The real estate licensee is not specifically involved with the title examination but can facilitate communication between the settlement agent and the seller or buyer.

Procedure

In a **title examination,** the prospective seller's chain of title is developed by searching through the grantee index backward in time to some predetermined point to establish the source of title for each owner in the chain. Then, for each grantor in the chain of title, the examiner searches the grantor's index from the date the grantor acquired title to the date it was transferred to the next grantor in the chain. This process, called *adversing the title*, is done to determine whether any person not in the seller's direct chain of title might have some adverse claim or interest recorded against the property to be conveyed.

Finally, the examiner will search other indexes to determine whether there are any unrecorded claims against the property, such as judgment liens, mechanics' liens, or tax liens. While real estate licensees do not perform a title search in the normal course of taking a listing, they should alert the parties' attorneys in the event of even the slightest hint of title issues.

Title examinations may be classified as full or limited searches. In a *full search*, the seller's title must be established for at least 60 years. A *limited search* is a title examination that goes back fewer than 60 years. Limited searches are appropriate for some loan assumptions and second mortgage closings, unless the second mortgagee requires lender's title insurance.

A **chain of title** consists of consecutive terms of ownership; a gap in the chain could be caused by an unrecorded deed, a name change, an unadministered estate, a foreign divorce decree, or some other circumstance. Unless the missing link can be reconstructed from reliable sources, the defect could destroy the closing.

Errors such as an erroneous legal description, a misspelled name, or an improper execution in a prior recorded deed in the seller's chain of title must be corrected before the closing can proceed. Where possible, these problems can be cured by a correction deed from the same grantor to the same grantee; the correction deed must be recorded. A correction deed may not be used to change a greater estate to a lesser estate, nor can it be used to change the identity of the grantor altogether. It is the responsibility of the seller to locate the parties, then to correct the deed.

Title Report

At a minimum, the title report should reveal

- title holder of record;
- legal description of property;
- existing lenders;
- other lienholders (such as mechanics' lienors, judgment lienors, and tax lienors);
- status of taxes;
- easements, covenants, and other restrictions;
- objections to marketability;
- other matters affecting title; and
- requirements for vesting marketable title in the purchaser.

TITLE INSURANCE

Settlement agents are required by Virginia law to advise purchasers and borrowers of the availability of owner title insurance and of the benefits of acquiring it. It is to the benefit of the purchaser to have title insurance because the premium paid is nominal compared with the potential cost an owner could incur in connection with a suit to quiet title or other litigation regarding a defect in title.

If the purchaser is obtaining a loan secured by a deed of trust on the property, the lender will require that a lender's title insurance policy be provided. This policy protects only the lender's interest and will diminish in protection as the loan is paid down.

The additional charge to obtain an owner's policy that protects the owner for the full value of the property is minimal compared with the amount of protection provided.

Title insurance offered by many companies has been expanded recently. The purchaser should contact the title insurance provider (usually through the settlement company) to obtain an advance copy of the types of policies, their costs, and options offered.

TITLE ISSUES

Judgment Liens

Judgments constitute liens against all real property that the defendant owns or subsequently acquires. If the seller denies being named in the judgment, and it is not certain that the judgment is against the seller, an affidavit to this effect may be sufficient to protect the purchaser.

Judgments against prior owners of property may remain as valid liens against the property despite the fact that the property has been subsequently conveyed. The purchaser should require that the seller satisfy all judgments against the property because they remain as liens against the property for 20 years and are subject to execution.

Deed of Trust

A real estate licensee should be aware that it is not unusual for a title examiner to discover an unreleased deed of trust on the property. Most often, this is due to the failure of the lender or closer to have a certificate of satisfaction or deed of release signed by the beneficiary and recorded in a timely manner. Unreleased deeds of trust often go unnoticed until the seller attempts to sell the property. When the lender was a bank or mortgage company and the lien was in fact paid off, it is relatively easy to have a certificate of satisfaction executed and recorded prior to closing. However, if an individual or private lender was involved, these situations can cause delays in the closing, primarily owing to the problems associated with locating the individual.

Mechanics' Liens

Reported mechanics' or materialmen's liens must be treated as adverse claims against the property. The purchaser should require that these liens be paid and satisfied of record or discharged by the filing of a proper bond at or prior to closing. Unreported liens are also of concern to the purchaser, who will take the property "subject to" all mechanics' and materialmen's liens for work or materials furnished within the last 90 days. For this reason, the purchaser should require that the seller provide an affidavit that there have been no improvements performed or materials supplied within the 90 days prior to the date of closing. This affidavit, commonly known as a *90-day letter*, is required by all lenders and title insurance companies.

Mechanics' liens are generally not covered by standard title insurance. However, insurance carriers will provide this coverage for an additional premium.

WET SETTLEMENT ACT

The Wet Settlement Act applies to transactions involving purchase-money loans secured by first deeds of trust on real estate containing not more than four residential dwelling units. The act applies only to lenders regularly engaged in making loans secured by real estate.

At or before the loan closing, the lender must disburse the loan proceeds to the settlement agent. The lender may not charge or receive interest on the loan until disbursement of the loan funds and the loan closing have occurred.

The settlement agent or attorney will have the deed, deed of trust, and any other necessary documents recorded and will disburse the settlement proceeds within two business days of settlement. A settlement agent or attorney may not disburse any loan funds prior to recording the deed of trust or other security instrument perfecting the lender's security instrument. As a result, the seller will not receive his or her equity, and the real estate professional will not receive a commission check at the closing. Rather, all funds will be disbursed after the documents are recorded by the settlement agent.

Any person who suffers a loss because of the failure of a lender or settlement agent to disburse funds as required by law is entitled to recover double the amount of any interest collected in addition to actual damages, plus reasonable attorney's fees from the party that failed to disburse the funds appropriately.

IN PRACTICE

Seller Bob is closing on the sale of a property in Virginia on Tuesday and expects to close on his new purchase in Maryland on Wednesday using the proceeds from the Tuesday closing in Virginia. Bob might not have access to the proceeds of Tuesday's Virginia closing in time for Wednesday's closing in Maryland because no disbursements can be made at the settlement table (closing) in Virginia until the transaction is recorded.

QUESTIONS

1. When is the seller of real property required to have marketable title?
   a. At the time the listing is taken
   b. When a sales contract is signed
   c. By the time the buyer's loan is approved
   d. At closing

2. *B* is purchasing property from *S*. Prior to closing, certain defects are found in *S*'s title. What is the status of the sales contract between these parties?
   a. It is automatically rescinded.
   b. Because the seller has a reasonable time to correct defects, the contract is still in effect.
   c. The buyer may, at his or her option, cancel the contract and recover the earnest money.
   d. The contract is in force, and the buyer must close the transaction and accept the transfer as long as the defects are curable.

3. According to the Consumer Real Estate Settlement Protection Act, the selection of a settlement agent is made by
   a. the seller.
   b. the buyer.
   c. either the buyer or the seller.
   d. either the buyer's or the seller's agent.

4. At the time of taking a listing, the listing agent will find it helpful to ask to see all documents concerning the property that the seller has available in order to do all of the following *EXCEPT*
   a. find out about unrecorded deeds.
   b. verify deed of trust loan numbers and payment status.
   c. learn of any liens that may not be recorded.
   d. to determine whether a seller has marketable title at the time a property is held out for sale.

5. A full title search goes back how many years?
   a. 20
   b. 40
   c. 60
   d. 80

6. Which of the following changes may not be accomplished by using a correction deed?
   a. A change from a fee simple to a life estate
   b. Correction of an erroneous legal description
   c. Respelling of a misspelled name
   d. Correcting the signature on an improperly executed deed

7. In cases where title must be cleared by having correction deeds signed, who is responsible for locating the parties who must sign?
   a. The buyer
   b. The seller
   c. The settlement attorney
   d. The real estate licensee who represents the owner

8. *T* has recently purchased a property from *J*. *T* has reason to believe that there is an outstanding judgment lien against *J*. Which of the following is *TRUE*?
   a. *T* has no need to worry because the property has been conveyed.
   b. *T* has no need to worry because *T* was not named in the judgment.
   c. *T* should be worried because judgment liens remain against the property.
   d. *T* should be worried because *J* has really bad credit.

9. In preparing for the settlement on *S*'s sale of property to *J*, it was discovered that an unreleased deed of trust is still shown on the county records. This most likely occurred because
   a. *S* never paid off the deed of trust.
   b. *S*'s lender neglected to have a deed of release signed and recorded.
   c. *S*'s original settlement attorney absconded with the funds.
   d. *S* still owes for county property taxes.

10. All of the following are protections offered to an owner insured by a standard title insurance policy *EXCEPT*

a. losses suffered because of defects in the record title.
b. hidden defects not disclosed by the public record.
c. the cost of defending the title against adverse claims.
d. mechanics' and materialmen's liens.

CHAPTER 10

Virginia's Real Estate License Law

The Code of Virginia 54.1, Chapter 21, is the section of the statute that governs the practice of real estate professionals. The purpose of the law is to protect the public interest against fraud, misrepresentation, dishonesty, and incompetence in real estate transactions.

The law designates the Real Estate Board (REB) as the authority with the power to enforce, amend, and promulgate rules and regulations for implementing the law.

Definitions [§54.1-2100 et seq. and 18 VAC 135-20-10]

Certain words and phrases are used throughout both the License Law and the Rules and Regulations of the REB. These words and phrases have specific, statutory meanings separate and apart from any definition they might have outside the real estate profession. Several of these definitions have been addressed in Chapter 1 and are repeated here for emphasis.

Active—Any broker or salesperson under the supervision of a principal or supervising broker performing real estate brokerage activities.

Actively engaged—A broker or salesperson having active licensure with a licensed real estate firm or sole proprietorship or sole proprietorship and active for an average of at least 40 hours per week. The REB may waive the 40-hour-per-week requirement at its discretion.

Associate broker—Any individual holding a broker's license other than the one designated as the principal broker.

Client—An individual who has entered into a brokerage relationship with a licensee.

Customer—An individual who has not entered into a brokerage relationship with a licensee.

Firm—Any sole proprietorship (nonbroker-owned), partnership, association, limited liability company (LLC), or corporation, other than a sole proprietorship (principal-broker-owned), that is required by regulation to obtain a separate brokerage firm license.

Inactive status—Any broker or salesperson who is not under the supervision of a principal broker or supervising broker, who is not affiliated with a firm or sole proprietorship, or who is not performing any real estate activities.

Independent contractor—A licensee who acts for or represents a client other than as a standard agent and whose duties and obligations are governed by a written contract between licensee and the client.

Licensee—Any person, partnership, association, corporation, or LLC that holds a license issued by the REB to act as a real estate broker or real estate salesperson.

Limited service representative—A licensee who acts for or represents a client with respect to real property containing from one to four residential units, pursuant to a brokerage agreement that provides that the limited service representative will not provide one or more of the duties of a standard agent.

Principal broker—The individual broker designated by each firm to ensure compliance with Chapter 21 of Title 54.1 of the Code of Virginia and to receive all communications and notices from the REB that may affect the firm and/or its licensees. In the case of a sole proprietorship, the licensed broker who is the sole proprietor has the responsibilities of the principal broker. The principal broker shall have responsibility for the activities of the firm and all of its licensees.

Principal to a transaction—Any party to a real estate transaction in the capacity of a seller, buyer, lessee or lessor, optionor or optionee, or licensor or licensee. The listing and selling brokers are not, by virtue of their brokerage relationship, principals to the transaction.

Real estate—As defined in the Virginia law, real estate includes condominiums, leaseholds, time-sharing, and any other interest in real property. Ownership of a cooperative apartment is also considered real estate ownership, even though the shares held by members of the co-op are construed as personal property.

Sole proprietor—Any individual, not a corporation, who is trading under his or her own name or under a fictitious or assumed name, as provided by the regulations. A licensed broker who is a sole proprietor shall have the same responsibilities as a principal broker. A sole proprietor who is not licensed must designate a licensed broker to perform the duties of a principal broker.

Standard agent—A licensee who acts for or represents a client in an agency relationship. A standard agent shall have the obligations as provided in Article 3 of Title 54.1 of the Code of Virginia that covers the law of agency as it relates to real estate and who shall be obligated to adhere to the Virginia Real Estate License Law.

Supervising broker—May be either the principal broker or an individual broker designated by the principal broker to supervise the provision of real estate brokerage services by associate brokers and salespersons assigned to an office.

THE REAL ESTATE BOARD (REB) [§54.1-2104, 2105]

The Virginia Real Estate Board (VREB) is 1 of 19 boards that regulate more than 30 occupations and professions. As of this edition, the Real Estate Board regulates over 70,000 practitioners, including salespersons, associate and principal brokers, and sole proprietors. The Department of Professional and Occupational Regulation's (DPOR's) mission is to serve and protect the public through

1. licensure of qualified individuals and businesses in professions that, if not regulated, may harm the public's health, safety, and welfare; and
2. enforcement of laws pertaining to professional conduct.

DPOR, a Commerce and Trade secretariat agency, is composed of practitioners and citizens appointed by the governor. DPOR licenses or certifies over 300,000 individuals and businesses ranging from architects and contractors to real estate practitioners and professional wrestlers.

The REB is composed of nine members. Seven members may be either brokers or salespersons with at least five consecutive years' experience immediately prior to appointment, and two are citizen (consumer) members. Appointments are made by the governor for a term of four years. Sitting members may be reappointed for one additional four-year term. Members of the REB select the chairperson.

Authority

The REB, by statute, may do all things necessary and convenient for carrying into effect the provisions of the law. REB's authority includes

- issuing and renewing real estate licenses;
- enforcing the license law;
- taking disciplinary action for violations of license law or rules and regulations by
  - suspending or revoking a license,
  - levying fines, or
  - denying license renewal;
- establishing requirements for real estate licensing;
- approving schools for teaching authorized courses for real estate brokers and salespersons;
- determining license fees; and
- waiving all or part of the prelicensing requirements if an applicant for licensure is currently licensed in another state or the District of Columbia.

In addition to administering the real estate license law, the REB has the responsibility of administering

- the Virginia Fair Housing Act;
- the Virginia Condominium Act;
- the Virginia Time-Share Act;
- the Virginia Real Estate Transaction Recovery Fund;

- the Virginia Cooperative Act; and
- The Virginia Property Owners Association Act.

There are some aspects of real estate practice with which the REB does *not* become involved. For example, the REB does not

- arbitrate disputes between salespersons and brokers;
- become involved in disputes between brokers;
- establish commission rates or commission splits; or
- standardize listing agreements, sales contacts, or many other forms used in the industry, although from time to time the REB may be charged with development of specific forms such as the disclosure forms required by the Virginia Residential Property Disclosure Act.

The REB could become involved in any of these matters in case of a violation of the license law or the rules and regulations.

WHO MUST HAVE A LICENSE? [§54.1-2106.1; 18 VAC 135-20-20]

Who must have a license is addressed in Chapter 1 and is repeated here for emphasis.

Any person, firm, partnership, association, LLC, corporation, or sole proprietorship (broker-owned or nonbroker-owned) who, for a fee, commission, or other valuable consideration, performs an act of real estate brokerage for others, is required by Virginia law to be a licensed real estate broker or salesperson. The phrase "act of real estate brokerage" includes selling or offering real estate for sale; buying or offering to buy real estate; negotiating the purchase or exchange of real estate; and renting, leasing, or negotiating a lease for real estate. A single performance of any one of these acts requires a real estate license.

A separate firm license is required for business entities such as

- sole proprietorships (nonbroker-owned),
- partnerships,
- associations,
- limited liability companies (LLCs), and
- corporations.

This firm license is *separate and distinct* from the broker licenses required of each partner, associate, LLC manager, or corporate officer of these business entities who actively participate in brokerage activities. A broker-owned sole proprietorship is not required to obtain a separate firm license unless operating under a fictitious name.

Operating Without a License

If the REB is aware of someone who is engaging in acts of real estate brokerage without a license, it will investigate the matter. If the suspicion is true, the REB may refer the matter to the Commonwealth attorney for action. Any penalty for such activities against the individual or firm will be determined by the courts. Operating without a license is considered to be a Class 1 misdemeanor with a penalty of up to $1,000 per violation. A third or subsequent violation within a single three-year period constitutes a Class 6 felony. The civil penalties against one person or business entity cannot exceed $10,000 per year. The Department of Professional and Occupational Regulation (DPOR) also has the authority to investigate unlicensed activity and to enforce licensure and regulatory provisions of Title 54.1 by instituting proceedings in general district or circuit courts.

REQUIREMENTS FOR LICENSURE [18 VAC 135-20-30 THROUGH 135-20-60]

The following general requirements apply to any person seeking licensure either as a salesperson or broker. The applicant must

- be at least 18 years old;
- have, at a minimum, a high school diploma or its equivalent;
- if licensed in another jurisdiction, be in good standing in every jurisdiction where licensed;
- have a good reputation for honesty, truthfulness, and fair dealing, and be competent to transact real estate business in such a manner as to safeguard the public interest;
- not have been found guilty of violating the fair housing laws of Virginia or any other jurisdiction;
- meet the current educational requirements by achieving a passing grade in all required courses before sitting for the licensing exam and applying for licensure;
- pass a written license examination approved by the REB within 12 months prior to applying for a license and follow all rules established by the REB or the testing service regarding the conduct of license applicants, including any written or verbal instructions communicated prior to the examination date or at the test site;
- be in good standing, and not have had a real estate license suspended, revoked, or surrendered in connection with a disciplinary action, or been the subject of disciplinary action in any jurisdiction;
- not have been convicted, in any jurisdiction, for a misdemeanor involving moral turpitude, sexual offense, drug distribution, physical injury, or any felony (a plea of *nolo contendere* [no contest] is considered a conviction); and
- follow all rules established by the REB with regard to conduct at the examination.

An applicant for a broker's license must meet additional educational requirements and must have been actively engaged as a real estate salesperson for 36 of the previous 48 months. Note that the definition of "actively engaged" means an average of 40 hours per week. The specific licensing requirements for a broker, salesperson, and reciprocal licenses are discussed later in this chapter.

If a license applicant has had a real estate license suspended, revoked, or surrendered in connection with a disciplinary action or has been subject to disciplinary action in any jurisdiction, the applicant must include a detailed explanation of the circumstances that caused the action along with his or her application for licensure.

If an applicant has been convicted of a misdemeanor involving moral turpitude, sexual offense, drug distribution, or physical injury, or any other felony, the following must be submitted with the license application:

- An official FBI record, the original state police criminal record, and certified copies of court papers relative to the conviction.
- A written account of the part that he or she played in the offense and the current status or resolution of the final conviction. If a prospective licensee is concerned about becoming licensed due to a past criminal conviction, the applicant must first meet the educational and testing requirements for licensure. The documentation is submitted with the license application.

Real Estate Examination

All initial applications for licensure must be made within 12 months of the examination date. Failure to apply within this time period will require retaking the exam.

Real Estate Salesperson

An applicant for licensure as a real estate salesperson must, in addition to the general requirements discussed above, have successfully completed a "Principles of Real Estate" or similar course approved by the REB. The course must contain four semester credit hours or a minimum of 60 classroom, correspondence, or other distance learning instruction hours prior to making application for the examination.

Real Estate Broker

Applicants for a real estate broker's license must meet the following requirements in addition to meeting the salesperson licensing requirements. An applicant must

- have been actively engaged as a real estate salesperson for 36 of the 48 months immediately preceding the date of application for licensure as a real estate broker, and
- have successfully completed 12 classroom or correspondence semester credit hours (four 45-hour courses, or 180 classroom hours) of study approved by the REB in such subjects as brokerage, real estate law, real estate investments, real estate finance, and real estate appraisal, or related approved subjects prior to the licensing examination. All applicants are required to complete the 45-hour brokerage course.

Concurrent Licenses

Brokers who are active in more than one legal entity, that is, who work for more than one brokerage firm, may apply for **concurrent licenses.** Concurrent licenses will be issued to brokers who provide written statements verifying that written notice of the applicant's concurrent status has been provided to the principal broker of each firm with which the applicant is or will be associated.

Concurrent licensure does not refer to persons holding licenses in multiple states.

Branch Office Licenses

A successful real estate broker often has offices in several different markets. When a broker maintains multiple offices within Virginia, a **branch office license** must be issued for each branch office. The application form must include the name of the firm, the location of the branch office, and the name of the branch office's supervising broker. The branch office license is maintained at the branch office. In addition, a roster of every salesperson and broker assigned to the branch shall be available to the public in each office. Typically, this roster is posted in the office lobby.

Active and Inactive Licenses

An **active license** means that the licensee is affiliated with or employed by a broker. The licensee's broker must certify his or her license application and agrees to be responsible for the licensee's brokerage activities. When the REB has approved the application, the license will be issued and sent to the principal broker. The licensee is now considered to have *active* status: He or she is licensed to engage in real estate activities and receives a "pocket card" as evidence of his or her status as a broker or salesperson. The principal broker is responsible for maintaining the licenses of every salesperson and broker (affiliated with or employed by the brokerage entity) at the main office of the firm.

Alternatively, an individual may satisfy all the licensing requirements and pass the license examination but choose to apply for **inactive license** status. Although the person has an inactive license, he or she is not affiliated with or employed by a broker and *may not* engage in acts of brokerage or earn compensation, *including referral fees*. The license of an inactive licensee is maintained by the REB.

Active to Inactive Status Any licensee may request that his or her license be placed on inactive status, which means that the licensee is no longer affiliated with or employed by *any* broker.

If a licensee changes from active to inactive status, it is the responsibility of the individual licensee to make application for the change and to request that the broker return the actual license. The REB, on receipt of the change of status application, notifies the former broker of the change request. If the broker has not yet returned the license of the individual involved in the change, the broker must do so by certified mail so that it is received by the REB within ten days of the date of notification.

No licensees shall engage in acts of real estate brokerage or earn compensation while their licenses are on inactive status.

Licensees and Professional Organizations. Licensees may become members of professional real estate organizations such as the National Association of REALTORS® and its state and local affiliates. However, only a duly licensed person or entity is authorized to engage in "acts of real estate brokerage" in Virginia.

Inactive to Active Status When an inactive licensee wishes to activate his or her license and affiliate with a broker, proper application must be made to have the license activated. This is accomplished by filling out an application form, then having the broker certify the application and mail the form with the proper fees to the REB. If a licensee has been on inactive status for three years or more, the licensee must meet educational requirements in effect at that time to be reinstated to active status. If the licensee was engaged in a real estate-related field while he or she was inactive and can demonstrate to the REB that the knowledge of real estate has been retained, the REB may waive the education requirements. If the licensee was on inactive status at the time the license was renewed, the licensee must submit evidence that he or she did successfully complete the required 16 hours of continuing education during the 24 months preceding reactivation.

Referral Agents

A **referral agent** is a real estate licensee who does not engage in real estate activities such as listing and selling property. As the title implies, a referral agent refers prospective buyers or sellers to the broker with whom the agent is affiliated. If a sale results from the referral, the broker may pay the licensee a fee for the referral. The referral agent's license is displayed either in the referral office or in the main office of the broker with whom he or she is affiliated. The REB considers a person acting in the capacity of a referral agent to be active, not inactive. A referral agent will be required to complete the mandatory 16 hours of continuing education within each two-year licensing cycle.

IN PRACTICE

Membership by licensed brokers in most local real estate associations affiliated with the National Association of REALTORS® (NAR) typically requires all licensees affiliated with the broker to maintain active membership in the REALTORS® association. Some REALTOR® association rules may technically exclude REALTOR® brokers from supervising (and including) non-REALTORS® in the same firm as their REALTOR® affiliated licensees. A referral company is typically a firm in which the principal broker and the affiliated licensees are not members of a REALTOR® association.

■ LICENSURE BY RECIPROCITY [18 VAC 135-20-60]

A person who holds a real estate license issued by another state may apply to the REB for a **license by reciprocity.** Applicants may obtain a Virginia real estate license by reciprocity if they

- are at least 18 years old;
- have, at a minimum, a high school diploma or its equivalent;
- have received the salesperson's or broker's license by passing a written licensing examination that is substantially equivalent to Virginia's examination;
- sign a statement verifying that they have read and understand Virginia License Law and the REB Rules and Regulations (reciprocal licensees must pass the Virginia portion of the licensing exam prior to their first renewal);
- are in good standing as a licensed broker or salesperson in their state and have not been subject to suspension, revocation, or surrender of their license in connection with a disciplinary proceeding;
- (for a salesperson's license) have been actively engaged in real estate practice for 12 of the preceding 36 months, or have met educational requirements substantially equivalent to Virginia's;
- (for a broker's license) have been licensed as a real estate broker and actively engaged as a broker or salesperson for 36 of the 48 months immediately prior to application; and
- satisfy the reputation and criminal record requirements demanded of licensees in Virginia.

Consent to Suits

One additional requirement for nonresidents is that they file an irrevocable *consent to suits and services*. A **consent to suits and services** is a binding legal agreement that allows the Director of the DPOR to accept *service* of any legal process or pleading on the nonresident licensee's behalf.

The service of legal documents on the director is as valid and binding on the licensee as if service had been made on the licensee in person. [§54.1-2111]

■ **FOR EXAMPLE** *J* is licensed in Maryland and wishes to also be licensed in Virginia. In case *J*'s actions result in potential harm to a member of the public, it will be necessary for the aggrieved party to be able to file a suit against *J*. The consent to suits and services form authorizes the Director of the DPOR to accept notice of the suit in *J*'s behalf. Otherwise, *J* might be able to legally avoid having court action taken against him.

■ LICENSURE OF BUSINESS ENTITIES [18 VAC 135-20-45]

A salesperson or associate broker may apply for a salesperson's license as a business entity. This business license is in addition to the individual license. The individual(s) participating under this concept still operates under the supervision of a principal broker. This concept is in response to the practice of several salespersons or associate brokers operating as a team or as an individual operating under his or her own business entity within the brokerage firm or sole proprietorship (broker-owned).

This business entity may take any form or name as long as the entity is authorized to do business in accordance with the requirements of Code of Virginia, §§59.1-69 through 59.1-76, which address transacting businesses under an assumed name. Every member or owner under this type of entity who actively participates in the brokerage business must be licensed as either a salesperson or broker.

Business entity license holders are reminded that all advertising must be under the direct supervision of the principal or supervising broker and in the name of the firm. The firm's licensed name must be clearly and legibly displayed on all advertising. Disclosure requirements include advertising by the firm that contains the firm's licensed name and address or advertising by a licensee that must contain the licensee's name, the name of the firm where the licensee is affiliated, and the firm's address.

■ **FOR EXAMPLE** Salespersons Mary and Jim are active with XYZ Realty, which holds a firm license. Mary and Jim wish to form a corporation and apply for a salesperson license as a business entity while still active with XYZ Realty. They form their corporation and meet the requirements for operating under a fictitious name. A separate salesperson license as a business entity is issued by the REB. Members of the new business entity still maintain their individual salesperson licenses and are under the supervision of their principal broker.

■ RENEWAL OF LICENSES [18 VAC 135-20-90 THROUGH 135-20-140]

The real estate licenses of salespersons, brokers, and firms expire every two years, on the last day of the month in which the license was issued. For a licensee to continue his or her professional real estate activities, the license must be renewed. Renewal requirements apply to active and inactive licensees alike.

The REB reserves the right to deny the renewal or reinstatement of any license for the same reasons that it would deny initial licensure or discipline a current licensee, or failure to pay imposed monetary penalties.

The Renewal Process

The REB mails renewal notices, usually to each licensee at the last known home address of that individual. Renewal notices for firms are mailed to the last known business address. *Failure to receive a notice of renewal does not relieve the licensee of the responsibility to renew.*

The applicant for renewal completes the application form and returns it to the REB, along with the required fee and any other documentation that may be required. The application form and fees must be *received* by the REB prior to the expiration date that appears on the license. (See Table 10.1.)

Failure To Renew and Reinstatement

If the licensee does not renew his or her license prior to expiration, the licensee must apply to have the license reinstated. Applicants for reinstatement of an active license must have completed the required continuing education hours.

The regulations allow for reinstatement of a license up to one year following expiration. If the application to reinstate is received within 30 days of expiration, there is no monetary penalty. However, from the 31st day up to one year, application for reinstatement is subject to the current reinstatement fee. The reinstatement fee is a flat fee and is *not* in addition to the normal renewal fees.

After 12 months, reinstatement is not possible under any circumstances, and the licensee must meet all educational and examination requirements in effect at that time and apply for licensure as a new applicant.

Once the license has expired, the licensee may *not* engage in any acts of real estate brokerage until the license has been reinstated. Licensees who engage in acts of real estate brokerage after their license has expired are legally subject to the penalties associated with operating without a license, including during the reinstatement period.

Continuing Education [18 VAC 135-20-100]

As a condition of renewing their licenses, all active real estate brokers and salespersons, whether or not they are Virginia residents, must complete one or more continuing education courses, totaling at least 16 hours during each licensing term for salespersons and 24 hours during each licensing term for brokers. Licensees who are called to active duty in the United States Armed Forces must complete the continuing education requirement within six months of their release. All active licensees renewing between July 1, 2007, and June 30, 2009, must complete an additional two hours of continuing education in Limited Service Agency.

The course or courses must be provided by an accredited university, college, community college, or other accredited institution of higher learning, or by an approved proprietary school, that is, a privately owned school, real estate professional association, or a related entity approved by the REB. The courses may be taken by correspondence or by other distance learning instruction.

Eight of the 16 hours must include the subjects of ethics and standards of conduct, fair housing (two hours), legal updates and emerging trends, real estate agency, and real estate contracts. The remaining eight hours shall be on other approved subjects. Licensees from other jurisdictions may substitute continuing education completed in their jurisdictions for the remaining eight hours. Approved subjects include but are not limited to

- property rights;
- contracts;
- deeds;
- mortgages and deeds of trust;
- types of mortgages;
- leases;
- liens;
- real property and title insurance;
- investment;
- taxes in real estate;
- real estate financing;
- brokerage and agency contract responsibilities;
- real property management;
- search, examination, and registration of title;
- title closing;
- appraisal of real property;
- planning subdivision developments and condominiums;
- regulatory statutes;
- housing legislation;
- fair housing;
- REB regulations;
- land use;
- business law;
- real estate economics;
- real estate investments;
- federal real estate law;
- commercial real estate;
- Americans with Disabilities Act;
- environmental issues impacting real estate;
- building codes and design;
- local laws and zoning ordinances;
- escrow requirements;
- ethics and standards of conduct; and
- common interest ownership.

Post-licensing Education

Post-licensing education (PL or PLE) is proscribed by the Real Estate Board as that education required to obtain the *first renewal* of a real estate salesperson license. Post-licensing education always takes place during the initial two-year term of the license. **Continuing education** (CE or CED) is proscribed by the Real Estate Board as that education required to obtain the *second and all subsequent renewals* of a real estate license.

Additional Broker Continuing Education

Post-licensing education and continuing education are *not* interchangeable. As of July 1, 2008, all new licensees are required to complete 30 hours of classroom, correspondence, or other distance learning in specified areas of (1) residential real estate, (2) commercial real estate, or (3) property management. This requirement must be completed within the first year (12 months) of obtaining a license. As of July 1, 2008, all brokers to whom active licenses have been issued by the board shall be required to satisfactorily complete courses of not less than 24 hours of classroom or correspondence or other distance learning instruction during each licensing term. Of the total 24 hours, the curriculum shall include:

- A minimum of eight required hours to include at least three hours of ethics and standards of conduct, two hours of fair housing, and the remaining three hours of legal updates and emerging trends, real estate agency, and real estate contracts;
- A minimum of eight hours of courses relating to supervision and management of real estate agents and the management of real estate brokerage firms as are approved by the board; and
- Eight hours of general elective courses as are approved by the board.

Licensees are responsible for retaining proof of completed continuing education for three years. A certificate of course completion issued by the school and containing the hours of credit completed is adequate proof of course completion. Failure by the licensee to provide course completion certification as directed by the REB will result in the license not being renewed and/or disciplinary action.

The REB requires that each school establish and maintain a record of continuing education for each student for a minimum of five years.

Any person who is *active* at the time of license renewal must complete the required course or courses as a condition of renewal. The courses *must* be completed prior to the date the license expires. An active licensee who does not complete the continuing education requirement prior to license expiration may complete the courses during the period of time allowed for license reinstatement (one year) but cannot reinstate the license until the continuing education courses are completed. Referral agents are considered active and therefore must complete the courses as a condition of renewal.

Any person who is *inactive* at the time of license renewal may renew his or her inactive license and is *not* required to complete the courses as a condition of renewal. However, when that licensee chooses to activate the license, he or she must document that the required continuing education courses have been completed within the past 24 months.

EXEMPTIONS FROM LICENSURE [§54.1-2103]

The law recognizes that under certain circumstances, individuals or business operations engaging in what could be considered an act of real estate brokerage may be entitled to exemption from the requirements of licensure. Those conditions include, but are not limited to, the following:

- Owners, lessors, and their employees dealing with their own property
- Persons acting as attorneys-in-fact under a power of attorney for final consummation of contracts for sale, lease, or exchange of real estate
- Attorneys at law in the performance of duties as an attorney at law, to include the sale of real estate, condemnation proceedings, and so forth
- Receivers, trustees in bankruptcy, administrators, executors, or other persons acting under court order
- Trustees under trust agreements, deeds of trust, or wills, or their employees
- Corporations managing rental housing when officers, directors, and members in the ownership corporation and the management corporation are the same persons and the management corporation manages no property for others

TABLE 10.1

Licensing Fees [18 VAC 135-20-80; 135-20-120]

Type of License	Application Fee	Renewal Fee
Salesperson by education and examination	$170*	$65
Salesperson by reciprocity	$170*	n/a
Salesperson's or associate broker's license as a business entity	$210*	$90
Broker by education and examination	$210*	$80
Broker by reciprocity	$210*	n/a
Broker concurrent license	$140	$80
Firm license	$270	$160
Branch office license	$190	$90
Transfer application	$60	n/a
Activate application	$60	n/a

*Each new licensee, whether salesperson or broker, must pay $20 into the Transaction Recovery Fund.

- Any existing tenant of a residential dwelling who refers a prospective tenant to the owner of the unit or to the owner's agent or employee and receives, or is offered, a referral fee from the owner, agent, or employee
- Auctioneers when selling real estate at public auction when employed by the owner (an auctioneer cannot advertise that he or she is authorized to sell real estate)
- Salaried residential property managers
- Appraisers, mortgage bankers, and loan officers in the normal practice of their profession

All real estate licensees are always required to comply with the REB regulations, even though they also may be in one of the exempt categories.

Rental Location Agents

Rental location agents provide a service to the real estate industry but are not required to maintain a real estate license. Rental location agents are no longer regulated.

License Application and Renewal Fees

The statute allows for the collection of fees associated with the issuance and renewal of licenses. The REB has the authority to set these charges. The purpose of these fees is to help defray the cost of administering the license law and to fund services provided by the REB to the real estate community throughout Virginia. The current fee structure is shown in Table 10.1.

OBTAINING A LICENSE

Once a license applicant has successfully completed the educational requirements, the applicant's next step is to take and pass an examination administered by the REB or a designated testing service. In Virginia, real estate licensing examinations are prepared by PSI Examination Services.

The application is sent to PSI. When PSI receives the application and the required application fee and registers the applicant into the system, the applicant may schedule the examination.

The examination is administered by computer, and applicants will know the results as soon as they have completed the exam. If the applicant passes, successful notification appears on the computer screen. License application forms for submittal to the REB will be available at the test center. If the applicant does not pass, unsuccessful notification appears on the screen. Registration forms for submittal to PSI to retake the examination will be available at the test center. There is no prescribed waiting period. All candidates also receive an official score report in writing at the test center. If the applicant fails one portion of the exam (state or national) that portion must be retaken and passed. All license applications must be received by the DPOR within one year of passing the exam. Exam results are confidential and are reported only to the applicant and to the DPOR.

More information and test application forms may be found on the following Web site:

WEB LINK

@

www.psiexams.com (click on Information, Virginia, VA Real Estate)

BROKERAGES [18 VAC 135-20-160 THROUGH 135-20-170]

There may be only *one* principal broker for each firm, regardless of the number of agents affiliated with that firm or the number of offices the firm operates.

Name of Business

A brokerage business may be known by any name that identifies the owner or owners, or it may use an assumed or fictitious name. If the firm chooses to operate under an assumed or fictitious name, the application for licensure of the firm must be accompanied by a certificate of ownership that has been filed with the clerk of the court in the jurisdiction in which the business operates. This fictitious or assumed name is the name by which the business will be known to the public.

Place of Business

Every licensed broker who is a resident of Virginia must maintain a place of business within the commonwealth. A **place of business** is defined as one where the business of real estate brokerage is normally transacted and where business calls can be directed and received. A place of business may be located in a private residence only if the business area is separate and distinct from the living quarters and is accessible to the public.

Office Supervision

Each place of business or branch office must be supervised by a supervising broker who is responsible for exercising reasonable and adequate supervision of the provision of real estate brokerage services by the associate brokers and salespersons assigned to that office. Two important factors are (1) the availability of the supervising broker to review and discuss contracts, brokerage agreements, and advertising, and (2) the availability of training and written procedures and policies providing clear guidance in areas specified by the REB.

The current emphasis is on the ability of the supervising broker to provide adequate supervision and training of those assigned to an office, rather than a physical presence in a specific location.

Signage

The broker may display a sign at his or her office(s). Any sign must state the name by which the brokerage is known to the public, that is, the name that appears on the license issued by the REB, and the words *Real Estate*, *Realty*, or the name of a generally recognized organization of real estate professionals. The signs must indicate clearly that the business being conducted is real estate brokerage.

Change of Location, Name, or Ownership

In the event the broker's main office changes location or the name of the brokerage changes, it is the principal broker's responsibility to advise the REB of the change within 30 days. The REB will issue new licenses for the remainder of the license period. This is necessary because the broker's name and business address appear on individual licenses.

If the location of a branch office changes, only the branch office license needs to be returned.

Salespersons and individual brokers are responsible for keeping the REB informed of their current home addresses and of any changes in their names or addresses within 30 days of the change.

Transfer and Termination of Active Status

When a salesperson or broker is discharged or in any way terminates active status, the principal broker must sign and note the date of termination on the license and return it by certified mail to the board so that it will be received within ten calendar days of the date of termination or status change. If the principal broker is discharged or terminates active status, the firm must notify the board and return the license by certified mail within three business days of termination.

Any licensee may transfer from one licensed real estate firm to another by completing and submitting to the board a transfer application signed by the new supervising broker along with the accompanying transfer fee. (See Table 10.1.)

All licenses are the property of the REB. All licenses must be returned to the REB on termination of the licensee, termination of the business entity, death of a licensee, status change, or change of name or address.

■ BROKER ESCROW ACCOUNTS [§54.1-2108; 18 VAC 135-20-180]

Any broker who holds money belonging to others pending consummation or termination of a real estate transaction must maintain an escrow account solely for those funds. There is, however, no requirement that a broker hold a buyer's earnest money deposit in the case of a sales transaction. In this situation, the money may be held by a settlement agent, an attorney, or even a seller. Who holds the earnest money deposit is a matter to be negotiated in the sales contract.

Other funds that require an escrow account include down payments, rental payments, security deposits, money from buyers or sellers for payment of settlement expenses, money advanced by the broker's client or expended on behalf of the client, and other funds received on behalf of the client or other person unless otherwise agreed in writing. If a fund is to be deposited in an escrow account, it must be deposited by the fifth business banking day following ratification of the sales contract or receipt of the lease, unless otherwise agreed in writing.

IN PRACTICE

A business banking day can be described as Monday through Friday with the exception of legal holidays as defined by the Federal Reserve Bank. Though many banks offer Saturday and even Sunday hours of operation, the Federal Reserve Bank is closed on weekends and legal federal holidays. A list of banking holidays is available at: *www.federalreserve.gov/releases/k8/default.htm.*

Establishing and Maintaining an Escrow Account

Each account established shall be opened and maintained in a federally insured depository in Virginia. When the account is opened, it must be made clear to the financial institution that the account is an escrow account. Each account—and all checks, deposit slips, and bank statements relating to it—must be labeled *Escrow* as part of the account name. The designation of the account as an escrow account precludes attachment of the funds by the broker's creditors. It also puts the financial institution on notice that this account contains funds that belong to people other than the broker who opened the account.

The principal broker will, and the supervising broker may, be held responsible for these accounts. The balance in the escrow account must at all times be sufficient to account for funds designated to be held by the firm.

Escrow Account Disbursal

Once deposited, no funds may be removed from the escrow account until the transaction is consummated unless agreed to, in writing, by all principals to the transaction. In the event that the transaction is not consummated, the broker or supervising broker shall hold funds in escrow until:

- consummation of transaction (i.e., settlement);
- all principals to the transaction agree, in writing, to the disposition;
- a court orders disbursement; or
- the broker can determine, in accordance with the specific terms of the contract, exactly who is the rightful recipient of the funds.

Broker Disbursal Options If the broker decides to distribute the funds according to the terms of the contract, he or she must first give written notice to the principal to the transaction who is *not* to receive the funds. Notice may be either hand-delivered or by certified mail with return receipt requested, addressed to the notice address set forth in the contract or to the last known address of the recipient including a statement that reads that "Payment will be made unless a written protest is received within 30 days of delivery of the notice."

If the payment is to be made within 90 days of the date of the nonconsummation of the contract, notice may be sent by receiptable e-mail or facsimile, if such information is provided in the contract.

No broker is required to make such determination, nor is a broker deemed to have violated any obligations to a client by making the determination.

Any money in the escrow account that will ultimately belong to the broker may be left in the account and not be considered commingling, provided that these funds are clearly identified in the account records and that these funds are removed from the account at periodic intervals of not more than six months. Withdrawals from the escrow account for payment of commissions shall be paid to the firm by a check drawn on the escrow account.

If necessary, the broker may use a nominal amount of personal funds to establish or maintain the escrow account and not be guilty of commingling, provided that any funds so used are clearly identified in the account records.

Interest-Bearing Accounts

There is no legal requirement that escrow funds be held in an interest-bearing account. If the escrow account does earn interest, the broker must disclose, in writing, to all parties involved exactly how any earned interest will be disbursed. Such disclosure shall be made at the time the contract or lease is written.

Property Management

Brokers acting as property managers need to maintain escrow accounts. They will be receiving monies as security deposits that will ultimately be returned to tenants. They also receive rental money that belongs to the property owner. Brokers who manage several different properties should establish separate accounts for each property, even if the properties are owned by the same person. A broker cannot use funds from one property for another or disburse monies from an escrow or property management escrow account unless there is sufficient money on deposit in the account.

RECORD KEEPING AND ESCROW FUNDS [§54.1-2108; 18 VAC 135-20-185]

The broker must maintain a bookkeeping system that accurately and clearly discloses full compliance with the requirements of these regulations. The records must include the following information:

- The source of the funds
- The date the funds were received
- The date the funds were deposited
- Where the funds were deposited
- The date money was disbursed from the account
- The name of the person or persons who received the money

Escrow account records must be maintained for three years from date of consummation or termination of the transaction.

Actions that constitute improper record keeping and maintenance of escrow funds by the principal or supervising broker include

- accepting any note, nonnegotiable instrument (such as a promissory note or postdated check), or anything of value not readily negotiable (such as jewelry), as a deposit on a contract, offer to purchase, or lease, without acknowledging its acceptance in the agreement;

- commingling any person's funds with the personal or business funds of a principal or supervising broker or his employees or any licensee with his own funds or those of his corporation, firm, or association;
- failure to deposit escrow funds in accounts designated to receive escrow funds within five business banking days of ratification of the sales contract;
- failure to have sufficient balances in an escrow account at all times;
- failure of the principal broker to report to the Real Estate Board within three business days of any circumstance where it is believed that the improper conduct of a licensee has caused an insufficient balance in an escrow account;
- failing to retain a complete and legible copy of each disclosure of a brokerage relationship, executed contract, listing or buyer agency agreement, closing statement, and other material documents related to a real estate transaction in the broker's control or possession for a period of three years from the date of the closing or ratification (if the transaction fails to close);
- failing to maintain, for a period of three years from the date of the closing or termination of a lease of the licensee's or conclusion of a licensee's involvement in a lease, a complete and accurate record of monies received and disbursed on behalf of others; and
- failing to account for or remit, within a reasonable time, any funds coming into the possession that belongs to others.

Protection of Escrow Funds

The mismanagement of escrow funds is the basis of many complaints filed with the REB. If the REB has reason to believe that a broker is unable to properly protect escrow funds, for whatever reason, it may petition the court to intercede. The court may bar the licensee from any further activity with the escrow account and may take whatever other actions are necessary to protect the funds. The court may appoint a receiver to manage the funds, pending a complete investigation by the REB. It is the court that makes the appointment, not the REB.

If, as a result of the investigation, it is determined that the licensee has been at fault or has mismanaged the escrow funds, he or she must pay the costs of the receiver. If the licensee has no funds to pay the receiver, the receiver will be paid from any monies in the escrow account that would normally be due the licensee. If no such funds are available, the REB shall determine whether the receiver will be paid from the Transaction Recovery Fund.

If the investigation determines that the licensee is not at fault, the receiver will be paid from the funds of the REB.

ADVERTISING [18 VAC 135-20-190]

REB regulations define **advertising** as all forms of representation, promotion, and solicitation related to real estate activity that is disseminated by any means to consumers. **Institutional advertising** refers to advertising where no specific real property is identified; for example, an ad placed by a real estate firm to solicit new agents.

All advertising must be under the direct supervision of the principal or supervising broker and in the name of the firm. The firm's licensed name must be clearly and legibly displayed on all advertising. Disclosure requirements include advertising by the firm that contains the firm's licensed name and address or advertising by a licensee that must contain the licensee's name, the name of the firm where the licensee is active, and the firm's address.

Activities that are prohibited include

- implying that property listed by the licensee's firm is actually for sale or rent by the owner or any unlicensed person;
- failing to include a notice that the owner is a real estate licensee if the licensee has any ownership interest in the property and is not using the services of a licensed real estate entity;
- failing to include the firm's licensed name on any sign outside each place of business;
- failing to obtain written consent from the principals involved before advertising a specific property; and
- failing to identify the type of services offered when advertising a property not actually listed by the person making the advertisement.

Online Advertising

Disclosure in the context of online advertising includes the name of the firm, the city and state where the firm's main office is located, and the jurisdiction in which the firm holds a license. In the case of advertising by a licensee, the name of the licensee, the name of the firm, the city and state where the licensee's office is located, and the jurisdiction in which the licensee holds a license must be clearly visible.

Online advertising for the purpose of any licensed activity that appears as a separate unit (for example, e-mail and Web pages) must contain the following disclosures:

- Web page: either a firm or licensee Web page must contain disclosure or a link to disclosure on the viewable page
- E-mail, newsgroups, discussion lists, bulletin boards: must include disclosure at the beginning or end of each message
- Instant message: disclosure is not required if the licensee has provided disclosure previously in another format
- Chat: disclosure is required prior to providing, or offering to provide, real estate services during the chat session
- Voice Over Net (VON): disclosure is required prior to advertising, or the disclosure text must be clearly visible on the same Web page
- Banner ads: a link to disclosure is required if disclosure is not included on the banner

DEATH OR DISABILITY [§54.1-2109]

If a sole proprietor or the only broker in a firm dies or becomes disabled, the REB may authorize an unlicensed individual to conclude the broker's business. The individual appointed may be an adult member of the broker's family, an employee of the broker, or some other suitable person. The person appointed may act only to conclude the business of the broker and may act in this capacity for a period of not longer than 180 days.

If the deceased was a sole proprietor or the only broker in the firm, two things happen by operation of law:

1. All listings are terminated.
2. The licenses of any licensees active with the broker or firm must be returned to the REB because there is no longer a broker to be responsible for licensees, who are not allowed to operate in their own names.

If the principal broker of a large real estate firm dies, the officers of the firm designate a new principal broker and immediately file the appropriate form with REB naming the new principal broker.

THE VIRGINIA REAL ESTATE TRANSACTION RECOVERY FUND [§54.1-2112 ET SEQ.]

Purpose of the Fund

The Virginia Real Estate Transaction Recovery Fund was established for the purpose of reimbursing parties who suffer monetary loss due to a licensee's improper or dishonest conduct.

Maintenance of the Fund

The establishment and maintenance of the fund is the duty of the Director of the DPOR. The cost of administering the fund is paid out of interest earned on deposits. The REB may, at its discretion, use part of the interest earned by the fund for research and education for the benefit of licensees.

Each new licensee, whether salesperson or broker, must pay $20 into the fund. Monies collected must be deposited into the fund within 30 days after receipt by the director.

The fund's minimum balance is $400,000. If the balance of the fund falls below $400,000, the REB may assess each active and inactive licensee a proportionate amount to bring the balance to the statutory minimum. No licensee may be assessed more than $20 during any two-year period ending on June 30 of even-numbered years. Licensees who fail to pay the assessment within 45 days of receiving the first notice are given a second notice. Failure to pay the assessment within 30 days of the second notice results in automatic suspension of the licensee's license. The license will be suspended until such time as the director receives the amount due. The REB has the power to assess all licensees at one time or on individual licensees' renewals.

At the close of each fiscal year, if the balance of the fund is more than $2 million, the excess amount over $2 million is transferred to the Virginia Housing Partnership Fund (see Virginia Housing Development Authority [VHDA] discussion in Chapter 11).

Claims Procedure

A person who files a claim for payment from the fund must first obtain a judgment against the licensee from a Virginia court of competent authority. After a licensee has been found guilty of misconduct, the injured party must take appropriate legal action against the licensee. Appropriate legal action includes

- forcing the sale of the licensee's assets to satisfy all or part of the claim;

- investigating any listings held by the licensee and determining any commissions that may be due;
- filing a claim in bankruptcy court, if the licensee has filed bankruptcy; and
- requiring the licensee to submit to interrogatories, if necessary.

If any portion of the claim remains unsatisfied, the individual may file a claim with the REB requesting payment from the fund for the unsatisfied portion of the claim within 12 months from the date of the final judgment.

The claim must be accompanied by an affidavit stating the licensee's improper conduct and the actions taken to recover damages from sources other than the fund.

A claimant must have pursued all legal means for possible recovery before a claim can be filed with the REB. On receipt of a claim, the REB will promptly consider the request and notify the claimant, in writing, of its findings.

Limitation on Recovery

No fund payment will be made to any of the following:

- Any licensee or a licensee's personal representative
- The spouse or child of any licensee against whom the judgment was awarded, or their personal representative
- Any financial or lending institution
- Any person whose business involves the construction or development of real property

The claim can be only for the difference between the original loss and any amount previously recovered through the legal process associated with the final judgment.

The amount of the claim is limited to actual monetary damages suffered in the transaction, court costs, and attorney's fees. The claim cannot include interest, punitive, or exemplary damages, even though these amounts may have been included in the judgment awarded by the court.

Funds Available

If at any time the amount of claims to be paid from the fund would deplete the fund to an amount below the statutory minimum of $400,000, the processing of all claims will be suspended. The REB will assess licensees as previously outlined. As funds become available to satisfy the pending claims, the claims will be paid in the order in which they were originally received.

In all cases, the REB may withhold payment of any claim for 12 months if it has reason to believe that additional claims may be filed. In the event that there are multiple claims against a licensee that exceed the maximum allowable payment from the fund, each claimant will receive a proportionate share of the total payment.

Monetary Limitations on Claims

Single Transaction In a single transaction, the maximum payment from the fund to all injured parties is $50,000. The maximum amount any single claimant may recover from the fund based on a single transaction is $20,000, regardless of the number of claimants.

Multiple Transactions If the same licensee is involved in multiple fraudulent transactions during any two-year period ending June 30 of even-numbered years, the maximum payment to all claimants combined is $100,000.

If a payment is made from the fund, the claimant must **subrogate** his or her rights to the REB. Subrogation permits the REB to take action against the licensee to recover the amount of claims paid due to the licensee's misconduct.

Penalty

Payment from the fund causes the licensee's license to be *immediately revoked.* The respondent may also be subject to other disciplinary action by the REB. The licensee may not apply for a new license until the fund has been repaid in full, plus interest at the judgment rate of interest from the date of payment from the fund.

Repayment to the fund does not guarantee that the license will be reissued. The REB may take disciplinary action against a licensee for a disciplinable violation whether or not he or she has reimbursed the fund.

STANDARDS OF CONDUCT

The regulations promulgated by the REB establish certain required standards of professional behavior expected of all real estate licensees in Virginia.

Disclosure of Interest [18 VAC 135-20-210]

If a licensee has any family, business, or financial relationship with any of the principals to the contract, all parties to the contract must be informed of the relationship in writing in the offer to purchase or lease. This requirement applies to any licensee who could be considered an "interested party" to the transaction.

Disclosure of Brokerage Relationships and Dual or Designated Agency [18 VAC 135-20-220]

Unless disclosure has been made previously, a licensee must disclose the party he or she represents to an actual or prospective buyer or seller who is not the client of the licensee and who is not represented by another licensee. In the case of both buyers and sellers, the disclosure must be made when "substantive discussions about specific property" take place. The written disclosure must be provided "at the earliest practical time, but in no event later than the time specific real estate assistance is first provided."

The disclosure must advise prospective buyers, sellers, landlords, or tenants of the duties of real estate brokers and salespersons under Virginia law, and it must encourage them to obtain relevant information from other sources.

A licensee who is acting as a dual or designated representative must obtain the written consent of all parties "at the earliest practical time." The disclosure may be made in conjunction with other required disclosures if it is conspicuous, printed in bold lettering, all capitals, underlined, or within a separate box.

IN PRACTICE

The REB's regulations do not contain a list of specific events that trigger the disclosure requirement. Common sense should tell the licensee when disclosure is required: If in doubt, disclose.

Provision of Records to the Board [18 VAC 135-20-240, 250]

A licensee must produce any document, book, or record concerning a real estate transaction in which the licensee was involved, or was required to maintain records, within ten days from the request by the REB. Any other inquiries made by the board must be responded to within 21 days.

Unworthiness and Incompetence [18 VAC 135-20-260]

Actions that constitute unworthy and incompetent conduct include the following:

- Obtaining a license by false or fraudulent representation—for instance, providing false information in the license application or cheating on the license examination. It is also improper for a currently licensed real estate salesperson to sit for the salesperson's licensing examination, or for a currently licensed broker to sit for the broker's examination (of course, a qualified, licensed salesperson may sit for the broker's exam).
- Holding more than one license as a real estate broker or salesperson in Virginia, unless permitted to do so by law. Only brokers may hold more than one Virginia license.
- Having been finally convicted or found guilty of a misdemeanor involving moral turpitude, sexual offense, drug distribution, physical injury, or any felony. Any plea of nolo contendere is considered a conviction.
- Failing to inform the board in writing within 30 days of pleading guilty or nolo contendere or being convicted or found guilty of any convictions as previously stated.
- Having had a license suspended, revoked, or surrendered in connection with a disciplinary action.
- Having been found guilty of violating the Virginia Fair Housing Act or any other local, state, or federal fair housing laws.
- Failing to act in such a manner as to safeguard the interests of the public, or otherwise engaging in improper, fraudulent, or dishonest conduct.

Conflict of Interest [18 VAC 135-20-270]

Actions constituting a conflict of interest include the following:

- Being active with, or receiving compensation from, a real estate broker other than the licensee's principal broker without the written consent of the principal broker.
- Acting for more than one party in a transaction without the written consent of all principals for whom the licensee acts. Dual agency is not illegal in Virginia, provided that the principals to the transaction know it and agree to it in writing.
- Acting as a standard agent or independent contractor for any client in a real estate transaction outside the licensee's brokerage firm or sole proprietorship. All of a licensee's, salesperson's, or associate broker's acts of real estate brokerage must be conducted in the name of the employing broker.

Improper Brokerage Commission [18 VAC 135-20-280]

Brokers may pay commissions or fees to any licensees affiliated with their firm. Brokers also may pay commissions or fees to other brokers (or firms), regardless of where those brokers are located.

Salespersons and associate brokers may receive compensation from only the licensee's principal broker at the time of the transaction.

The performance of all real estate acts or the use of information gained as a result of such performance must be done with the consent of the principal broker. No licensee may act as an employee of a real estate settlement services company or provide real estate settlement services to clients or customers of the firm without the written consent of the broker.

Licensees are prohibited from receiving kickbacks from a third party who provides services or goods necessary to fulfill a contract, such as an appraiser, a home inspector, or a surveyor, when one of the principals to the contract is paying for the services unless full written disclosure is made to the principal. The principals must be informed, in writing, of any "finder's fees" or commissions paid to the licensee.

Licensees should be careful not to interpret the foregoing as a "license" to accept kickbacks as long as the principals are informed, in writing, of any "finder's fees" or commissions paid to the licensee. Additionally, licensees are reminded that all commissions and/or fees are required to be paid directly to the broker first. No licensee may receive a commission or fee from anyone other than his or her principal broker.

IN PRACTICE

When recommending services or third-party vendors such as lenders, appraisers, or home inspectors, licensees should be careful to offer clients and customers *options* for services or vendors from which to choose. This will avoid the appearance that the licensee is "steering" the client or customer to any one service or vendor for personal gain.

Options for home inspection services:

1. ABC Home Inspectors
2. Professionals Inspections, Inc.
3. Best Inspections Company

Other options include, but are not limited to the Yellow Pages, Internet search engines, and recommendations of informed and satisfied recipients of these types of vendor services.

Similarly, a licensee may not personally pay for services required by the terms of a real estate contract without written disclosure of the payment to the principals. For instance, a buyer might be short of the cash needed to pay for a survey of the property. If the licensee agrees to pay for the survey personally, there could be accusations later that the survey was inferior or not done by a competent professional surveyor unless all of the principals agree to the arrangement. The licensee has a personal interest in the transaction being completed; offering to pay for one of the steps necessary for completion could appear to be self-serving.

A listing contract or lease that provides for a "net" return to the seller/lessor is not allowed in Virginia. (See Chapter 2, page 17.)

Finally, no licensee may charge money or other valuable consideration *to*, or accept or receive money or valuable consideration *from*, any person or entity *other than the licensee's principal* for expenditures made on the principal's behalf without the written consent of the principal.

Improper Dealing [18 VAC 135-20-290]

Actions that constitute improper dealing include

- entering into a brokerage relationship that does not have a specific, definite termination date (most listing and buyer representation agreements include a blank space in which the date may be inserted);
- offering property for sale or lease without the owner's knowledge and consent, or on terms other than those authorized by the owner;
- placing *any* sign on *any* property without permission (this regulation could include the placement of directional signs on the property of someone other than the seller); and
- advertising property for sale, rent, or lease in any newspaper, periodical, or sign without including in the advertisement the name of the firm or sole proprietorship.

Misrepresentations and Omissions [18 VAC 135-20-300]

The regulations prohibit specific actions as misrepresentations or omissions. They are

- using "bait and switch" tactics by advertising or by offering real property for sale or rent with the intent not to sell or rent at the price or terms advertised, unless the advertisement or offer clearly states that the property advertised is limited in specific quantity and the licensee or registrant did in fact have at least that quantity for sale or rent;
- failing to disclose material information related to the property that is reasonably available to the licensee—a dual representative may not disclose confidential information to either client;
- failing to promptly present *every* written offer, rejection, or counteroffer to the buyer and seller;
- failing to include the *complete* terms and conditions of the real estate transaction in any offer to purchase or rent, including identification of all those holding any deposits;
- knowingly making any false statement or report, or willfully misstating the value of any land, property, or security for the purpose of influencing a lender regarding applications, advance discounts, purchase agreements, repurchase agreements, commitments of loans, or to change the terms or time limits for any of these items without the written consent of the principals;
- making *any* misrepresentation; and
- making a false promise through agents, salespersons, advertising, or other means.

Delivery of Instruments [18 VAC 135-20-310]

Actions constituting improper delivery of instruments include

- failing to promptly deliver complete and legible copies of any written listings, offers to lease, offers to purchase, counteroffers, addenda, and ratified agreements to each party in a transaction—anyone who signs his or her name to a document is entitled to a copy;
- failing to provide timely, written notice of any material change in the transaction to all parties;
- failing to deliver a complete and accurate statement of money received and disbursed by the licensee, duly signed and certified by the principal or supervising broker (or his or her authorized agent), to the seller and buyer at the time a real estate transaction is completed. However, if the transaction is closed by a settlement agent other than the licensee (or his or her broker), and if the financial disclosure is provided on the applicable settlement

statement, the licensee is not required to provide a separate statement of receipts and disbursements; and

- refusing or failing without just cause to surrender any document or instrument to the rightful owner on demand.

Principal and Supervising Broker's Responsibility for Licensees [18 VAC 135-20-330]

A principal or supervising broker is liable for the unlawful acts of a real estate salesperson, employee, partner, or affiliate of a principal or supervising broker only if the REB finds that the principal or supervising broker knew or should have known of the unlawful act or violation.

Effect of Disciplinary Action on Subordinate Licensees [18 VAC 315-20-340]

If a principal broker's or sole proprietor's license is revoked or suspended, or if renewal is denied, the licenses of any and all individuals affiliated with or employed by the affected firm are automatically ordered returned to the REB until such time as they are reissued on the written request of another sole proprietor or principal broker. That is, affiliated licensees must either transfer or become inactive.

COMPLAINT PROCEDURE

Compliance and Investigations Process

The Compliance & Investigations Division of the Department of Professional and Occupational Regulation (the Department) reviews complaints to determine whether the Department is authorized to process the complaint. The Department will only process complaints against individuals or businesses that are subject to the laws or regulations of regulatory boards within the Department.

Complaint Analysis and Resolution (CAR)

This section of DPOR is responsible for the receipt, processing, and analysis of all complaints coming into the Department regarding real estate regulants. Upon review, the Complaint Analysis and Resolution Section may close the file, investigate the complaint, resolve the matter by a consent order, or refer the case to Alternative Dispute Resolution or Investigations for further action.

Complaints must be in writing; forms for filing a complaint can be found online at: *www.dpor.virginia.gov* under the link "Compliance & Investigations."

A complaint can be handled in a variety of ways:

- Investigation
- Informal resolution through a Compliance or Consent Order
- Alternate dispute resolution (uses conciliation and mediation)
- Adjudication

Possible Solutions/ Options

A complaint may be

- closed;
- resolved by Complaint Analysis and Resolution through Compliance or a Consent Order;
- referred to staff for technical review regarding violations and/or offering a Consent Order; or
- referred to Adjudication Division for an Informal Fact-Finding Conference (IFF).

The Adjudication Section

The Adjudication Section reviews files referred from Complaint Analysis & Resolution or Field Investigations that there is probable cause of a violation of the Board's regulations and/or laws. The Adjudication Section is responsible for conducting Informal Fact-Finding Conferences (IFF), which includes scheduling the IFF, sending the Notice, presenting the IFF, and providing support to the Presiding Officer or Board member at the IFF in preparing the Summary.

Informal Fact-Finding Conference

The IFF is a hearing conducted at the offices of DPOR; it is presided over by an REB member and supported by DPOR staff.

IFF Process

The presiding board member

- listens to the testimony of participants,
- asks questions,
- reviews additional information presented,
- leaves the record open for additional evidence to be presented or collected,
- maintains control of the conference by avoiding an adversarial proceeding, and
- remains neutral.

After considering the testimony and evidence, the presiding board member will offer a Consent Order or prepare a Summary and Recommendation.

Consent Order

The regulant accepts responsibility without contest (no appeal possible) and submits to the judgment recommended by the presiding board member. The Consent Order is presented at the full board meeting for approval. The board may

- accept the consent order as presented,
- reject the consent order,
- make a counteroffer, and
- remand it to an IFF.

IFF Review and Recommendations

The presiding board member can recommend the following:

- Probation
- Revocation
- Suspension
- Denial of renewal
- Fines
- Any other remedy granted by statute or regulations (e.g., education, examination, or reprimand)

Complaints not resolved or closed are referred to Adjudication Section for an IFF.

REB Board Meetings

It is important to note that all disciplinary decisions come before the full REB for review and approval. REB scheduled meetings (there are approximately eight per year) are open to the public. IFF participants are afforded an opportunity to address the full board at these meetings and may speak for five minutes, but no new evidence may be presented. The board carefully considers the IFF Summary and Recommendation, which outlines thoughts, analysis, and credibility issues and makes its final decision.

Possible Outcomes

- IFF Summary and Recommendation: accept, reject, or modify violations and/or sanctions
- Consent Order: accept, make counteroffer, ask for exhibits, or request an IFF (if one has not been held)

If the REB finds the licensee guilty, it may impose a monetary penalty of up to $2,500 for each violation. The REB may also suspend, revoke, or deny renewal of the respondent's license. The REB's decision is final, although the licensee may appeal the decision through the Court of Appeals. In all of these proceedings, the accused has the right to be represented by legal counsel.

Automatic License Suspension or Revocation

There are two instances in which disciplinary action may be taken against a licensee and his or her license may be suspended or revoked without review or a hearing:

1. If a licensee does not pay the assessment to the Transaction Recovery Fund, his or her license will be automatically *suspended*.
2. If a payment is made from the Transaction Recovery Fund, the license of the respondent will be automatically *revoked*.

QUESTIONS

1. Which of the following is an accurate description of the Real Estate Board?
   a. Seven members: six licensees and one consumer
   b. Seven members: five licensees and two consumers
   c. Nine members: either licensed brokers or salespersons
   d. Nine members: seven licensees and two consumers

2. Is it possible to become licensed in Virginia without taking the Virginia real estate license examination?
   a. No
   b. Yes, if the person is licensed to practice law in Virginia
   c. Yes, because any person who is currently licensed in another jurisdiction and meets all requirements for reciprocity may be licensed in Virginia
   d. Yes, if the person is an appraiser

3. Which of the following is a requirement to obtain a real estate salesperson's license in Virginia?
   a. Successful completion of 12 credit hours of real estate law, investments, finance, and appraisal
   b. An associate degree or certificate in real estate from an accredited college, university, or proprietary school
   c. U.S. and Virginia citizenship
   d. Successful completion of a course of 60 classroom, correspondence, or distance learning hours in general principles of real estate

4. All of the following are requirements for a broker's license *EXCEPT*
   a. a college degree or certificate in business, finance, management, appraisal, or real estate.
   b. 12 semester hours of designated real estate courses.
   c. three years of experience as a salesperson.
   d. not have violated Virginia's fair housing laws or those of any other state.

5. A broker's business is growing, and now she wants to open a branch office. Which of the following is *TRUE*?
   a. The office must have an escrow account.
   b. The office may be managed by a salesperson with three years of experience.
   c. The office must have a separate license.
   d. The branch office will display the licenses of all salespersons and associate brokers assigned to that particular office.

6. A licensed salesperson may hold a concurrent license with more than one Virginia broker under which of the following circumstances?
   a. Under no circumstances
   b. With the permission of his or her sales manager
   c. With the written consent of the brokers being represented
   d. With the permission of the REB

7. A licensee who allows his or her license to expire has how long to reinstate the license without monetary penalty?
   a. Up to 15 days
   b. Up to 30 days
   c. No more than 365 days
   d. One year from the last transaction

8. A licensee was out of town on vacation. When she returned on October 10, she found her license renewal notice and realized that her license had expired on July 31. If she wants to remain licensed, she *MUST*
   a. reapply for a new license as a new applicant.
   b. meet the current educational requirements.
   c. apply for reinstatement of her license and pay the current reinstatement fee.
   d. apply to have her license placed on inactive status.

9. How often are real estate licenses renewed in Virginia?
   a. Annually, in the month issued
   b. Every two years, in the month of the licensee's birthday
   c. On June 30 of each even-numbered year
   d. Biennially, on the last day of the month in which issued

10. All of the following statements are correct regarding an active licensed broker who has been licensed in Virginia since 1975, *EXCEPT*
    a. the broker may be licensed in more than one legal real estate entity.
    b. the broker is exempt from the continuing education requirements on the basis of having been licensed for more than 15 years.
    c. the broker may contract to be a property manager.
    d. the broker's office may be located in his or her home under certain circumstances.

11. Yore Realty opens its first office in Richmond. Which of the following is a permissible sign to place in front of the office?
    a. "Yore office"
    b. "Yore House: We Serve Richmond's Homeowners"
    c. "Yore Realty"
    d. "Yore: A Member of the Greater Richmond Chamber of Commerce"

12. A salesperson decides to retire. When the salesperson terminates his or her affiliation, what must he or she do?
    a. Give the broker an official letter of termination that he or she can send to the REB
    b. Nothing; the broker is responsible for notifying the REB of the change
    c. Return all customer cards to the employing broker
    d. Return his or her license, along with a letter of termination, to the REB

13. If a broker establishes an account to hold money belonging to others, which of the following is *CORRECT*?
    a. All checks, deposit slips, and bank statements must include the word *Escrow* as part of the account name.
    b. Accounts may be labeled either "Trust" or "Escrow."
    c. The account cannot be in the same bank as the broker's personal checking account.
    d. An individual account is required for each transaction.

14. Earnest money deposits may be distributed from the broker's escrow account in any of the following situations *EXCEPT*
    a. at settlement on the property.
    b. when all parties to the transaction agree to disbursement.
    c. when requested by one party's attorney.
    d. when the broker determines distribution according to the contract.

15. A broker manages three properties for the same owner. One property is in need of emergency repairs, but there is not enough money in the management account to cover the cost. The broker borrows money from the escrow account of one of the other properties to make the repairs. Which of the following is *TRUE*?
    a. The broker has acted properly by safeguarding the client's interest.
    b. Such action is proper because all properties are owned by the same person.
    c. The broker is in violation of regulations for improperly handling escrow funds.
    d. The broker must use personal funds for repairs if there is not enough money in the management account.

16. Every Virginia real estate office is required to
    a. maintain escrow account records for five years.
    b. keep transaction records for three years.
    c. display signage at the office location.
    d. employ at least one salesperson.

17. What must appear on all "For Sale" signs placed on property by a broker?
    a. The broker's phone number
    b. The name of the person who listed the property
    c. The selling price of the property
    d. The name of the broker

18. Broker *D* has developed her own Web page to advertise her listings for sale. Online disclosure requirements require that she include on each page
    a. her full name and address.
    b. her name and her firm's name.
    c. her name and her firm's name and address.
    d. her name, her firm's name and address, and the jurisdiction in which her firm is licensed.

19. A licensed salesperson is selling her own condominium and advertises it as follows: "For Sale By Owner: 3 bed. condo unit in high rise. Call 987-6543 for details. Owner licensed." Based on these facts, which of the following is *TRUE*?
    a. Because the salesperson is acting in a private capacity, she is exempt from the advertising laws.
    b. The advertisement is proper because the owner has disclosed her licensee status as required by law.
    c. Virginia's advertising regulations do not apply to condominiums.
    d. The ad should have included her office number and broker.

20. Seller *S*'s listing broker commits a fraudulent act in connection with the sale of a property on March 15, 2007. On March 30, the transaction closes. On November 1, *S* sues the broker, alleging fraud. On December 20, the jury finds in favor of *S*. When must *S* file a claim with REB to recover money from the Transaction Recovery Fund?
    a. The request must be filed within 30 days following the illegal activity—in this case, by April 15, 2007.
    b. Within one year after having been awarded a judgment by the courts—in this case, by December 20, 2008.
    c. Within one year of filing suit—in this case, by November 1, 2008.
    d. Within two years of the date of closing—in this case, by March 30, 2009.

21. What is the minimum balance of the Virginia Real Estate Transaction Recovery Fund?
    a. $800,000
    b. $600,000
    c. $750,000
    d. $400,000

22. After proper investigation, a payment is made from the Transaction Recovery Fund owing to the improper activities of *H*, a licensee. What happens when the payment is made?

a. *H*'s license is automatically suspended.
b. The REB takes no further action if *H* repays the fund within 30 days.
c. *H*'s license is automatically revoked.
d. *H* is subject to a fine of $2,000.

23. A licensed salesperson obtains a listing. Several days later, the salesperson meets prospective buyers at the property and tells them, "I am the listing agent for this property, and so I'm very familiar with it." Under these circumstances, the salesperson

a. has failed to properly disclose his or her agency relationship.
b. has properly disclosed his or her agency relationship with the seller.
c. is in violation of REB regulations, because the listing belongs to the broker.
d. has created a dual agency, which is a violation of REB regulations.

24. A broker is convicted on May 1 of possession and distribution of a controlled substance. Both the crime and the conviction took place in the state of Maryland. On June 15, the broker calls the REB and leaves a message informing the REB of the conviction. Based on these facts, which of the following is *TRUE*?

a. The broker has properly informed the REB within 60 days after the conviction, and the broker's license may be renewed.
b. Both the conviction and the broker's failure to notify the REB within 30 days violates REB regulations.
c. Because the conviction did not occur in Virginia, it is not evidence of unworthy conduct.
d. The conviction is evidence of both improper dealing and fraud.

25. When a salesperson lists and sells property that he or she owns, it is important that the listing agreement include all of the following information, *EXCEPT*

a. the name of the employing broker.
b. a definite date on which the listing will expire.
c. a disclosure of licensure status.
d. the net amount that the seller will receive from the sale.

26. Several weeks after a closing, an associate broker received a thank-you letter and a nice bonus check from the seller of the house. The associate broker cashed the check because he felt it was earned. In this situation, which of the following is *TRUE*?

a. The associate broker may accept the bonus because he is licensed as an associate broker.
b. Accepting the money is allowed if more than 30 days have elapsed since the closing.
c. The associate broker may accept the money if his broker permits him to do so.
d. Accepting the money is a violation of REB regulations.

27. Under the terms of a sales contract, the seller is required to provide a termite certificate. The seller requests that the salesperson order one. The salesperson does so, knowing she will receive a referral fee from the pest control company. Is this a violation of the license law?

a. No, if the fee is less than $25
b. No, if the fee is disclosed in writing to the parties to the contract
c. Yes, a salesperson may not receive a referral fee
d. Yes, special fees may be paid to the salesperson only by the seller

28. *W*, an airline pilot, told M, a broker, about some friends who were looking for a new home. M contacted the friends and eventually sold them a house. When may M pay *W* for the valuable lead?

a. As soon as a valid sales contract is signed by the parties
b. Only after the sale closes
c. After the funds are released from escrow
d. M may not pay *W* for the lead.

29. When a sole proprietor has his or her license suspended for two years, what effect does this have on the associate brokers and salespeople affiliated with the proprietor?
   a. The affiliates' licenses will be revoked, subject to reinstatement after one year.
   b. The affiliates' licenses will be also be suspended for a two-year period.
   c. The suspension has no effect on the affiliates.
   d. The affiliates' licenses must be returned to the REB.

30. When a salesperson is alleged to have violated the license law, possibly resulting in disciplinary action, which of the following statements is *TRUE*?
   a. An investigation will be conducted by the REB.
   b. The salesperson is entitled to a jury trial before any action can be taken.
   c. The salesperson's license will be temporarily suspended until the REB can schedule a formal hearing.
   d. The employing broker also is charged with the same violation.

31. Bob is a licensee with QRT Realty and his individual practice is growing. Bob wants to hire an assistant to help him with paperwork, answer calls, and show properties on Sundays only. Bob will be able to do this as long as the assistant
   a. has a valid real estate license and becomes affiliated with Bob's firm.
   b. is a member of the local MLS.
   c. joins Bob's broker's real estate association.
   d. abides by the REALTOR® Code of Ethics.

32. Gatto and his wife are both new licensees with WYZ World Realty. They want to set up a team and advertise themselves as Team Gatto. They have applied for and received a salespersons' entity license, and their new signs read

    Team Gatto
    Real Estate Services
    Cell# 123-456-7890

    What information is missing from their sign?
   a. Gatto's home phone number
   b. The name of the broker or firm with whom Gatto and his wife are affiliated
   c. The broker's license number
   d. The broker's telephone number

33. Yolanda became licensed on January 1, 2008. It is now December 31, 2008 and Yolanda has failed to take any continuing education classes. What must she do if she is to remain licensed in 2009?
   a. Complete 16 hours of continuing education and apply for reinstatement
   b. Complete 32 hours of continuing education
   c. Complete 30 hours of post-licensing education and apply for reinstatement
   d. Complete 30 hours of continuing education

34. Phuong lives in Maryland, is a licensed broker/owner in Maryland, and has just obtained a broker's license by reciprocity in Virginia. Larry lives in Virginia, is licensed in Virginia and a close friend of Phuong, and wants to work for Phuong in Virginia. What must Phuong do if Larry is to affiliate with her and sell real estate in Virginia?
   a. Phuong must move to Virginia.
   b. Phuong must establish a brokerage in Virginia.
   c. Because Phuong holds a broker's license in Maryland, she need only acquire office space in Virginia from which Larry may operate.
   d. Phuong must hire a broker in Virginia.

35. The minimum balance of the Virginia Real Estate Transaction Recovery Fund is $400,000. What is the maximum amount allowed to remain in the recovery fund at the end of each fiscal year?
   a. $400,000
   b. $800,000
   c. $2,000,000
   d. $1,000,000

36. A licensed salesperson begins working with a buyer without a signed buyer representation agreement. Upon showing the buyer the first property, the agent states, "I am not the listing agent, but I think this property is just the one for you." Under these circumstances, the salesperson

a. has failed to properly disclose his or her agency relationship.
b. has properly disclosed his or her agency relationship.
c. is in violation of REB regulations, because he does not have a signed buyer representation agreement.
d. has created a dual agency, which is a violation of REB regulations.

37. A salesperson lists his broker's home for sale and publishes it in the local MLS. It is important that the salesperson disclose

a. the name of his broker.
b. the fact that both he and his broker are licensees.
c. the commission he will earn.
d. that he is an independent contractor.

38. Licensee Bob (a salesperson) is convicted of a crime on September 15. Which statement is *TRUE?*

a. By September 30, Bob must notify the REB of his conviction.
b. The jurisdiction in which Bob was convicted will automatically notify the REB.
c. By the end of October, Bob must notify the REB of his conviction.
d. Bob must notify the REB within 30 days of his conviction.

39. Mary, a licensee in Virginia, has made a buyer referral to a licensee in Texas. Upon the closing of sale in Texas, Mary receives a referral fee in the form of a check from the Texas broker for $2,500. Which is *TRUE?*

a. Mary can deposit the check.
b. Mary must give the check to her broker, even if it is made payable to her.
c. Mary cannot receive a referral fee because she is not licensed in Texas.
d. Mary can cash the check and give her broker his share of their mutual commission split.

40. Larry is a Maryland resident and a licensed broker in Maryland. He is also licensed as a broker in Virginia. In order for him to transact real estate in Virginia, Larry must

a. affiliate with a Virginia real estate firm.
b. do nothing additional to transact business in Virginia.
c. open a Virginia real estate firm.
d. Either 1 or 2

41. In question 40 above, Larry will also be required to file a(n)

a. Interstate Disclosure Waiver.
b. Consent to REB Licensure form.
c. consent to suits and services.
d. waiver to suits and services.

42. Tiko was licensed on July 5, 2008. She must complete 30 hours of postlicensing education

a. within two years of becoming licensed.
b. by July 5, 2010.
c. by December 31, 2008.
d. within the first 12 months of becoming a licensee.

43. Kim is a licensed broker whose license was last renewed on January 25, 2006. How many hours of continuing education will she be required to complete to renew her license?

a. 16
b. 30
c. 24
d. 28

44. John is an attorney in Virginia and also holds a salesperson's licensee. Mila, also a salesperson licensee, wants to go in with John and form a real estate firm. Which one of them can be the managing broker of the firm?

a. John
b. Mila
c. Neither
d. Both, if the responsibility is shared equally

11
CHAPTER

Real Estate Financing Principles

This chapter primarily discusses the financing of single-family residential real estate in Virginia. It does not address commercial or more sophisticated transactions, but many of the concepts addressed apply to such transactions.

PURCHASE CONTRACTS AND FINANCING

A licensed real estate broker or agent who has negotiated a sale may prepare a routine contract for the transaction. If a first deed of trust loan is to be obtained, the contract usually is made contingent on the purchaser's obtaining the loan. The real estate licensee must be careful in describing the loan because of the complexity of the terms for prevailing loans. The seller may add the provision that the purchaser must apply for the loan promptly and, should the purchaser not notify the seller by a certain date that loan approval has been obtained, the contingency shall be deemed waived. Typically, preprinted real estate contracts provide that the purchaser has a specified number of days from the date of the contract in which to apply for financing. The contract should specifically state what type of financing is contemplated: cash, assumption, seller financed, FHA, VA, or conventional loan obtained through an institutional lender.

The contract should provide a ceiling on the interest rate the borrower will accept. If this condition is not included, the purchaser could be bound by the contract even if the interest rate rises several percentage points between the date the contract is ratified and the date the purchaser locks in the interest rate with a lender. The lack of an interest rate cap could end up significantly increasing the cost of the home for the buyer.

If an existing loan is to remain on the property, the contract should specify whether it will be assumed or whether title will be taken subject to the existing loan.

INSTITUTIONAL FINANCING

Conventional Loans

In Virginia, deeds of trust, rather than mortgages, are the instruments primarily used in residential sales transactions. In the deed of trust there are three parties: the borrower, the lender, and a trustee (a neutral third party) who holds the deed of trust for both the borrower and the lender. Nearly every type of financial institution makes conventional deed of trust loans.

In Virginia, the note and deed of trust give the lender, in the event the borrower should default, the right to declare the entire debt due and payable. In that situation, the power of sale clause in the deed of trust gives the trustee the right to sell the property (foreclose) without going to court, hence the term *nonjudicial foreclosure* is most commonly associated with the deed of trust.

By signing the note and deed of trust, the borrower waives various rights, including the right to a court hearing.

It is extremely important that the borrower fully understand the nature of the note and deed of trust.

The note and deed of trust are generally prepared by the lender. Standard forms are available for specialized loans such as those insured (e.g., FHA) or guaranteed (e.g., VA) by the government. The note is not usually recorded, although the deed of trust should always be promptly recorded.

The note and deed of trust should be signed in the exact manner and in the same name as the title is held. No witnesses are necessary. The deed of trust must be **acknowledged,** that is, notarized, to permit its recordation in the land records of the circuit court where the property is located. Further, VA and FHA notes and notes to be sold out of state require notarization with a seal. Good sources of information on residential financing are available on the Internet at the following Web addresses:

WEB LINK @

http://www.hud.gov/ (for FHA)
http://www.va.gov/ (for Veterans Administration)
http://www.fanniemae.com (for Fannie Mae)
http://www.freddiemac.com (for Freddie Mac conventional loan products)

Late Charges

Many conventional first deed of trust loans contain a provision for a late charge if a monthly payment is not made within a certain period of time after the due date (referred to as a *grace period*). The fact that a late charge may be collected must be disclosed in the loan's truth-in-lending statement. In Virginia, late charges may not exceed five percent of the installment due and cannot be collected unless the payment is not made within seven calendar days after the due date. Most lenders permit 15 days. The late charge must be specified in the contract between the lender and the borrower. Late charges in excess of the statutory amount are void only with regard to the excess amount; an inflated late charge does not affect the underlying obligation.

Other Charges

In addition to such charges as points, late charges, and escrows, Virginia law permits lenders to charge a *loan origination fee* for granting a loan.

Other allowable closing costs are the fees charged for title examination, title insurance, recording charges, taxes, hazard insurance, mortgage guarantee insurance, appraisals, credit reports, surveys, document preparation, real estate tax service fees, lender inspection, and attorney or settlement agent charges for closing the loan and settlement on the property.

The lender generally requires a house location survey. The survey must be current (within the past six months), and the survey must be done by a certified land surveyor.

HELOCS OR CREDIT LINE DEEDS OF TRUST

Sometimes called *credit line deeds of trust*, a HELOC (Home Equity Line of Credit) permits the note holder to make advances from time to time secured by the real estate described in the deed. In today's market most HELOCs are second trusts and are many times made at the same time as the first trust with the same lender. The total amount of advances may not exceed the maximum credit line extended to the borrower. Virginia law permits credit line deeds of trust, subject to certain rules. The trust document must identify itself as a credit line deed of trust on the front page in capital letters and underscored type. The phrase THIS IS A CREDIT LINE DEED OF TRUST gives notice that the note holder named in the deed of trust and the grantors and other borrowers identified in the deed have an agreement.

From the date of the recording of a credit line deed of trust, the lien has priority over all other deeds, conveyances, and other instruments or contracts in writing that are unrecorded at that time and of which the note holder has no knowledge. The credit line deed of trust also has priority over judgment liens subsequently docketed. However, if a judgment creditor gives notice to the note holder at the address indicated on the credit line deed of trust, the deed of trust has no priority over the judgment for any advances or extensions of credit subsequently made under the deed of trust.

IN PRACTICE

Most HELOCs are second mortgages. An increasing number, however, are first mortgages. Using a HELOC as a substitute for a first mortgage is risky. Because the balance of a HELOC may change from day to day, depending on draws and repayments, interest on a HELOC is calculated daily rather than monthly.

For example, on a standard six percent mortgage, interest for the month is 0.06 divided by 12, or 0.005, multiplied by the loan balance at the end of the preceding month. If the balance is $100,000, the interest payment is $500.

On a six percent HELOC, interest for a day is 0.06 divided by 365, or 0.0001643, which is multiplied by the average daily balance during the month. If this is $100,000, the daily interest is $16.43, and over a 30-day month interest amounts to $492.90; over a 31-day month, it is $509.33.

DUE-ON-SALE CLAUSES

Loans that contain a **due-on-sale clause,** also called an *alienation clause,* are not assumable unless the lender chooses to waive the due-on-sale clause. Due-on-sale clauses are enforceable in Virginia. When a loan containing a due-on-sale clause is made on real property comprising not more than four residential dwelling units, the deed of trust must contain the following language, either in capital letters or underlined:

> *NOTICE—The debt secured hereby is subject to call in full or the terms thereof being modified in the event of sale or conveyance of the property conveyed.*

PURCHASE-MONEY FINANCING AND SELLER FINANCING

Purchase-money financing occurs when a mortgage or deed of trust is given as part of the purchaser's consideration for the purchase of real property. Purchase-money financing may be provided by a third party such as an institutional lender or the seller. When provided by the seller, it commonly refers to a seller "taking back" a second trust in lieu of cash to make up the difference between the first trust from the institutional lender and the selling price for the property.

FOR EXAMPLE *T* wants $100,000 for his property. The purchasers are able to secure a $70,000 loan secured by a first deed of trust from an institutional lender. Because they have only $10,000 in cash available for a down payment, they ask *T* to accept a purchase-money deed of trust (seller financing) for $20,000. The rate and terms must be agreed on between *T* and the purchasers.

A purchase-money deed of trust has priority over other claims or liens against the purchaser except for property tax or IRS tax liens.

DEFERRED PURCHASE-MONEY DEED OF TRUST

Sellers having no immediate need to take the full amount of the proceeds of a sale may choose to defer the income of the sale and obtain an installment tax treatment by creating an annuity in the form of a deferred purchase-money deed of trust, held by the seller. One advantage to sellers is that they usually receive a substantial down payment. Such an arrangement may be prohibited, however, if there is to be a first deed of trust to an outside (institutional) lender. A purchase-money deed of trust held by the seller should state that it is granted to secure *deferred purchase money,* while a purchase-money deed of trust to a third (institutional lender) party states that it is granted to secure *purchase money.* If it is a second deed of trust, it can be for a short term with a balloon payment at the end. The first lender's guidelines must be followed. If it is subordinated, the purchase-money second deed of trust should include a provision that any default in a senior encumbrance or lien will also be considered a default on a second deed of trust.

■ **FOR EXAMPLE** *J* wants $400,000 for his property but does not want to take the proceeds of the sale in one tax year. *J* offers to take back financing in the form of a deferred purchase-money deed of trust. *J* will accept a $20,000 down payment from the purchasers and hold a note for $380,000 that balloons in ten years. The rate and terms must be agreed on between *J* and the purchasers.

■ RELEASES

Whenever the borrower pays off any note, a marginal release is made on the face of the instrument wherever the document is recorded. Alternatively, a certificate of satisfaction or a partial satisfaction form is filed in the deed books in the clerk's office in the county where the land is located.

■ VIRGINIA HOUSING DEVELOPMENT AUTHORITY

The Virginia Housing Development Authority (VHDA) was created in 1972 by the Virginia General Assembly. Its purpose is to make housing more affordable for those with low or moderate incomes. Currently, VHDA is self-supporting, and funding for its programs is provided by the private sector through the sales of VHDA bonds. Federal and state tax dollars are not used to fund VHDA lending programs.

A board of commissioners composed of ten members appointed by the governor provides for oversight.

The Virginia Housing Partnership [Revolving] Fund was created to address the serious shortage in the Commonwealth of safe and decent residential housing at prices that persons and families of low and moderate incomes can afford. Housing developments and housing projects funded through the fund are intended to provide additional affordable housing opportunities for low-income and moderate-income Virginians by preserving existing housing units, by producing new housing units, and by assisting persons with special needs to obtain adequate housing. The fund is administered and managed by the VHDA.

Basic VHDA services include the following:

- Single-family loan programs. Creative and lower interest rate loans for low- to moderate-income homebuyers who have not had an ownership interest in their primary residences during the three years prior to making application for the loan.
- Multifamily loan products. Mortgage loans to developers of multifamily projects (primarily for rentals for low-income and moderate-income tenants).
- Administration of the federal low-income housing Tax Credit Program.
- Administration of the federal Section 8 rent subsidy programs.
- Virginia Housing Fund. Loans for multifamily housing that will serve low-income and moderate-income residents in difficult situations or locations.
- Administration of some functions of the Virginia Housing Partnership Fund.

VHDA offers a variety of different loan programs, including those made in conjunction with FHA and VA. VHDA's new Flexible/Alternative program allows for

100 percent loan-to-value financing. A Homeownership Education course may be required of first-time buyers, depending on their credit score.

Specific guidelines for the various VHDA loan products may be obtained from a local lender or by contacting VHDA headquarters in Richmond or online at the following Web address:

WEB LINK @

www.vhda.com

VHDA also builds and operates residential housing, nursing care facilities, and nursing homes providing medical and related facilities for the residence and care of the elderly.

FORECLOSURE

There are three ways to foreclose a deed of trust in Virginia:

1. Decree of court (strict foreclosure)
2. Conveyance of the property by the grantors and the trustees to the beneficiary in consideration of the debt ("deed in lieu of foreclosure")
3. Sale by the trustee pursuant to a power of sale ("trustee sale")

Although an exhaustive discussion of foreclosure procedures is not necessary here, it is important for licensees to be aware that bankruptcy of the mortgagor is an automatic stay of foreclosure. If a lien is foreclosed, that is, no bankruptcy was granted, the lien and all inferior liens are wiped out. Superior liens, however—those that have priority over the foreclosed lien—are not affected. A purchaser takes the property subject to any prior liens.

VA and FHA Loans

Foreclosure of VA and FHA loans is subject to certain additional requirements. For instance, the loan must have been in default for three months prior to the commencement of foreclosure; notices must be given to both the debtor and the insuring agency; and the lender must take affirmative steps to avoid foreclosure, including personal interviews and acceptance of partial payments.

Trustee's Powers and Duties

Virginia is a **title theory** state.

Legal title to the property conveyed by the deed of trust is vested in the trustee for the benefit of the note holder. The trustee can act only in a manner authorized by statute or the express or implied terms of the trust.

The **trustee** is the agent for both the **grantor** (the homeowner) and the **beneficiary** (the lender) and is bound to act impartially between them. The trustee is obliged to seek every possible advantage to the trust in the course of any sale. This includes using all reasonable diligence to obtain the best price possible. The trustee may adjourn the sale from time to time to meet any unexpected occurrences, but the readvertisement of the sale must be in the same manner as the original advertisement.

If it is clear at the sale that the property will be sold for a grossly inadequate or sacrificial price, it is the trustee's duty to adjourn the sale. In addition, if the trustee knows of facts that might keep bidding low, such as a cloud on title, he or she must adjourn the sale and remove the hindrance.

By statute, the trustee must ascertain whether there are any real estate tax liens against the property being sold. The trustee is obligated to pay the taxes out of the proceeds of sale and give the tax lien priority over the deed of trust. In addition, the purchaser is required to see that the taxes are paid. If the taxes are not paid, the trustee may be liable personally and the purchaser takes the land subject to the tax lien (though not personally liable for its payment). The trustee should also pay the prorated portion of the current year's real estate taxes.

Caveat Emptor

The rule of *caveat emptor* ("let the buyer beware") applies in foreclosure sales, with regard to both the quality of title and the condition of the property.

Advertisement

The terms of the deed of trust will determine how the property is advertised. Even if the number of advertisements meets the terms, Virginia law provides that the sale may take place no earlier than the eighth day after the first advertisement and no later than 30 days after the last advertisement.

Conflict of Interest

A trustee may not purchase the property held in trust without written permission from the trustor. The trustee is bound by law to secure the highest possible price for the property, while a purchaser seeks to procure the property at the lowest possible price. The trustee's duty to the trust transcends any potential personal interest he or she may have or acquire in the property.

Auction

The sale must be held in accordance with the terms of the deed of trust, which specifies the time, manner, and place of sale. Unless the deed of trust states otherwise, the sale is held at the property itself, near the circuit court building, or at some other place selected by the trustee in the city or county in which the property is located.

At the sale, the trustee sells the property to the highest bidder, and the successful purchaser executes a memorandum of sale. The trustee obtains the deposit from the purchaser.

Trustee's Deed

The trustee cannot convey a greater interest than the deed of trust gives authority to sell. The sale is subject to encumbrances that have priority over the deed of trust. Accordingly, the trustee's deed should contain only a special warranty of title. However, the form of the deed and the title conveyed must conform to the manner in which the property was advertised.

Disbursement of Proceeds

The trustee must apply the proceeds of sale in the following order:

1. Discharge the *expenses of executing the trust,* including a commission to the trustee of five percent of the gross proceeds
2. *Discharge all taxes, levies, and assessments* with costs and interest, if they have priority over the deed of trust

3. Discharge, in the order of their priority, any *remaining debts and obligations* secured by the deed of trust and any liens of record inferior to the deed of trust, with interest
4. Render the *residue of the proceeds to the grantor* (foreclosed mortgagor) or his or her assigns

When the sale is made under any recorded deed of trust, the trustee must file a report and accounting with the commissioner of accounts within four months of the sale.

USURY

A **usurious transaction** is a contract for the loan of money at a greater rate of interest than allowed by law. Virginia law provides that loans secured by a first deed of trust on real estate may be lawfully enforced with *no limitation on the amount of interest,* if that arrangement is properly stated in the instrument or separate agreement. The contract generally is considered to be the promissory note. Most prudent lenders insert the rate in the note.

The law provides that disclosure of charges may be contained in an interest disclosure statement if such disclosure is not otherwise specified in the note. It further provides that an interest rate that varies in accordance with any exterior standard or that cannot be ascertained from the contract without reference to exterior circumstances or documents is enforceable as agreed in the signed contract. For instance, a note providing for an interest rate of three percent above the stated prime rate of a specific bank would be enforceable.

Allowable Interest Rates

Where the seller in a bona fide real estate transaction takes back a purchase-money deed of trust, the promissory note may provide for *any rate of interest agreed to by the parties.* Usury is not applicable to such a transaction because the interest rate is considered a time-price differential and thus part of the purchase price.

QUESTIONS

1. When borrowers sign a note and deed of trust, what have they agreed to regarding a court hearing if they default?
   a. To request the hearing within 30 days of default notice
   b. To permit the lender to set the place and time of the hearing
   c. To waive the hearing
   d. To abide by the court's ruling without appeal
2. The responsibility for preparing the note and deed of trust involved in a closing belongs to the
   a. seller's broker.
   b. settlement attorney.
   c. lender.
   d. buyer.
3. Which of the following statements is *TRUE* regarding a loan that is sold outside Virginia?
   a. The note must be acknowledged and recorded.
   b. The note must be notarized with a seal.
   c. The deed must be notarized.
   d. A loan secured by Virginia property may not be sold out of state.
4. What is the maximum late charge that may be assessed on a mortgage loan payment?
   a. No limit if the charge is stated in the loan contract
   b. Five percent
   c. Ten percent
   d. 15 percent
5. M purchased a house with a conventional first deed of trust loan. M's annual payment is $18,540, with monthly payments due on the tenth of each month. The loan has no provision for a grace period. If M makes a payment on June 18, can her lender legally impose a late charge?
   a. Yes, but no more than $154.50
   b. Yes, but no more than $77.25
   c. Yes, but no more than an amount equal to one month's interest
   d. No, late fees on conventional first deeds of trust are illegal in Virginia.
6. A deed of trust that permits the borrower to receive advances from time to time up to a maximum amount secured by real property is referred to as a(n)
   a. conventional loan.
   b. escrow credit loan.
   c. mortgage loan deed of trust.
   d. credit line deed of trust or a HELOC (Home Equity Line of Credit).
7. On a first deed of trust, what is the maximum interest that may be charged?
   a. No limit if the rate is stated in the loan agreement
   b. 18 percent per year
   c. 20 percent per year
   d. Two percent per month
8. What is the primary purpose of the Virginia Housing Development Authority?
   a. To encourage more housing development in Virginia
   b. To make housing more affordable for low-income and moderate-income buyers
   c. To obtain funds from state tax dollars
   d. To replace VA and FHA funding in Virginia
9. *B* is granted a $40,000 maximum credit line deed of trust. He borrows $15,000 against it and then receives notice that a judgment for $10,000 has been docketed against him. *B* then withdraws $12,000 to pay other creditors; this amount is a new advance against his credit line deed of trust. The judgment creditor forecloses. Assuming the sale of the property brings enough money, what is the order in which the various amounts will be paid?
   a. $15,000, $10,000, $12,000
   b. $15,000, $12,000, $10,000
   c. $27,000, $10,000
   d. $10,000, $27,000

10. A sales contract on a Virginia property is signed on Monday, May 1. Closing takes place on Friday, June 10, and the deed of trust is recorded on Tuesday, June 15. The borrower's first payment is due on August 30. When is the soonest that the broker may receive his or her commission check?

a. May 1
b. June 15
c. June 10
d. August 30

11. Hortense and Zavier's combined income is $150,000. They intend to use financing available through VHDA to purchase a modest one-bedroom condominium in Prince William County. What will be the probable outcome of their application?

a. VHDA will force them to purchase a more expensive property.
b. They will not be able to use 100 percent financing.
c. They make too much income to qualify for a VHDA loan.
d. Their loan application will be moved to the bottom of the waiting list.

12. Which statement is *TRUE* about a credit line deed of trust, or a HELOC (Home Equity Line of Credit)?

a. It allows the note holder to make advances from time to time secured by the real estate described in the deed.
b. It has no priority over other deeds, conveyances, and other instruments or contracts in writing that are unrecorded at that time and of which the note holder has no knowledge.
c. The total amount of advances may exceed the maximum credit line extended to the borrower.
d. They are never second trusts.

13. Who or what must be paid first from the proceeds of a sale at foreclosure?

a. The expenses of executing the trust, including a commission to the trustee
b. All taxes, levies, and assessments with costs and interest, if they have priority over the deed of trust
c. Any remaining debts and obligations secured by the deed of trust
d. The grantor

14. Purchase-money financing offered by the seller is usually called

a. variable rate financing.
b. seller take-back.
c. seller back-up financing.
d. conventional first trust.

15. In writing a purchase contract a licensed real estate broker or agent should insure that if a first trust is to be obtained

a. the contract is made contingent on the purchaser's obtaining the loan.
b. the contract provides a ceiling on the interest rate the borrower will accept.
c. the contract states what type of financing is contemplated.
d. All of the above

CHAPTER 12

Leasing

LEASING REAL ESTATE IN VIRGINIA: PRINCIPLES

Leases and landlord–tenant relationships are governed by Title 55, Chapter 13 [§§55-217 through 55-248] of the Code of Virginia, Table of Contents, Title 55, Chapter 13, which can be found at the following Web address:

WEB LINK
@

http://leg1.state.va.us/cgi-bin/legp504.exe?000+cod+TOC55000000013000000000000

Sale of Rental Property

When property that is currently being rented is sold, the new owner stands in the same legal relationship to the lessee as did the previous owner. Likewise, the lessee may have the same benefits of the lease as were enjoyed with the previous owner "except the benefit of any warranty in deed or law." [§55-218]

Appointment of Agent by Nonresident

A nonresident of Virginia who owns real property consisting of four or more rental units (whether residential or commercial) must appoint a Virginia resident as agent for the purpose of receiving any notices, service of process, or other legal paper that would otherwise have been served on the owner. If an agent is not appointed, or if the one appointed cannot be found, the Secretary of the Commonwealth serves as agent. The secretary forwards any papers to be served on the owner to the owner's home address.

Termination of a Lease

Virginia law requires different notice periods, depending on the length of the lease being terminated. The notice periods are a

- *three-month* notice to terminate a year-to-year lease,
- *30-day* notice to terminate a month-to-month lease, or
- *120-day* written notice to terminate a month-to-month lease, where the termination is due to rehabilitation of the property or a change in the property's use (such as conversion to a condominium).

If a definite termination date has been established, no notice is required.

Tenant Holdover

A tenant who, through no fault of his or her own, is unable to vacate the premises at the end of the lease term is not legally held to another full term of the lease. Rather, the tenant is liable to the lessor only for use and occupation of the premises and for any loss or damage suffered by the lessor. There may, however, be further legal issues.

Right of Reentry

If a tenant's rent is in arrears or the tenant has breached the lease, the landlord may post a written eviction notice in a conspicuous location on the premises. The notice shall be in lieu of a demand and reentry; on proof to the court that the rent claimed was due and no sufficient distress was put upon the premises, or that the terms of the lease were broken before the service of the eviction notice and that the landlord had power to reenter, the landlord will be due all rent in arrears and regain possession of the unit.

Written Act of Reentry

Publication and recordation and certification of eviction proceedings shall be made by the sheriff to the appropriate court jurisdiction.

Desertion

If a tenant whose rent is in arrears deserts the premises, the landlord may post a written notice in a conspicuous location on the premises requiring that the tenant pay the rent. A month-to-month tenant has ten days after the notice is posted; a yearly tenant has one month.

If the tenant fails to pay, the landlord may enter the premises, and the tenant's rights are ended. Nonetheless, the tenant still owes the rent up to the time of the landlord's reentry.

Failure to Pay Rent

For residential tenants, Virginia law specifies that failure to pay defaulted rents within five days of receiving notice results in the tenant's forfeiture of the right to possession.

Destruction of Premises

In some states, if the improvements on leased land are destroyed, the lessee is still bound by the terms of the lease and must continue paying full rent. Virginia has reversed and repealed this common-law doctrine. Tenants who are not at fault in the destruction of the improvements are entitled to a reduction in the amount of rent until the improvements are rebuilt and the tenants' previous use of the property can be restored.

A tenant's obligation to leave the property in good condition at the end of the lease terms is not an obligation that requires that the tenant rebuild in the event of destruction that was not his or her fault. Similarly, landlords are also under no positive duty to rebuild destroyed premises. Tenants are entitled to have the rent reduced in proportion to the diminished value of the leased premises. Tenants must be able to prove to the court that the destruction was not their fault and that the leased premises have been diminished in value to them.

Seizure of Tenant Property (Distress)

Goods belonging to a tenant may be seized for nonpayment of rent for up to five years after the rent is due, whether or not the lease has ended. The seizure is made by a sheriff or other officer, based on a warrant issued by a judge or magistrate. The warrant is based on a petition from the lessor. The lessor's petition must show (1) the grounds for believing that the rent is due and (2) the exact amount owed. The lessor must post a bond.

A copy of the **distress warrant** (the order of seizure) is given to each defendant, along with a copy of the bond. The goods subject to seizure may include anything on the premises belonging to the tenant (including any assignees' or subtenants' goods) or goods that have been removed within the 30 days prior to seizure. If any of the goods seized are subject to a prior lien, the lessor's proceeds may be based only on the interest the tenant actually had in the personal property. Any sublessee is liable only to the extent that he or she owed money to the original tenant.

The seizure of a tenant's property arises from enforcing a landlord's lien, which is a statutory right. The landlord's lien relates back to the beginning of the tenancy, not merely to the time the rent became delinquent.

If seizure of the tenant's property is made for rent due and any irregularity or unlawful act is performed during the proceeding by or for the landlord, the tenant may sue to recover damages from the landlord. However, the distress warrant itself is still lawful, and the tenant still owes the rent, despite any improper enforcement actions.

Prevention of Forfeiture

If a tenant who has been served with a "pay or quit" notice pays the arrears before his or her case comes to trial, the tenant will hold the tenancy just as he or she did before the proceedings began, without a new lease or conveyance. This could be looked upon as a sort of "right of redemption," similar to a debtor's right to recover property prior to a foreclosure sale. However, a tenant may exercise this right only once in any 12-month period.

Rent Control

In 1950, the Virginia General Assembly declared that federal rent control is no longer necessary in the state.

VIRGINIA RESIDENTIAL LANDLORD AND TENANT ACT

Title §55, Chapter 13.2 of the Code of Virginia, the Residential Landlord and Tenant Act [VRLTA], was established to

- simplify and revise the laws for the rental of dwelling units,
- simplify and revise the rights of landlords and tenants,
- encourage the parties to maintain and improve the quality of housing, and
- provide a single body of law for landlord and tenant relationships.

Limitations

As the title implies, the act concerns itself with residential property. Not everyone or every residential property is subject to the act. The act does *not* apply to the following:

- Property owners who are natural persons (or their estates) who rent no more than ten single-family residences. Also, the act does not apply to owners who do not rent more than four single-family residences or condominium units that are located in any city or county that has either an urban county executive form or county manager plan of government.
- Nonresidential rentals
- Residence at an institution if incidental to detention or the provision of medical, geriatric, educational, counseling, religious, or similar services
- Occupancy under a possession agreement by the purchaser of a property, that is, an option contract
- Occupancy by a member of an organization in a portion of a structure operated for the organization
- Occupancy in a hotel, motel, or similar location for not more than a 30-day period if occupied continuously
- Occupancy by an employee of a landlord whose right to occupancy is a requirement or benefit of employment (such as a property manager)
- Occupancy by an owner of a condominium unit or holder of a proprietary lease in a cooperative
- Occupancy in HUD-regulated housing, where regulation is inconsistent with the statute
- Occupancy by a tenant who pays no rent

Notwithstanding the limitations (exemptions) above, a landlord may make any of these applicable in the rental agreement.

All apartments, regardless of the number owned and rented, are subject to the VRLTA. Duplexes are considered to be apartments if there are common areas and/or utilities (such as one furnace).

Application Fees

The landlord may charge a prospective tenant a fee at the time the tenant applies to lease a dwelling. If the fee exceeds $32 and the tenant does not rent the property, the landlord will refund all fees in excess of the landlord's expenses and damages (costs incurred for preparing the dwelling for occupancy, holding an unoccupied unit, etc.) within 20 days. If the application fees were made by cash, certified check, cashier's check, or money order, the refund will be made within ten days of the applicant's failure to rent if such failure was due to the landlord's rejection of the application.

Unsigned or Undelivered Leases

If a written lease is not signed by either the lessor or the lessee but the agreed rent is paid and accepted, the rental agreement is binding on both parties. Similarly, even if a lease is never delivered but the rent payments are accepted, the lease remains binding.

In such cases, if the term of the lease provides for a term longer than one year, it is effective only for one year.

Security Deposits

The landlord may require that the tenant provide a security deposit at the time the property is leased. The **security deposit** is to protect the landlord against unpaid rents or damage—other than normal wear and tear—caused by tenants and/or pets during the lease period.

The security deposit may not exceed an amount equal to two months' rent. The deposit must be returned to the tenant within 45 days after the tenant vacates the property. If the landlord intends to withhold a portion of the security deposit to cover damages or losses, the tenant must be provided a written itemized list of such deductions. The landlord is required to make a final inspection of the dwelling within 72 hours of the termination of the lease. The landlord must notify the tenant of the date and time of the inspection, and the inspection must be at a reasonable time. The tenant has the right to be present during the landlord's inspection, but must advise the landlord in writing of the intent to be present.

Interest on Security Deposits

No interest shall be due and payable unless the security deposit has been held by the landlord for a period exceeding

- 13 months after the effective date of the rental agreement; or
- after the effective date of any prior written or oral rental agreements with the same tenant, for continuous occupancy of the same dwelling unit.

Such security deposit earning interest begins accruing from the effective date of the rental agreement, and such interest shall be paid only upon termination of the tenancy, delivery of possession, and return of the security deposit. Pet damage deposits are treated the same as security deposits.

When property or money is held as security deposit for more than 13 months, it shall accrue interest at an annual rate equal to four percentage points below the Federal Reserve Board discount rate as of January 1 of each year. Pet damage deposits are treated the same as a security deposit.

However, no interest shall be due and payable unless the security deposit has been held by the landlord for a period exceeding 13 months after the effective date of the rental agreement or after the effective date of any prior written or oral rental agreements with the same tenant, for continuous occupancy of the same dwelling unit.

Such security deposit interest, which begins accruing from the effective date of the rental agreement, shall be paid only on termination of the tenancy, delivery of possession, and return of the security deposit.

To calculate interest owed on security deposits taken in prior years, a schedule of the interest rates since July 1975 is available at VRLTA, §55-248.15:2. (See Table 12.1)

TABLE 12.1

Interest Rates Since 1975

Time Period				Interest Rate
1. Jul 1	1975	through Dec 31	1979	3.0%
2. Jan 1	1980	through Dec 31	1981	4.0%
3. Jan 1	1982	through Dec 31	1984	4.5%
4. Jan 1	1985	through Dec 31	1994	5.0%
5. Jan 1	1995	through Dec 31	1995	4.75%
6. Jan 1	1996	through Dec 31	1996	5.25%
7. Jan 1	1997	through Dec 31	1998	5.0%
8. Jan 1	1999	through Jun 30	1999	4.5%
9. Jul 1	1999	through Dec 31	1999	3.5%
10. Jan 1	2000	through Dec 31	2000	4.0%
11. Jan 1	2001	through Dec 31	2001	5.0%
12. Jan 1	2002	through Dec 31	2002	0.25%
13. Jan 1	2003	through Dec 31	2003	0%
14. Jan 1	2004	through Dec 31	2004	1.0%
15. Jan 1	2005	through Dec 31	2005	2.25%
16. Jan 1	2006	through Dec 31	2006	4.25%
17. Jan 1	2007	through Dec 31	2007	5.25%

Prepaid Rent

A tenant may offer and a landlord may accept prepaid rent. A landlord who accepts prepaid rent must deposit the total amount in an escrow account and withdraw the monthly installments as they come due. **Prepaid rent** means rent paid more than one month in advance of the rent due date.

Insurance

The landlord can require that the tenant pay the cost of premiums for both renter's insurance and damage insurance. In the case of damage insurance, the cost of premiums is not considered as a security deposit but rather as rent. The landlord cannot require that the tenant pay both security deposit and premiums if the amount exceeds two months' rent. Similarly, in the case of renter's insurance, the cost of premiums is not considered a security deposit but rather rent. If premiums are paid prior to the tenancy, the total of all payments for security deposits and renter's insurance as well as damage insurance shall not exceed two months' rent. Otherwise, the landlord may charge additional monthly rent to cover the costs. For both types of insurances, the tenant may elect to obtain separate policies.

More information on damage insurance and renter's insurance can be found at the following Web site:

WEB LINK @

http://leg1.state.va.us/cgi-bin/legp504.exe?000+coh+55-248.7:2+400008

Landlord's Obligations

The landlord has certain obligations under the law; they are described below.

Disclosure of Ownership. The landlord must disclose to the tenant the name and address of the property owner or anyone authorized to manage the property or otherwise act on behalf of the owner. The disclosure must be in writing and provided to the tenant prior to the beginning of the tenancy. If the property is sold, the tenant must be supplied with the name, address, and telephone number of the purchaser. If the property is being converted to a condominium or cooperative, or if the tenant will be displaced due to the demolition or rehabilitation of the property within the next six months, the tenant is entitled to written notice of the situation.

Confidentiality. Neither the landlord nor managing agent shall release information that the landlord possesses about a tenant or prospective tenant to a third party unless the tenant or prospective tenant has given prior written consent or unless the information is

- a matter of public record;
- a summary of the tenant's rent payment record, including the amount of the tenant's periodic rent payment;
- a copy of a material noncompliance notice that has not been remedied, or a termination notice given to the tenant and the tenant did not remain in the premises thereafter;
- requested by a local, state, or federal law-enforcement or public safety official in the performance of his or her duties;
- requested pursuant to a subpoena in a civil case;
- requested by a contract purchaser of the landlord's property, provided the contract purchaser agrees in writing to maintain the confidentiality of such information; or
- otherwise provided in the case of an emergency.

Inspection of Premises Within five days of tenant occupancy, the landlord will provide the tenant with a written report that itemizes existing damages to the premises. The tenant has five days after receipt of this report to object in writing. The landlord may also adopt a policy that allows the tenant to prepare a written report of the move-in inspection. In this case, the landlord has five days after receipt to object. The landlord may also provide for a joint move-in inspection report that will be signed by both the landlord and the tenant.

Disclosure of Mold Landlords must use reasonable efforts to prevent the accumulation of moisture and mold growth and promptly respond to tenant written notices about such conditions.

Within five days of occupancy by the tenant, the landlord shall disclose, in writing, the existence of any visible evidence of mold in the dwelling. This disclosure will be included in the move-in report. The tenant may either accept the dwelling as is or terminate the occupancy. If the landlord's disclosure states that there is no visible evidence of mold, the tenant has five days after receiving the report to otherwise object in writing.

Military Airport Zone Disclosures. Title §55-248 Chapter 12.1 covers required disclosures for properties located adjacent to a military air installation. The landlord of property in any locality in which a military air installation is located, or any person authorized to enter into a rental agreement on the landlord's behalf, shall provide to a prospective tenant a written disclosure that the property is located in a noise zone or accident potential zone, or both, as designated by the locality on its official zoning map.

Disclosure shall be provided prior to the execution by the tenant of a written lease agreement or, in the case of an oral lease agreement, prior to occupancy by the tenant. The disclosure shall specify the noise zone or accident potential zone in which the property is located according to the official zoning map of the locality.

An inaccurate disclosure made regarding the location of the noise zone or accident potential zone shall be deemed as nondisclosure unless the inaccurate information is provided by an officer or employee of the locality in which the property is located.

Failure to disclose gives the tenant rights of termination in the first 30 days of occupancy.

Maintenance. The landlord shall

1. comply with the requirements of applicable building and housing codes materially affecting health and safety;
2. make all repairs and do whatever is necessary to put and keep the premises in a fit and habitable condition;
3. keep all common areas shared by two or more dwelling units of the premises in a clean and structurally safe condition;
4. maintain in good and safe working order and condition all electrical, plumbing, sanitary, heating, ventilating, air-conditioning, and other facilities and appliances, including elevators, supplied or required to be supplied by the landlord;
5. maintain the premises in such a condition as to prevent the accumulation of moisture and the growth of mold, and to promptly respond to any written notices from a tenant;
6. provide and maintain appropriate receptacles and conveniences, in common areas, for the collection, storage, and removal of ashes, garbage, rubbish and other waste incidental to the occupancy of two or more dwelling units and arrange for the removal of same; and
7. supply running water and reasonable amounts of hot water at all times, reasonable air-conditioning if provided, and heat in season, except where the dwelling unit is so constructed that heat, air-conditioning, or hot water is generated by an installation within the exclusive control of the tenant or supplied by a direct public utility connection.

The landlord shall perform foregoing duties imposed in accordance with law; however, the landlord shall only be liable for the tenant's actual damages caused by the landlord's failure to exercise ordinary care.

Note: The landlord and tenant may agree in writing that the tenant perform the landlord's duties specified in 3, 6, and 7 above and also specified repairs, maintenance tasks, alterations and remodeling, but only if the transaction is entered into in good faith and not for the purpose of evading the obligations of the landlord, and if the agreement does not diminish or affect the obligation of the landlord to other tenants in the premises.

If a landlord fails to maintain the property, the failure is considered to be a violation of the terms of a lease. A tenant whose landlord fails to properly maintain the premises must notify the landlord of the violation in writing. The landlord then has 30 days to correct the problem. Emergency situations warrant quicker action on the part of the landlord.

Tenants who choose to remain in a property, even though a violation has not been corrected, should continue to make rental payments within five days of the rental due date. However, the payments should be deposited with the general district court. To terminate a lease, a tenant must file a claim with the general district court.

House Rule Changes During the period of occupancy, the landlord may adopt additional minor changes to the rules and regulations. However, changes to "house rules" may not alter the terms and conditions of the lease. For instance, a change in the hours the swimming pool is open or a requirement that parking decals be displayed on vehicles would be appropriate house rule changes; a change in the number of persons permitted in each unit would not be an appropriate midlease change. The landlord must give reasonable written notice of any rule changes.

Rule changes that substantially alter the rental agreement are valid only if the tenant agrees in writing to the changes. The tenant may refuse to accept the changes and insist on being bound only by the conditions of the original lease. However, at the expiration of the rental agreement, the tenant must either accept the changes or vacate the property.

Right to Access The landlord must give the tenant reasonable notice of intent to enter the property, except in the case of an emergency. The tenant cannot deny a landlord's reasonable request, provided the landlord does not abuse the right. If the landlord abuses the right of access, the tenant may seek an injunction from the circuit court.

The landlord shall give the tenant 24 hours' notice to enter the premises and perform nonemergency-type maintenance. In the event that nonemergency maintenance requires that the tenant vacate the premises, the landlord shall give the tenant 30 days' written notice to vacate to a comparable dwelling selected by the landlord and at no cost to the tenant for a period not exceeding 30 days.

Access Following Entry of Certain Court Orders. A tenant who has obtained an order from a court of competent jurisdiction granting the tenant possession of the premises to the exclusion of one or more cotenants or authorized occupants may provide the landlord with a copy of that court order and request that the landlord either

- install a new lock or other security devices on the exterior doors of the dwelling unit at the landlord's actual cost or
- permit the tenant to do so, provided that
  - — installation of the new lock or security devices does no permanent damage to any part of the dwelling unit, and a duplicate copy of all keys and instructions of how to operate all devices are given to the landlord;
  - — upon termination of the tenancy, the tenant will be responsible for payment to the landlord of the reasonable costs incurred for the removal of all devices installed and repairs to all damaged areas;
  - — a landlord who has received a copy of a court order in accordance with this provision shall not provide copies of any keys to the dwelling unit to any person excluded from the premises by such order;
  - — this provision shall not apply when the court order excluding a person was issued *ex parte* (i.e., based on one party's request without hearing from the other side).

Noncompliance by Landlord If the landlord violates the lease agreement or is in violation of any provision affecting health and safety, the tenant may notify the landlord in writing of the violations and state that the lease agreement will terminate on a date not less than 30 days after the notice if the violations are not corrected in 21 days. If the violations cannot be corrected, a written notice will be given to the landlord stating that the lease agreement will terminate upon a date not less than 30 days after notice is given. If the landlord adequately corrects the violations, the lease agreement will not terminate. In certain situations, the tenant may be able to recover damages, reasonable attorney fees, injunctive relief, and security deposits.

Tenants' Obligations

In addition to the lease provisions, the tenant has additional responsibilities under the law, as described below.

Condition of Property A tenant must comply with all applicable building and housing codes that materially affect health and safety. A tenant must keep the leased premises as clean and safe as conditions permit. Garbage must be removed regularly. The facilities and equipment (including heating, plumbing, electrical, sanitary, air conditioning, and appliances) must be used in a reasonable manner. Tenants may not destroy or remove any part of the premises or permit anyone else to do so, either through negligence or deliberate act.

Behavior Tenants must conduct themselves in a manner that will not disturb neighbors. Each tenant is expected to abide by all reasonable rules and regulations established by the landlord. A landlord may also serve notice to a guest of a tenant banning them from the premises for conduct violating the terms and conditions of the rental agreement or of local, state, or federal law.

Noncompliance by Tenant If the tenant violates the terms of the lease or is in violation of the tenant's responsibility to maintain the dwelling so that it materially affects health and safety, the landlord may notify the tenant of the violation in writing and state that the rental agreement will terminate on a date not less than 30 days after notice is given unless the tenant corrects the violation within 21 days. If the violation can be satisfied by repairs or by payment for damages and the tenant takes action to correct the violation, the leased agreement shall not be terminated. If the tenant fails to take action within 14 days, the landlord may enter the property, correct the problem, and charge the tenant for any costs incurred. In an emergency, the landlord may enter and correct the violation as promptly as necessary.

For tenant violations that cannot be corrected, the landlord will notify the tenant in writing of the violation and state that the rental agreement will terminate on a date not less than 30 days after notification. For violations that involve a criminal or willful act, cannot be corrected, and pose a threat to health and safety, the landlord may terminate the rental agreement immediately and proceed with actions to obtain possession. The court hearing for possession will be held within 15 calendar days from the date the tenant was notified.

Nonpayment of Rent If rent payments are not received when due, the landlord may take the following actions:

- *Five-day pay-or-quit notice*. The landlord may issue a written notice giving the tenant five days to pay the rent or vacate the property.
- *Unlawful detainer warrant*. The landlord may begin eviction proceedings immediately after issuing this warrant. The tenant remains obligated to pay the rent.
- *Eviction*. If full payment of rent is not received within five days, the landlord may file suit to have the tenant evicted. The landlord may not remove or exclude the tenant from the property or deny essential services until such time as the court takes eviction action.

Note: Recent legislation has passed to expedite the process for removing tenants from rental property. The unlawful detainer process now requires an initial hearing within 21 days, and the execution of the writ of possession by the sheriff should occur within 15 calendar days from the date received.

Acceptance of Rent with Reservation

Provided the landlord has given written notice to the tenant that the rent will be accepted with reservation, the landlord may accept full payment of all rent and receive an order of possession from a court of competent jurisdiction pursuant to an unlawful detainer action. The landlord must include this written notice in the termination notice given to the tenant or in a separate written notice given to the tenant within five business days of receiving the rent. The landlord shall continue to accept the rent with reservation until the alleged violation has been remedied or the matter has been adjudicated in a court of competent jurisdiction.

Detainer Action. A landlord or apartment complex brings a detainer action to evict a tenant who has not paid the rent or has possibly violated the lease. The landlord usually gets a judgment for "possession" of the apartment plus back rent and attorney fees.

Returned Checks If the tenant issues a check that is returned for insufficient funds, the landlord may give notice requiring payment in cash, cashier's check, or certified check within five days. If payment is not received, the landlord may proceed as with nonpayment of rent.

Security Devices Tenants may install security equipment at their own expense. At the request of the landlord, the property must be restored to its original condition on termination of the lease. Tenants must provide the landlord with complete operating instructions along with keys, codes, and passwords for any equipment installed.

Absence from the Property If a tenant plans to be absent from the property for more than seven days, the landlord may enter the property for the purpose of protecting it. If the terms of the lease require tenant notification of extended absences, and if the tenant fails to advise the landlord, the tenant may be responsible for any damage that occurs during the absence.

Automatic Renewal Clauses

Many leases contain **automatic renewal clauses.** The clause specifies that the lease will automatically renew under the same terms and conditions unless either party gives written notice within a specific number of days prior to the termination date. Any changes, such as a rent increase, must be agreed to in writing by the tenant. Failure to agree to any changes constitutes notice to vacate. In the event that all terms and conditions, including rent, remain unchanged, the renewal of a rental agreement is considered to be a new agreement.

Early Termination by Military Personnel

Any member of the armed forces of the United States and any member of the National Guard serving on full-time duty or as a Civil Service technician with the National Guard may, through the procedure detailed below, terminate his rental agreement if the member

- has received permanent change of station orders to depart 35 miles or more (radius) from the location of the dwelling unit;
- has received temporary duty orders in excess of three months' duration to depart 35 miles or more (radius) from the location of the dwelling unit;
- is discharged or released from active duty with the armed forces of the United States or from his full-time duty or technician status with the National Guard; or
- is ordered to report to government-supplied quarters resulting in the forfeiture of basic allowance for quarters.

Tenants who qualify to terminate a rental agreement under these circumstances must do so by giving the landlord a written notice of termination to be effective on a date stated in the notice. This date cannot be less than 30 days after the date on which the next rental payment (after the date on which the written notice is given) is due and payable. The termination date must be no more than 60 days prior to the date of departure required by the official orders or any supplemental instructions for interim training or duty prior to the transfer. Prior to the termination date, the tenant must furnish the landlord with a copy of the official notification of the orders or a signed letter, confirming the orders, from the tenant's commanding officer.

The landlord may not charge any liquidated damages.

Subleases and Assignment

If the lease allows the tenant to either sublet or assign with the landlord's approval, the landlord must approve or disapprove the written application of the prospective sublessee or assignee within ten business days. Failure to respond within this time period constitutes approval of the sublessee or assignee.

Abandoned Dwelling(s)

If a landlord cannot clearly make the determination that a tenant has abandoned the dwelling unit (perhaps some personal property is left behind), the landlord would serve notice on the tenant in accordance with Section 55-248.6 of the VRLTA requiring that the tenant give written notice within seven days to the landlord that the tenant intends to remain in occupancy of the dwelling unit. If the tenant does not give written notice to the landlord within the seven-day period, on the eighth day the landlord may treat the premises as abandoned.

Disposal of Abandoned Property

Once it is determined that the property is abandoned, the landlord may dispose of the property as he or she sees fit or appropriate, provided ten days' written notice has been given to the tenant. Any funds received from the sale of the abandoned property may be used to offset debts owed by the tenant, including the cost of moving and storing the abandoned property. Excess funds are treated as a security deposit.

Disposal of personal property abandoned by the tenant after a termination of lease agreement should be consistent with the disposal of personal property after eviction.

Disposal of Property of Deceased Tenants

If a tenant, who is the sole occupant of the dwelling unit, dies, and there is no person authorized by order of the circuit court to handle probate matters for the deceased tenant, the landlord may dispose of the personal property left in the premises, or in a storage area provided by the landlord, provided the landlord has given at least ten days' written notice to

- the person identified in the rental application, lease agreement, or other landlord document as the authorized person to contact in the event of the death of the tenant; or
- the tenant if no such person is identified in the rental application, lease agreement, or other landlord document as the authorized contact person. The notice given under clause (i) or (ii) shall include a statement that any items of personal property left in the premises would be treated as abandoned property and disposed of, if not claimed within 30 days.

Note: While the second option above might appear nonsensical, the possibility exists that a person unknown to the landlord has been duly authorized by the tenant and could act on behalf of the tenant's estate upon receiving the notice among the pieces of mail sent to the tenant's address.

Prohibited Lease Provisions

Virginia law does not permit the following provisions in residential leases:

- An agreement to waive any rights granted by Virginia law
- A confession of judgment or *cognovit* clause—an agreement by the tenant to permit an attorney to enter a confession of judgment against him or her in the event of a lawsuit arising out of the lease
- An agreement to pay the landlord's attorney fees (with certain exceptions)

- An agreement to limit the landlord's liability to the tenant or indemnify the landlord for the liability or any attendant costs
- An agreement to waive rights pertaining to the 120-day conversion or rehabilitation notice
- An agreement for occupancy in public housing to restrict lawful possession of firearms unless required by federal law
- An agreement that results in the tenant paying a security deposit, a bond, or a commercial insurance policy premium (purchased by the tenant) that exceeds two months' periodic rent (aggregate)

Any of these provisions, if included in a residential lease, is unenforceable. The inclusion of an unenforceable provision does not, however, void the lease.

Retaliatory Action

A landlord may not retaliate against a tenant who sues or otherwise seeks to enforce his or her legal rights or rights under the lease. Rent increases, a decrease in service, or termination of the lease are all barred retaliatory actions. The tenant is protected from retaliation if the landlord has notice of any of the following:

- The tenant has complained to the government about building code violations or conditions dangerous to health or safety
- The tenant has made a complaint to or filed suit against the landlord for violation of any provision of the VRLTA
- The tenant has organized or has become a member of a tenants' organization
- The tenant has testified against the landlord in court
- The tenant has complained about possible fair housing law violations

Cable, Satellite, and Other Television Facilities

No landlord shall demand or accept payment from any tenants in exchange for access of tenant to cable, satellite, or other television facilities unless the landlord is itself the provider of the service. The landlord may not discriminate in rental charges between tenants who receive any such service and those who do not.

A landlord may require that the provider of cable, satellite, and other television facilities and the tenant bear the entire cost of the installation, operation, or removal of the facilities incident thereto. Additionally, a landlord can demand or accept reasonable indemnity or security for any damages caused by such installation, operation, or removal.

The act does not prevent a landlord from increasing rent to bring the property into line with prevailing market rentals for similar property. A landlord is also free to decrease services. The changes, however, must apply equally to all tenants.

MANAGEMENT RESPONSIBILITY

A property manager shares the owner's responsibility for ensuring that landlord–tenant relations comply with the VRLTA. As the owner's agent, a property manager could be liable for any violations, especially fair housing and tenants' rights issues.

QUESTIONS

1. G, who lives in Virginia, is acting as resident agent for *T*, who lives in Los Angeles. *T* owns an apartment building in Alexandria. When a tenant is injured on the premises and decides to sue *T*, G is on an extended vacation and cannot be located when the notices are served. Who will receive these notices?
   a. The sheriff
   b. The president of the tenants' association
   c. *T*, the owner
   d. The Secretary of the Commonwealth

2. *H* owns the Cherry Run apartment complex, which has fallen into disrepair. *H* decides to repair and renovate the buildings and convert them to condominiums. How much notice is required to terminate the tenants' month-to-month leases?
   a. 30 days
   b. 60 days
   c. 90 days
   d. 120 days

3. A tenant rents farmland, a barn, and a house. The buildings are destroyed by a fire caused by lightning. Must the tenant still pay rent and abide by all the terms of the lease?
   a. Yes, based on common law principles governing ground leases.
   b. Yes; any damage to or destruction of the leased premises is the tenant's responsibility.
   c. No; destruction of the improvements terminates a ground lease.
   d. No; if the tenant is not at fault, he or she is entitled to release from the lease or a reduction in rent until his or her use of the land is restored.

4. A one-year lease period begins on April 1, 2007. The tenant stops paying rent on July 1, the notice to quit is received on August 1, and the landlord's lien is recorded on December 15. When does the landlord's lien attach to the tenant's property?
   a. April 1, 2007
   b. July 1, 2005
   c. August 6, 2005
   d. April 1, 2006

5. Four months before her lease expires, *V* abandons her apartment, stops paying rent, and disappears. *V* leaves her furniture and an expensive entertainment center behind. If the landlord sells the apartment's contents at a "garage sale," which of the following is *TRUE*?
   a. *V*'s obligation to pay rent for the lease term ends if the sale nets an amount equal to the outstanding rent.
   b. Because the landlord failed to obtain a distress warrant, *V* is relieved of all obligations under the lease and is entitled to damages.
   c. *V* may be entitled to damages for the landlord's unlawful seizure, but because the seizure was for rent due, *V* is not relieved of the obligation to pay the outstanding rent.
   d. The landlord acted improperly; no seizure of a tenant's property is lawful until the lease has ended.

6. A prospective tenant applies for a lease in the Seven Hills apartment building and pays the mandatory $125 application fee. If the tenant decides *NOT* to sign a lease, what happens to the application fee?
   a. The fee may be kept by Seven Hills.
   b. The fee must be returned to the prospective tenant within 20 days.
   c. The fee must be returned to the prospective tenant, less a ten percent charge to cover paperwork.
   d. All sums in excess of the landlord's actual expenses must be returned to the prospective tenant.

7. A landlord, who is subject to the VRLTA, charges $750 per month for an apartment. What is the maximum amount the landlord can require as a security deposit?
   a. $750
   b. $1,000
   c. $1,500
   d. $2,250

8. *B* entered into a one-year lease on July 1, 2004, with the right to continue on a month-to-month basis after the lease expires. *B* gave the landlord a one-month rent security deposit. In accordance with the terms of the lease, *B* gives proper notice and vacates the property on October 31, 2005. How much interest will accrue on *B*'s one-month rent security deposit?
   a. None
   b. Four months' interest
   c. 12 months' interest
   d. 15 months' interest

9. During a crime wave, a tenant decides to install a burglar alarm in a rented house. Does the tenant need to inform the landlord?
   a. No; the tenant has full right of possession during the lease.
   b. No; only tenants in multiunit apartment buildings are required to inform a landlord about a security system.
   c. Yes; the tenant must also give the landlord instructions and passwords.
   d. Yes, but the cost of the system may be deducted from the rent.

10. Sgt. *T* rented an apartment at Happy Villas four months ago. He has now been reassigned to a different airbase with orders to move in 30 days. His landlord may charge him for damages of
    a. one month's rent.
    b. seven months' rent.
    c. one-half of one month's rent.
    d. nothing because he is military.

11. How soon must the landlord disclose in writing the existence of any visible evidence of mold in the dwelling?
    a. Within three days of occupancy
    b. Within 48 hours of occupancy
    c. When the lease is signed
    d. Within five days of occupancy

12. Virginia law requires a three-month notice (90 days) to terminate a year-to-year lease. How many days' notice more or less than 90 days are required to terminate a month-to-month lease?
    a. 60 days' less notice
    b. 30 days' more notice
    c. Five days' more notice
    d. 61 days' less notice

13. The tenant, after having received a notice from the landlord regarding abandonment, has how many days to give written notice to the landlord that the tenant intends to remain in occupancy of the dwelling unit?
    a. 14 days
    b. Five days
    c. Seven days
    d. Ten days

14. What types of insurance premiums can the landlord require a tenant to pay?
    a. Auto insurance and renter's insurance
    b. Renter's insurance
    c. Damage insurance
    d. Both 2 and 3

15. Kendra lives in Fairfax County, Virginia, and has just won the Virginia Lottery. She intends to purchase outright four homes for members of her family and allow them to live rent-free. Additionally she is purchasing outright two condominium units for investment, which she intends to rent. All of the properties are in Fairfax County. Why will Kendra's properties *NOT* be subject to the VRLTA?
    a. The VRLTA does not apply to properties that have no mortgages.
    b. Only two of Kendra's properties will be subject to a lease.
    c. Kendra owns fewer than ten properties in Virginia.
    d. The VRLTA does not cover properties purchased for family use.

CHAPTER 13

Fair Housing and Ethical Practices

The Virginia Fair Housing Law, Title 36, Chapter 5.1 [§36-96.1], states that it is the policy of the Commonwealth to provide for fair housing throughout the Commonwealth to all its citizens, regardless of race, color, religion, national origin, sex, elderliness, familial status, or handicap. All discriminatory practices in residential housing transactions are prohibited. Fair housing in Virginia is also covered by the Virginia Administrative Code, 18 VAC 135-50-70, effective September 10, 2003.

Virginia's Fair Housing Law has been ruled substantially equivalent to the federal fair housing law. It is an exercise of the state's police power for the protection of the peace, health, safety, prosperity, and general welfare of the people of Virginia.

■ FAIR HOUSING BOARD

Fair Housing Board Created [§54.1-2344]

Title 54.1 Chapter 23.2, §§54.1-2343 and 54.1-2344, relates to the Department of Professional and Occupational Regulation (DPOR) and the creation of the Fair Housing Board.

A Fair Housing Board was created at DPOR in 2003 to administer and enforce the provisions of the Fair Housing Law. In the past, such authority was vested with the Real Estate Board (REB). The Fair Housing Board shall establish, by regulation, an education-based certification or registration program, as the Board deems appropriate. The Fair Housing Board has no authority to discipline persons licensed by the REB who violate the Fair Housing Law; this authority will remain with the REB.

Additional information about the Virginia Fair Housing Law can be found at the following Web site:

WEB LINK

@

http://leg1.state.va.us/cgi-bin/legp504.exe?000+cod+54.1-2344

Membership, Terms, Chairman, and Powers and Duties

The Fair Housing Board is composed of 11 members, to be appointed by the governor, as follows:

- One representative of local government
- One architect licensed in accordance with Chapter 4 [§54.1-400 et seq.] of this title
- One representative of the mortgage lending industry
- One representative of the property and casualty insurance industry
- One representative of the residential property management industry not licensed in accordance with Chapter 21 [§54.1-2100 et seq.] of this title
- One contractor licensed in accordance with Chapter 11 [§54.1-1100 et seq.] of this title
- One representative of the disability community
- One representative of the residential land lease industry subject to Chapter 13.3 [§55-248.41 et seq.] of Title 55
- Three citizen members selected in accordance with §54.1-107

The initial terms of Board members are as follows: four members are appointed for a term of four years, four members are appointed for a term of three years, and three members are appointed for a term of two years. Thereafter, all terms of Board members are for terms of four years.

Protected Classes

The Virginia Fair Housing Law prohibits discrimination in housing and real estate activities on the basis of

- race,
- color,
- religion,
- national origin,
- sex,
- elderliness,
- familial status, or
- handicap.

Definitions

Certain terms in the Fair Housing Law have specific legal definitions.

Dwelling A dwelling refers to all or part of any building or structure designated or intended for use as a residence by one or more families. The term also includes vacant land offered for sale or lease for the construction or location of any residential building or structure.

Elderliness For purposes of the Fair Housing Law, an **elderly person** is any individual who has attained his or her 55th birthday.

Familial Status The Fair Housing Law protects *individuals* under the age of 18 who live with either

- a parent or other person having legal custody or
- the designee of a parent or other person having custody with the written permission of the parent or other person.

The definition also includes pregnant women and people who are in the process of securing legal custody of a minor.

IN PRACTICE

J, K, L, and *M* (related adults including one 19-year-old) have applied to rent a small one-bedroom apartment and have been turned down by the landlord based on a reasonable occupancy standard. Accepting the reasonable occupancy standard, they then claim that they are a family under "Familial Status" and are entitled to rent the unit as a family regardless of the occupancy standard.

The law protects individuals, not families (per se), and does not apply in this situation. However, if one party was a minor, the law would apply under familial status.

Handicap A person is considered **handicapped** if he or she suffers from a physical or mental impairment that substantially limits one or more of his or her major life activities. Having a record of such an impairment, or being regarded as having such an impairment, also constitutes a handicap under the Fair Housing Law. The law does apply to individuals in a recognized drug treatment program. The term does not apply to current, illegal use of or addiction to a controlled substance as defined by law. Transvestites are specifically excluded from the definition of handicap.

EXEMPTIONS

As with the federal law, there are some exemptions in Virginia, as follows:

- A single-family residence sold or rented by the owner is exempt from the statute, as long as the owner owns no more than three such homes at the time. In the case of a sale where the owner was not residing in the home at the time of the sale or was not the resident of the home prior to the sale, the exemption applies to only one sale within any one 24-month period.
- Rooms or units in one- to four-family structures are exempt if the owner occupies one of the units and does not use discriminatory advertising.
- Religious organizations, institutions, associations, or societies may limit the sale or rental of property they own or operate for other than commercial purposes to persons of the same religion. Such organizations may give preference to their members, as long as membership in the organization is not restricted on the basis of race, color, national origin, sex, elderliness, familial status, or handicap.
- Private, state-owned, or state-supported educational institutions, hospitals, nursing homes, religious organizations, and correctional institutions may, for personal privacy reasons, require single-sex occupancy of its owned and operated single-family residences, rooms, and units. Single-sex restrooms in such dwellings or buildings are not illegal.
- Private membership clubs that provide lodging that they own or operate for other than commercial purposes may give preference to their members.

Advertising for Shared Dwellings

An individual who intends to share his or her living quarters with another may advertise on the basis of sex, but only on the basis of sex. For example, an ad could say, "Females only need apply," but it could not say "Christian females" or "white females."

Single-Family Occupancy

Certain restrictive covenants and zoning laws exist that restrict housing in an area to single-family housing. According to Virginia Fair Housing law, a family care home, foster home, or group home in which no more than eight persons reside who are mentally ill, retarded, or developmentally disabled, together with resident counselors or staff, is considered single-family occupancy for zoning purposes. For purposes of restrictive covenants, there is no maximum number of residents.

A condominium unit owners' association may, if permitted by the bylaws, restrict the number of occupants in any unit, as long as the limitation is reasonable and not more restrictive than the local zoning ordinance.

Housing for Elderly Persons

It is legal to discriminate on the basis of age to permit housing for elderly persons. Housing is exempt from the familial status protection if it is provided under a state or federal program designed to assist the elderly, or if it is intended for and solely occupied by persons at least 62 years of age, or if it has at least one person 55 years of age or older in 80 percent of the occupied units. Qualified housing in this second category must provide the elderly with important housing opportunities and adhere to published policies and procedures that demonstrate the intent to provide such housing.

Criminal Background

People who have been convicted of the illegal manufacture or distribution of controlled substances are not protected by the fair housing law.

Rental applications may require the disclosure of any criminal convictions, and applicants may be required to consent to and to pay for a criminal background check. A building manager or property owner may refuse to rent a dwelling to an individual who has a record of prior criminal convictions involving harm to persons or property, and whose presence would pose a threat to the health or safety of others.

Similarly, the law's protections do not make it unlawful for an owner to deny or limit residential rentals to persons who pose a clear and present threat of substantial harm to others or the premises.

IN PRACTICE

Local counties, cities, and towns may enforce legislation adopted prior to 1991 that is *more restrictive* (protective of more classes) than either the state or the federal law. Any amendments to the local legislation, however, must conform to the state's law. Because licensees often practice in more than one jurisdiction within the state, they must be aware of all local legislation that differs from federal and state laws.

Impact for Real Estate Licensees

It is illegal for real estate licensees to be involved in discriminatory housing practices in any way. While licensees should be aware of the exemptions in order to fully comply with the law, it is of more vital importance that they comply with the law's nondiscriminatory intent. The law [§36.96.2A] states that *this exemption shall not apply to or inure to the benefit of any licensee of the Real Estate Board, regardless of whether the licensee is acting in his personal or professional capacity.*

UNLAWFUL DISCRIMINATORY HOUSING PRACTICES

In Virginia, it is illegal for anyone to commit any of the following discriminatory acts on the basis of a person's race, color, religion, national origin, sex, elderliness, familial status, or handicap:

- Refusing to sell or rent a dwelling to any person who has made a bona fide offer to do so, or refusing to negotiate the sale or rental of a dwelling
- Discriminating against any person in the terms, condition, or privileges of the sale or rental of a dwelling, or in providing services or facilities
- Making, printing, or publishing any notice, statement, or advertisement with respect to the sale or rental of a dwelling that indicates an actual or intended preference, limitation, or discrimination
- Falsely representing that a dwelling is not available for inspection, sale, or rental
- Denying membership or participation in a multiple-listing service (MLS), real estate brokers' organization, or any other service, organization, or facility related to the business of selling or renting dwellings
- Including any discriminatory restrictive covenant in the transfer, sale, rental, or lease of housing, or honoring any discriminatory restriction
- Inducing or attempting to induce the sale or rental of a dwelling by representations regarding the entry or prospective entry into the neighborhood of protected persons
- Refusing to sell, rent, or negotiate with anyone on the basis of their own handicap, that of anyone who will be residing in the dwelling, or that of anyone associated with them
- Discriminating in the terms, conditions, or privileges of the sale or rental of a dwelling or in its services or facilities on the basis of an individual's handicap, or that of anyone associated with the individual

IN PRACTICE

The use of words or symbols associated with a particular religion, national origin, sex, or race is considered prima facie evidence of an illegal preference. The use of such words or symbols may not be overcome by a general disclaimer that no discrimination is intended.

Special Rule Regarding Handicapped Persons

Handicapped individuals, that is, persons with disabilities, must be permitted to make reasonable modifications, at their own expense, of existing premises to make the premises fully accessible to the individual. A landlord may make modification of rented premises conditional on the tenant's agreement to restore the premises to their original condition (reasonable wear and tear excepted) if it affects the value of the property.

It is unlawful to refuse to make reasonable accommodations in rules, practices, policies, or services in order to afford handicapped individuals equal opportunities to use and enjoy a dwelling. For instance, a "no pets" policy should be flexible enough to accommodate service animals, such as a guide dog or an assistance monkey.

New multifamily dwellings, that is, those with four or more units, must be designed and constructed in such a way that the public use and common areas are readily accessible to handicapped persons. All ground-floor unit doors must allow passage by persons in wheelchairs and contain light switches, electrical outlets, and environmental controls that are accessible by persons in wheelchairs. Kitchens and bathrooms must be designed for full maneuverability. In buildings with elevators, all units must meet the accessibility requirements.

Lending Institutions

The Fair Housing Law also applies to lending institutions and other businesses involved in residential real estate transactions. It is unlawful to discriminate in the availability, terms, or conditions of real estate financing on the basis of race, color, religion, national origin, sex, elderliness, familial status, or handicap. Discrimination on the basis of financial qualification is permitted, however.

If any lending institution is found to be engaging in unlawful discriminatory practices, the Fair Housing Law forbids state, county, city, or municipal treasurers or other government officials to deposit public funds in the institution. Existing deposits of public funds must be withdrawn from offending lenders, although the action may be deferred for one year to avoid financial loss to the state, county, city, or agency. If the lender corrects its practices, there is no prohibition against the deposit of public funds.

The Virginia Fair Housing Law also applies to those who are involved indirectly in the sale or rental of real property, such as newspapers and other publications. Appraisers cannot include any discriminatory information in appraisal reports.

ENFORCEMENT OF THE FAIR HOUSING LAW

Persons who feel that their rights under the Fair Housing Law have been violated may take action against the party alleged to have discriminated. *Complaints involving persons licensed by the REB* must be filed with the REB, which is empowered to initiate and receive complaints against licensees, investigate alleged violations, and resolve conflicts either by conference and conciliation or by issuing a charge and referring the matter to the attorney general for action.

A complaint must be filed with the REB within one year of the occurrence or termination of the alleged discriminatory practice.

In any action brought under the Virginia Fair Housing Law, the burden of proof is upon the complainant. The REB must acknowledge receipt of the complaint and advise the claimant of time limits and choices of forums for hearing the complaint.

Know Days

Accused persons must be notified of the allegation and of their legal rights within ten days. Proceedings must commence within 30 days after receiving the complaint. The investigation should be completed within 100 days. While the investigation may take longer than 100 days in some circumstances, no investigation may take more than a year from the date of the complaint.

The REB may issue subpoenas, interview witnesses, and request the production of documents in the course of its investigation. During the investigative period, it is possible for the complainant and respondent to enter into a conciliation agreement, subject to REB approval.

If reasonable cause exists to believe that a discriminatory housing practice has occurred or is about to occur, the REB must seek resolution by conciliation or forward the charge to the attorney general for civil action. If no reasonable cause exists, the case will be dismissed.

Penalties

If the case results in civil action by the attorney general, the court may

- award preventive relief by temporary or permanent injunction, restraining order, or other necessary order;
- award other appropriate relief, including compensatory or punitive damages;
- assess civil penalties (in cases involving zoning or land use ordinances, patterns, or practices of discrimination or the breach of a conciliation agreement) of up to $50,000 for a first violation and up to $100,000 for any subsequent violation; and
- award the prevailing party reasonable attorney's fees and costs.

Whether or not a complaint has been filed with the REB, a civil action may also be initiated by an injured person in a U.S. district court or state court within two years after the occurrence or termination of an alleged discriminatory housing practice. If a civil action is filed at the same time a complaint is filed with the REB, the REB will delay action until the court rules. If a conciliation agreement is breached, a civil action may be filed within two years of the breach.

Actions Against Licensees

If any real estate licensee is found guilty of violating the Fair Housing Law, the REB will take appropriate steps to consider suspension or revocation of the license or to take other disciplinary action.

QUESTIONS

1. Which of the following is protected by the Virginia Fair Housing Law?
   a. Marital status
   b. Familial status
   c. Source of income
   d. Dietary restriction
2. All of the following are protected by the Virginia Fair Housing Law's provisions for the handicapped or elderly *EXCEPT* a
   a. 55-year-old recovered heroin addict.
   b. 62-year-old cocaine user.
   c. paralyzed veteran.
   d. mentally ill person.
3. An owner may discriminate on the basis of religion in selling or renting his or her own property in which of the following situations?
   a. The ad clearly states that religion is a criterion.
   b. The broker is fully informed of the religion criterion.
   c. The owner already owns four other properties rented to persons of the same religion.
   d. The owner is a religious organization or institution.
4. M was looking for someone to share her house. She placed the following advertisement in the local paper: "Share lovely town house. Large wooded lot, near transp, shops, and recreation. $650 per mo. Female only." Which of the following is *TRUE*?
   a. The ad is a violation of the Fair Housing Law because it discriminates against males.
   b. The ad violates the Fair Housing Law's prohibition against sexual discrimination.
   c. The ad is legal because M is sharing her own home.
   d. The newspaper is now subject to a civil action for publishing a discriminatory ad.
5. A building manager receives a lease application from *T*, a prospective tenant. The application discloses that *T* served time in prison for income tax evasion. *T* now has regular income from a manufacturing job and otherwise meets the building's qualification standards. Can the building manager lawfully refuse to rent an apartment to *T*?
   a. No; the Fair Housing Law prohibits discrimination on the basis of prior criminal record.
   b. No; *T* 's criminal conviction did not involve harm to persons or property.
   c. Yes; the Fair Housing Law permits a building manager to refuse to rent to any convicted criminal.
   d. Yes; the fair housing law does not apply to actions by building managers.
6. When a young couple just recently immigrating from El Salvador attempted to rent an apartment, they were told that no units were available, when in fact there were at least four available at that time. The rental company was guilty of
   a. nothing; it has the right to say what it pleases.
   b. nothing; it has the right to limit rentals to U.S. citizens.
   c. unlawful discriminatory housing practice of false representation.
   d. discrimination based on age.
7. A "no pets" policy would have to be waived in all of the following cases *EXCEPT*
   a. M has two small cats that have lived with her for ten years.
   b. *H* is legally blind and needs a guide dog.
   c. *J* is hearing impaired and requires the service of a small dog that responds to alarms, doorbells, etc.
   d. *D* suffers from mild paralysis and needs the assistance of a spider monkey.

8. Two people apply for a mortgage loan from Mighty Mortgage Company: *R*, a 65-year-old blind male with no income or savings, and *S*, a 35-year-old black female with no debts and a six-figure income from her law practice. Based on these facts alone, if both *R* and *S* are turned down, Mighty Mortgage has most likely committed unlawful discrimination against
   a. *R* only.
   b. *S* only.
   c. both *R* and *S*.
   d. neither *R* nor *S*.

9. Investigations of fair housing complaints must be completed within how long after a complaint is filed?
   a. 30 days
   b. 60 days
   c. 100 days
   d. One year

10. A civil action brought by the attorney general for a first violation of the Virginia Fair Housing Law could subject a guilty party to a monetary civil penalty of
    a. up to $10,000 for a first offense.
    b. up to $25,000 for a first offense.
    c. up to $50,000 for a first offense.
    d. actual damages and legal fees only.

11. Lei, a licensee with RTU Realty in Prince William County, has been charged with a violation of the Virginia Fair Housing Law. Lei's case will be heard before the
    a. Real Estate Board.
    b. Fair Housing Board.
    c. local real estate association board.
    d. County Fair Housing Board.

12. The Fair Housing Board Consists of 11 members. How many citizen members are appointed to the board?
    a. Two
    b. Three
    c. Five
    d. One

13. According to the Virginia Fair Housing Law, a family care home could exist in a community zoned for single-family homes. What other types of homes could qualify under the Virginia Fair Housing Law?
    a. A foster home
    b. A group home in which no more than eight persons reside who are mentally ill, retarded, or developmentally disabled, together with resident counselors
    c. None of the above
    d. 1 and 2

14. Under the Fair Housing Law, what symbol or logo would be deemed discriminatory if printed on a licensee's business card?
    a. HUD's Equal Housing symbol
    b. The REALTOR® logo/symbol
    c. A local MLS's logo/symbol
    d. A religious cross or symbol

15. Kirsten wants a tenant to share her single-family home. Kirsten is very religious and does not drink or smoke. Which one of the following ads may she run in the local newspaper?
    a. SF House to share, $650 per month, male nonsmoker only.
    b. SF House to share, $650 per month, white female nonsmoker only.
    c. SF House to share, $650 per month, Lutheran nonsmoker only.
    d. SF House to share, $650 per month, religious nonsmoker only.

APPENDIX A

Practice Examination

1. Salesperson *S* represents Seller *K* and Salesperson *B* represents Buyer *J* in the same transaction. *S* and *B* both work for Broker *N*. In this situation, *S* is known as a(n)
   a. associate broker.
   b. subagent.
   c. single agent.
   d. designated agent.

2. Who of the following *MUST* hold a real estate license in Virginia?
   a. An attorney preparing an abstract of title
   b. A local multiple-listing service company
   c. An officer of a limited liability company who specializes in listing commercial property
   d. A business executive selling her company's surplus acreage

3. The duties that an agent owes to his or her client are established by
   a. statute.
   b. common law.
   c. the agent's broker.
   d. the agent's client.

4. All of the following are ways to terminate a brokerage relationship *EXCEPT*
   a. default by either party.
   b. death of the salesperson.
   c. expiration of the agreement.
   d. mutual agreement by the parties to terminate.

5. The residential property disclosure statement must contain notice to purchasers regarding Megan's Law advising them of the source for information on
   a. registered sex offenders.
   b. agency representation.
   c. known property defects.
   d. stigmatized property.

6. If the seller gives the buyer the required residential property disclosure statement three days after the contract is signed, when can the buyer terminate the contract?
   a. Within 15 days of date sent, if e-mailed
   b. Within ten days, if hand-delivered
   c. Within five days of postmark, if mailed
   d. Under the doctrine of caveat emptor, the buyer cannot terminate the contract.

7. If a married woman with three children dies intestate, how would her property be distributed?
   a. To her husband under laws of dower and curtesy
   b. One-third to her husband, the remaining two-thirds to her children equally
   c. One-half to her husband, the other half to her children equally
   d. Two-thirds to her husband, the remaining third to her children equally

8. *J* is an unmarried homeowner of a $475,000 mansion. What is the total maximum value of *J* 's homestead exemption?
   a. $4,750
   b. $5,000
   c. $237,500
   d. $475,000

9. When *D* died, he left his wife $10,000 and all of the rest of his property to his two children. *D*'s wife renounced the will in order to claim her elective share of his augmented estate. She will now be entitled to
   a. all of his estate.
   b. one-half of his estate.
   c. one-third of his estate.
   d. none of his estate, but she may continue to live there.

10. *H*, M, and *R* are joint tenants. M sells his tenancy to *T*. Which of the following is *TRUE* of this situation?
   a. *H*, *R*, and *T* are now joint tenants.
   b. *H*, *R*, and *T* are now tenants in common.
   c. *H* and *R* are tenants in common with a joint tenancy with *T*.
   d. *H* and *R* are joint tenants with a tenancy in common with *T*.

11. *S* and *J* are tenants in common, and *J* dies intestate. What happens to *J*'s interest?
   a. It passes to *J*'s heirs.
   b. It passes to *S* as a sole owner.
   c. It passes to *J*'s heirs with *S* as a joint interest.
   d. It passes to *J*'s heirs if the property is sold.

12. *K* owns an individual unit in a condominium building and wants to sell it. Which of the following documents does *K* need to show prospective buyers before *K* can sell the unit?
   a. A list of any past suits or judgments against the condominium association
   b. A copy of the balance due on *K*'s deed of trust loan
   c. A copy of the current bylaws and rules and regulations
   d. A plat map indicating the location of the condominium building

13. *A* and *B* have recently signed a contract to purchase a town house in a development governed by a Property Owner's Association. They will be able to cancel this contract if they
   a. change their minds.
   b. cancel any time prior to closing.
   c. cancel within three days of receiving the POA disclosure packet.
   d. cancel within 14 days of receiving the POA disclosure packet.

14. The following is what kind of legal description? *All those certain lots, pieces or parcels of land, situated in the city of Roanoke, Virginia, known, numbered and designated on the Plat of Hampton Square and recorded in the clerk's office of the Circuit Court of the City of Roanoke, Virginia, in Map Book 26, page 7, as Lots No. 9 and 10.*
   a. Metes and bounds
   b. Rectangular survey
   c. Government survey
   d. Lot and block

15. What is the most common description of real estate in Virginia?
   a. Combination of metes and bounds and government survey
   b. Combination of metes and bounds and lot and block
   c. Combination of lot and block and government survey
   d. Combination of rectangular survey and government survey

16. If a contractor records a mechanic's memorandum of lien on September 15, 2007, how long does he or she have to file a suit to enforce it?
   a. Until October 15, 2007
   b. Until December 31, 2007
   c. Until March 15, 2008
   d. Until September 15, 2008

17. If all of the following liens are recorded against a property and the bank forecloses, which will be paid first?
   a. Real estate tax lien
   b. Mechanic's lien
   c. Deed of trust lien
   d. Vendor's lien

18. *P* owns a house in severalty and wishes to sell it. His broker tells him that his wife, *N*, will need to sign the contract even though she does not own the property. Why would this be the case?
   a. *N* is required to sign the contract under the Statute of Frauds.
   b. *N* is required to sign the contract to convert the equitable title into legal title.
   c. *N* is required to sign the contract so that the title is "marketable."
   d. *N* is required to release any future interest in the property she might hold.

19. An implied warranty against structural defects on new construction continues for how long?
    a. Six months after the date of transfer of title or the buyer's taking possession
    b. One year after the date of transfer of title or the buyer's taking possession
    c. Two years after the date of transfer of title or the buyer's taking possession
    d. Five years after the date of transfer of title or the buyer's taking possession

20. All of the following are requirements for a valid deed *EXCEPT*
    a. the signature of the grantee.
    b. consideration.
    c. accurate legal description of the property.
    d. delivery and acceptance of the deed.

21. *F* buys *T*'s home for $250,000. The state recordation tax rate is $0.33 per $100 and the grantor tax rate is 0.5 percent. Which of the following is a correct statement of the state grantor and recordation taxes to be paid?
    a. *F* will pay $373.75; *T* will pay $373.75.
    b. *F* will pay $224.25; *T* will pay $250.
    c. *F* will pay $825; *T* will pay $1,250.
    d. *F* will pay $149.50; *T* will pay $299.00.

22. M was very careful to execute a will leaving her beachfront condominium to her favorite niece, *S*. *S* will receive title to the property
    a. after the will has gone through probate court.
    b. anytime she wants to file with the clerk's office.
    c. immediately after the will is read.
    d. as soon as she pays the next month's condo fee.

23. The Virginia requirement that a deed of trust be recorded and all settlement proceeds be distributed within two days of the date of settlement is covered under what statute?
    a. Fair Lending Act
    b. Residential Deed of Trust Act
    c. Statute of Frauds
    d. Wet Settlement Act

24. All of the following information is found on a title report *EXCEPT*
    a. easements and covenants.
    b. buyer's full legal name.
    c. status of taxes.
    d. existing lenders.

25. A gap in the chain of title could be caused by any of the following *EXCEPT*
    a. a deed for one transfer of the property was never recorded.
    b. the seller was divorced in a foreign country.
    c. the name of the party on the deed was changed but never recorded.
    d. the property was sold to a relative for $1 with a recorded deed.

26. Under Virginia Real Estate License Law an "independent contractor" is
    a. anyone practicing real estate in Virginia.
    b. a salesperson who must pay federal taxes on estimated quarterly basis.
    c. a licensee representing a client other than as a standard agent.
    d. a person contracted with to add a deck to the property.

27. How is the selection of Real Estate Board members made?
    a. Elected by the public
    b. Selected by Virginia Association of REALTORS®
    c. Appointed by the governor
    d. Volunteers from real estate community

28. *H* completes his real estate salesperson course on June 20, 2007. He then takes and passes the Virginia licensing exam on July 15, 2007. How much time does *H* have to apply for his license before being required to retake the exam?
    a. Until December 20, 2007
    b. Until January 15, 2008
    c. Until June 20, 2008
    d. Until July 14, 2008

29. If a licensee is found guilty of a violation of the license law or rules and regulations, the Real Estate Board may take all of the following disciplinary actions *EXCEPT*
    a. impose a prison sentence of no more than one year.
    b. levy fines.
    c. deny license renewal.
    d. suspend or revoke a license.

30. The Real Estate Board's activities include which of the following activities?
    a. Arbitrates disputes between salespersons and brokers
    b. Issues real estate licenses
    c. Recommends commission rates and commission splits
    d. Approves standardized listing agreements and sales contracts

31. *K*'s license is about to expire, so she signs up for some continuing education classes. She takes two hours of Virginia real estate laws and regulations, two hours of ethics and standards of conduct, two hours of real estate taxes, and two hours of escrow requirements. Assuming *K* successfully completes these courses, will she have met her renewal education requirements?
    a. Yes, because she has completed at least eight hours of continuing education.
    b. No, because she has failed to take a course on federal real estate laws.
    c. No, because she has failed to take a course on the Americans with Disabilities Act.
    d. No, because she has failed to take a course on fair housing laws and complete a total of 16 hours of continuing education.

32. *J* accidentally let his salesperson's license expire, but two months later is ready to renew it. What does *J* need to send to the Real Estate Board for his renewal fee?
    a. The current annual fee for a salesperson renewal
    b. The current annual fee for reinstatement
    c. The current annual fee for renewal plus the current fee for reinstatement
    d. The current annual fee for renewal plus reinstatement plus $100 fine

33. Salesperson *R* is getting married and will be changing her last name. When should she inform the REB?
    a. Within 30 days of the wedding
    b. Within 45 days of the wedding
    c. Within 60 days of the wedding
    d. Before her license renewal deadline

34. Salesperson *R* decides to leave Broker *K*'s firm and work at Broker *M*'s firm. How should the Real Estate Board be notified of this change?
    a. *R* should file a "Change of Brokerage" form with the REB.
    b. *K* should give *R*'s license to M.
    c. *R* should fill out the application for the change, obtain M's signature, and send with fee to the REB.
    d. *R* and *K* should file a "Termination of Brokerage" form with the REB.

35. C has a Virginia salesperson's license, but she is currently holding it in inactive status. She decides to sell her home with the help of a local brokerage firm. Should she disclose her license status to potential buyers?
    a. Yes, because disclosure is required regardless of an inactive license status
    b. No, because the local brokerage firm will be earning the commission from the sale
    c. No, because disclosure is not required when a licensee sells his or her own home
    d. No, because disclosure is not required when a license is inactive

36. Salesperson *W* finds a buyer for a home he has listed. The buyer gives *W* an earnest money cashier's check for $2,000. A sales contract is ratified. What should *W* do with the check?
    a. Keep it until closing
    b. Deposit it in his escrow account within three business banking days
    c. Deposit it in his escrow account within five business banking days
    d. Immediately give it to his broker

37. The name of the broker must appear in all advertising *EXCEPT* a(n)
   a. newspaper Open House ad placed by a salesperson.
   b. For Rent ad placed on a grocery store bulletin board by a salesperson.
   c. cable TV ad paid for by a salesperson.
   d. salesperson selling as For Sale By Owner with disclosure that owner is licensed.

38. If the Real Estate Transaction Recovery Fund falls below $400,000, how much money may the Real Estate Board assess each licensee?
   a. $20 from each salesperson; $40 from each broker
   b. $20 from each inactive licensee; $40 from each active licensee
   c. $20 from each salesperson and broker, inactive or active
   d. $40 from each salesperson and broker, inactive or active

39. All of the following actions are considered improper delivery of instruments *EXCEPT* failing to
   a. promptly deliver complete and legible copies of any written contracts to each party in a transaction.
   b. maintain all signed documents for a period of three years.
   c. deliver a complete and accurate statement of money received and disbursed by a licensee.
   d. provide timely, written notice of any material change in the transaction to all parties.

40. Which of the following statements is *true* regarding institutional financing in Virginia?
   a. Mortgage loans, rather than deeds of trust, are the instruments primarily used in residential sales transactions.
   b. VA and FHA notes require notarization to be valid.
   c. Late charges on a loan may not exceed three percent of the installment due.
   d. Due-on-sale clauses are prohibited in Virginia.

41. One of the primary functions of the Virginia Housing Development Authority (VHDA) is to
   a. build housing for low/moderate-income people.
   b. research new methods of housing development.
   c. provide housing financing for residents of Virginia.
   d. enforce Fair Housing and RESPA regulations.

42. A foreclosure of a deed of trust could be achieved without court action or sale of the property through which of the following?
   a. Strict foreclosure
   b. Deed in lieu of foreclosure
   c. Trustee sale
   d. Equitable foreclosure

43. G has just purchased a rental property that has four months to go on the current lease. The present tenants now have the right to
   a. continue their lease under current terms.
   b. move out immediately.
   c. sue the former owner for breaking the terms of their lease.
   d. demand repainting and recarpeting by the new owner.

44. F entered into a one-year lease on October 1, 2006, with the right to continue on a month-to-month basis after the lease expires. F gave the landlord a security deposit. In accordance with the terms of the lease, F gives proper notice and vacates the property on December 31, 2007. How much interest will accrue on F's security deposit?
   a. None
   b. Two months'
   c. 12 months'
   d. 15 months'

45. The Virginia Residential Landlord and Tenant Act protects the rights of both landlords and tenants and applies to
   a. all properties advertised for rent.
   b. hotels offering two-week rentals.
   c. all apartment building rentals.
   d. occupancy by a property manager employed by the landlord.

46. If a tenant leaves one couch and two chairs in his apartment after the lease has ended, is the landlord allowed to sell it?

a. Yes, provided the tenant is given ten days' written notice
b. Yes, within one week of the lease's termination date
c. No, Virginia includes a nonabandoned property clause in all leases
d. No, the furniture remains the property of the tenant

47. Which one of the following is protected by Virginia's Fair Housing Law?

a. A 58-year-old AIDS victim
b. A 45-year-old homosexual
c. A 35-year-old transvestite
d. A 51-year-old veteran

48. *T* will be in violation of the Virginia Fair Housing Law if he refuses to rent his two-bedroom apartment for any of the following reasons *EXCEPT*

a. the couple applying are from Nigeria.
b. the couple has two small children.
c. the applicant is 65 years old.
d. the applicants do not have adequate income.

49. All of the following apartment building accommodations for handicapped persons are considered reasonable requests *EXCEPT*

a. allowing a blind person to have an assistance monkey in a "no pets" building.
b. allowing a paralyzed person to install railings in his or her bathroom.
c. removing walls along a corridor of a common area to make the hallway wide enough for wheelchair access.
d. giving first-floor unit preferences to a wheelchair-bound person.

50. If an alleged fair housing discriminatory act has taken place, how long after the occurrence of the act does the injured party have to file a complaint with the REB?

a. Three months
b. Six months
c. Nine months
d. One year

51. *J* is a listing agent with WRX Realty and has agreed to represent buyer *T* in the sale of his own listing without a disclosure to *T* (the buyer). *J* is now a(n)

a. dual agent.
b. designated agent.
c. undisclosed dual agent.
d. buyer agent.

52. Vika is an agent with TUV Realty and has listed a property for sale in Homestead Acres. At an open house, an unrepresented buyer decides to purchase Vika's listing and declines representation. How may Vika proceed with this sale?

a. Represent the seller only and treat the purchaser as customer
b. Disclose, represent the seller only, and treat the purchaser as a customer
c. Disclose dual agency and represent both parties
d. Ask her broker to designate an agent to represent the buyer

53. *Q* is affiliated with "Just For You Realty" and has just passed the broker's exam. *Q* intends to remain affiliated with the same firm with his new license. How much will *Q*'s new license cost him?

a. $150
b. $210
c. $250
d. $60

54. Mary and Jake have just wed, Mary for the second time. They are purchasing a home together and have agreed to an arrangement that will allow Mary to will her share of the property to her grandchildren upon her demise. How should Jake and Mary take title?

a. Tenancy by the entirety
b. Tenants in common
c. Joint tenants
d. None of the above

55. Cato has a house for rent and has placed the following ad on the supermarket bulletin board: SF house for rent, $2,200 per month, no children, no smokers, no old folks. If Cato is found guilty of discrimination, what is the maximum amount he could be fined?

a. $100,000
b. $50,000
c. $75,000
d. $25,000

56. VHDA funding comes from

a. Fannie Mae.
b. the U.S. government.
c. the Virginia General Fund.
d. bonds sold through the private sector.

57. Giles has lived in Virginia since moving here from Pennsylvania 30 years ago and has amassed a portfolio of 20 rental properties. He is now returning to Pennsylvania and will manage his holdings from there. What requirement does Virginia impose on him?

a. Giles must leave a forwarding address.
b. Giles must sell all of his properties.
c. Giles must place his properties with a nonresident trust management firm.
d. Giles must appoint a resident agent.

58. When must a landlord pay interest on a security deposit?

a. After 12 months
b. After six months
c. After 15 months
d. After 13 months

59. A landlord asks for two months' security deposit on all rentals and requires all tenants to pay the cost of renters and damage insurance (premiums) available from the landlord. If the premiums total $100 per year per unit and all units rent for $995 per month, what is the maximum the landlord can receive as a security deposit?

a. $2,090
b. $1,790
c. $1,890
d. $1,990

60. Which applicant could a landlord safely decline renting?

a. A wheelchair-bound person wishing to live on the top floor of a three-story walkup
b. A handicapped person requiring major modifications for living and accessibility
c. An ex-drug user currently in a rehab program
d. A blind veteran with no guide dog

61. Colonel Jackson owns a nicely furnished condo and has been posted to an embassy abroad where he will have a completely furnished apartment. He decides to rent his condo fully furnished but wants more than two months' security to cover the cost of possible damage to some expensive pieces of art. What should the colonel do?

a. Require a bond secured by not more than two months' security
b. Require the tenant secure and pay the premiums for damage insurance
c. Advertise for adult tenants only, no children
d. Either 1 or 2

62. Jennifer wants to hire George, a licensed agent, to help her find a specific property, but she does *NOT* want an agency relationship with him. George will probably work for Jennifer as a(n)

a. buyer agent.
b. dual agent.
c. standard agent.
d. independent contractor according to a written contract between George and Jennifer.

63. Artimus is thinking about getting a real estate license. His plan is to affiliate with a broker and use the marketing skills of his unlicensed wife Corliss to expand his practice. What will Corliss be able to do?

a. Show properties when Artimus is available
b. Show properties when Artimus is NOT available
c. Assist one of Artimus's buyers in filling out a contract
d. Design and mail brochures for Artimus

64. Peter wants to sell his house himself and is *NOT* licensed. What are Peter's options?
    a. Peter must disclose that he is not licensed.
    b. Peter must have a license to sell his own house.
    c. Peter must hire a licensed agent to sell his own house.
    d. Peter may sell his house himself; a license is not required.

65. *K* wants to sell her house herself and is licensed. What must *K* do?
    a. *K* must disclose that she is licensed.
    b. *K* must have a license to sell her own house.
    c. *K* must hire a licensed agent to sell her own house.
    d. *K* may sell her house herself; a license is not required to sell her own property.

66. Landlord Bob is also a licensee and has had a fair housing complaint filed against him. Bob's hearing will be held before
    a. the nine-member Real Estate Board.
    b. the 11-member Fair Housing Board.
    c. the eight-member Real Estate Board.
    d. a combined session of both the Fair Housing and Real Estate Boards.

67. A multidenominationally owned religious home for the elderly may exclude which of the following persons?
    a. A Buddhist
    b. A Catholic
    c. A retired Presbyterian minister
    d. An avowed atheist

68. At foreclosure, when can the payment of tax liens become subordinate?
    a. If they do not have priority over the deed of trust
    b. Never
    c. If the highest bidder refuses to take the property subject to the tax lien
    d. If the sale does not bring enough proceeds to pay both

69. Zoë is handicapped and needs the skills of her service spider monkey, Misha. How much may her landlord charge as a pet deposit if the monthly rent is $1,550?
    a. $310
    b. $155
    c. $1,550
    d. None of the above

70. Under what circumstances may a landlord ask questions related to a disability?
    a. If the applicant is in a wheelchair on making the application.
    b. If the applicant is applying for housing designated or designed for people with a disability
    c. If the housing is designated for people with a particular disability
    d. Both 1 and 2

APPENDIX B

Answer Key: Chapter Quizzes

CHAPTER 1
Real Estate Brokerage and Agency

1. (c) By Virginia statutory definition, a salesperson may perform all of the functions listed except serve as a managing broker.
2. (a) An individual who wants to sell her own house does not need a real estate license.
3. (c) Since there can only be one principal broker, all others are associate brokers whether or not they are in a managerial or supervisory position.
4. (d) An "agency" relationship could best be described as one in which a licensee acts for or represents another person in a real estate transaction.
5. (c) Routine services that do not create an agency relationship are referred to as *ministerial acts*.
6. (c) A licensee is not required to always be obedient to the client's demands.
7. (c) Revealing to a seller that your client could probably pay more violates the statutory duties owed to your client.
8. (a) A brokerage relationship can be terminated by any of the reasons listed except one party unilaterally "firing" the other party.
9. (d) When both buyer and seller are represented by agents from different firms, no agency disclosure is required.
10. (d) In this scenario, both seller and buyer are (potential) clients of the broker. The broker's only legal option is to make designated agents of both M and T; the broker remains the dual agent.
11. (c) A roster of salespersons and brokers assigned to the branch office should be made available at the branch office on request by any member of the public.
12. (c) When a licensee acts as an independent contractor and not as a standard agent, a written agreement and not the statute governs the relationship between the licensee and the client.
13. (d) Robert doesn't have to make an agency disclosure to Sally because she is already in an agency relationship with another agent.
14. (c) The seller is not liable for misrepresentations made by a licensee.
15. (c) Because no specific property was discussed, no disclosure was required.

CHAPTER 2
Seller and Buyer Agency Agreements

1. (b) When a broker and seller enter into an exclusive-right-to-sell listing, a definite termination date is required.
2. (a) Based on these facts, you must decline this listing agreement because the clause violates REB regulations, which state that net listings are prohibited.
3. (b) July 1, 2008, would be the correct way to enter the termination date on a listing form.

4. (b) The builder's obligations are not cancelled by the issuance of a real property disclosure statement.
5. (b) The seller is not required to disclose a recent death on the property.
6. (c) That the seller recently died of AIDS is expressly forbidden to be disclosed on the Residential Property Disclosure Statement form.
7. (b) The responsibility for obtaining information regarding released sexual offenders in a community rests with the buyer.
8. (d) A sale by a real estate licensee of a two-unit residential property is exempt from the Residential Property Disclosure Act.
9. (c) The broker must disclose the cracked foundation, but disclosing the suicide could constitute a breach of duty to the client.
10. (a) Known adverse material defects of the property must be disclosed by the seller.

CHAPTER 3
Interests in Real Estate

1. (c) A change in a county ordinance does not constitute the exercise of eminent domain by the process of condemnation.
2. (a) For condemnation purposes, *just compensation* means fair market value at the time of the taking.
3. (b) A genuine but ineffective effort to purchase must be made before a condemnation suit is initiated.
4. (a) Dower and curtesy rights in Virginia have been abolished.
5. (c) *J* dies intestate. This means that she died without executing a will.
6. (d) A 52-foot sailboat purchased during the marriage cannot be excluded from G's augmented estate.
7. (b) The total maximum value of *P*'s homestead exemption is $6,500, which includes $5,000 plus $500 for each dependent.
8. (d) The householder is entitled to keep the $5,000 exemption in addition to the family bible, wedding rings, and burial plots.
9. (d) Inconvenience is not a basis for an easement by necessity.
10. (b) The new use is hostile, and if not stopped within 20 years, it could become an easement by prescription.

CHAPTER 4
Forms of Real Estate Ownership

1. (c) B or *J* can void the contract, but E is bound.
2. (a) A joint tenancy is created in Virginia by an act of the parties.
3. (b) G and B own real property as joint tenants with right of survivorship. G dies owing money to creditors. B owns the property and is not liable to the creditors.
4. (d) B and M own land as tenants by the entirety. B signs a contract to sell his share of the property to *J*. Based on these facts, all of the following are true *except* that M is now the sole owner of the land.
5. (d) Virginia is not a community property state.
6. (a) M and H are partners in a successful accounting practice. They are in the process of purchasing a small office condominium for their practice. They would not be able to take title as tenants by the entirety.
7. (b) Corporate seal and signatures of corporate officers are necessary for a corporation to convey property by deed.
8. (c) When a person wants to create a condominium, the word *condominium* must appear in the name of the property.
9. (b) Contracts for the *initial* purchase of a condominium may be rescinded without penalty ten days after the later of contract ratification or receipt of the POS (Public Offering Statement).
10. (a) If a condominium unit owner fails to pay the owners' association's assessment against his or her unit, the owners' association may place a lien against the unit.
11. (c) Of the owners, 80 percent are needed to dissolve the condominium status of the property.
12. (a) After hand-delivery of the documents, B will have three days to cancel the contract.

13. (b) If *J* should decide to rescind the contract, March 9 is the latest date when *J* may do so without incurring a penalty.
14. (b) When the owner's interest in a time-share includes either a freehold interest or an estate for years, it is a time-share estate.
15. (c) If she decides to make an offer on the property, she will have seven days after ratification of the contract to cancel the contract without penalty.
16. (b) The statute of limitations on any action for misrepresentation of information as it applies to time-shares is two years.
17. (c) M can cancel her contract within three days after receiving the POA disclosure packet.
18. (b) S is six months behind in his POA fees. The association has the right to place a lien on the property.
19. (b) Both the Condominium Act and the Property Owner Association Act have a set limit of $325 that may be charged for preparation of the required document packet.
20. (d) The REB is not charged with the administration of the Virginia Residential Property Disclosure Act.
21. (c) In a condominium, the unit owner obtains a fee simple interest in an individual unit but not in the common elements of the condominium.
22. (d) *J* can postpone the settlement pending receipt and acceptance of the update.
23. (d) The POA documents *cannot* be waived.
24. (a) The time for rescission of the contract has passed.
25. (c) A couple engaged to be married is planning to purchase a home prior to the wedding. They cannot take title as tenants by the entirety because they are not yet married.

CHAPTER 5
Legal Descriptions

1. (d) The description does not enclose a parcel of land.
2. (d) The fact that Block F has only six lots and the street address is Lot 5 is enough correct information to permit identification. The deed is valid.
3. (c) *J* prevails regarding access to the creek because the survey supersedes errors in the plat.
4. (a) A lender may use the services of either licensed or exempt surveyors, but the lender cannot require that a particular surveyor conduct the survey.
5. (d) The survey for 1234 Grand Avenue shows the location of the house, the garage, the fence, utility lines, and the children's playhouse in the backyard. This is most likely an as-built survey.

CHAPTER 6
Real Estate Taxes and Other Liens

1. (a) Tax rates and assessments must be uniformly applied to similar properties.
2. (b) For real estate tax purposes they will be classified differently, according to use.
3. (d) Land owned by handicapped persons is not exempt from property taxes.
4. (b) Taxes on new construction are estimated from the date of the certificate of occupancy.
5. (a) In Virginia, the buyer owns a property (for real estate tax purposes) on the date of sale.
6. (c) Property tax liens have first priority.
7. (c) This improvement most likely will be paid for by a special assessment.
8. (c) A mechanic may wait no more than 90 days after the work was done before filing a mechanic's lien.
9. (b) A mechanic has six months to enforce a lien by filing suit.
10. (d) A creditor on a judgment must enforce the judgment within 20 years once it is rendered.

CHAPTER 7
Real Estate Contracts and Documentation

1. (d) The sale is unenforceable under the Statute of Frauds, but the parties are free to comply with its terms.
2. (a) A general power of attorney may not be used in a real estate transaction.

3. (a) If the contract is silent on the issue, only the buyer is liable under his or her equitable title interest.
4. (c) *D* is liable owing to the implied warranty against structural defects.
5. (d) An oral lease for a term of less than one year, as in this case, is enforceable.
6. (a) A licensee who agrees merely to prepare a sales contract for a fee may be guilty of practicing law without a license.
7. (c) An actual contract used for the purchase and sale of real property may take any form.
8. (c) A sales contract would not contain the ages of the parties to the contract.
9. (b) By the provisions of Virginia Code Section 55-512 this packet must be delivered to the seller within 14 days of the request.
10. (a) When requesting the disclosure packet, payment may accompany the request.

CHAPTER 8
Transfer of Title

1. (c) Failure of all grantors to sign would most likely invalidate a deed.
2. (d) The heir will not win because a person is presumed competent unless a court has ruled otherwise.
3. (b) Kendra's original sale of Blackacre was voidable by her *because she was a minor at the time of the original sale*, and she may recover the property from Herb.
4. (d) The lender's permission should be obtained for a borrower to execute a power of attorney for a real estate transaction.
5. (a) Any affidavits or sworn statements the seller is required to deliver at the closing must be signed by the seller.
6. (b) A property sold for $675,600. The Buyer will pay $2229.48; $675,600 × (0.0008 + 0.0025) = $2229.48. The Seller will pay $3,378; $675,600 × (.005) = $3,378.
7. (c) The seller would be expected to pay grantor tax of $0.50 per $500 of purchase price.
8. (c) All of the people listed are entitled to prevail on a claim of title by adverse possession *except* a person who has been entering an orchard and taking apples every October since 1972.
9. (b) M will receive title to the property after the will has gone through probate.
10. (b) The witnesses signed the will; therefore, the will is valid.

CHAPTER 9
Title Records

1. (d) The seller of real property is required to have marketable title at closing.
2. (b) Because the seller has a reasonable time to correct defects, the contract is still in effect.
3. (b) According to the Consumer Real Estate Settlement Protection Act, the selection of a settlement agent is made by the buyer.
4. (d) The listing agent is not required to determine whether a seller has marketable title at the time a property is held out for sale.
5. (c) A full title search goes back 60 years.
6. (a) A change from a fee simple to a life estate may *not* be accomplished by using a correction deed.
7. (b) In cases where title must be cleared by having correction deeds signed, the seller is responsible for locating the parties who must sign.
8. (c) *T* has recently purchased a property from *J*. *T* has reason to believe that there is an outstanding judgment lien against *J*. *T* should be worried because judgment liens remain against the property.
9. (b) Discovery that an unreleased deed of trust still shows on the county records is most likely because S's lender neglected to have a deed of release signed and recorded.
10. (d) Mechanics' and materialmen's liens are not protections offered to an owner insured by a standard title insurance policy.

CHAPTER 10
Virginia's Real Estate License Law

1. (d) The Real Estate Board consists of nine members: seven licensees and two consumers.
2. (c) Any person who is currently licensed in another jurisdiction and meets all requirements for reciprocity may be licensed in Virginia.
3. (d) Successful completion of a course of 60 classroom, correspondence, or distance learning hours in general principles of real estate is a requirement to obtain a real estate salesperson's license in Virginia.
4. (a) A college degree or certificate in business, finance, management, appraisal, or real estate is not a requirement for a broker's license.
5. (c) A broker's business is growing, and now she wants to open a branch office. The office must have a separate license.
6. (a) A licensed salesperson may under no circumstances hold a concurrent license with more than one Virginia broker.
7. (b) A licensee who allows his or her license to expire has up to 30 days to reinstate the license without monetary penalty.
8. (c) If she wants to remain licensed, she must apply for reinstatement of her license and pay the current reinstatement fee.
9. (d) Real estate licenses are renewed in Virginia biennially, on the last day of the month in which issued.
10. (b) An active licensed broker who has been licensed in Virginia since 1975 is *not* exempt from the continuing education requirements on the basis of having been licensed for more than 15 years.
11. (c) Yore Realty opens its first office in Richmond. "Yore Realty" is a permissible sign to place in front of the office.
12. (b) A salesperson decides to retire. When the salesperson terminates his or her affiliation, the broker is responsible for notifying the REB of the change.
13. (a) If a broker establishes an account to hold money belonging to others, all checks, deposit slips, and bank statements must include the word *escrow* as part of the account name.
14. (c) Earnest money deposits may not be distributed from the broker's escrow account when requested by one party's attorney.
15. (c) The broker may not borrow money from the escrow account of one of the other properties to make the repairs.
16. (b) Every Virginia real estate office is required to keep transaction records for three years.
17. (d) The name of the broker/firm must appear on all "For Sale" signs placed on property by a broker.
18. (d) Broker *D* has developed her own Web page to advertise her listings for sale. Online disclosure requirements will require that she include on each page her name, her firm's name and address, and the jurisdiction in which her firm is licensed.
19. (b) Based on these facts, the advertisement is proper because the owner has disclosed her licensee status as required by law.
20. (b) *S* sues her broker. The jury finds in favor of *S*. *S* must file a claim with REB to recover money from the Transaction Recovery Fund within one year after having been awarded a judgment by the courts in her case.
21. (d) The minimum balance of the Virginia Real Estate Transaction Recovery Fund is $400,000.
22. (c) When the payment is made, *H*'s license is automatically revoked.
23. (a) Under these circumstances, the salesperson has failed to properly disclose his or her agency relationship.
24. (b) Based on these facts, both the conviction and the broker's failure to notify the REB within 30 days violate REB regulations.
25. (d) The listing agreement may not include the net amount that the seller will receive from the sale.
26. (d) In this situation, accepting the money is a violation of REB regulations because monies must be paid through the broker.

27. (b) This is not a violation of the license law if the fee is disclosed in writing to the parties to the contract.
28. (d) M may not pay W for the lead.
29. (d) When a sole proprietor has his or her license suspended for two years, all licenses affiliated with the proprietor must be returned to the REB.
30. (a) When a salesperson is alleged to have violated the license law, possibly resulting in disciplinary action, an investigation will be conducted by the REB.
31. (a) Bob will be able to do this as long as the assistant has a valid real estate license and becomes affiliated with his firm.
32. (b) The name of the broker or firm with whom Gatto and his wife are affiliated is missing from their sign.
33. (c) Yolanda must complete 30 hours of continuing education and apply for reinstatement.
34. (b) Phuong must establish a brokerage in Virginia.
35. (c) The maximum balance is $2,000,000.
36. (a) The salesperson has failed to disclose his agency relationship.
37. (b) The salesperson must disclose that the owner is a licensee.
38. (d) Bob must notify the REB within 30 days of his conviction.
39. (b) Mary must give the check to her broker.
40. (d) Larry must affiliate with a real estate firm or open his own firm.
41. (c) Larry will be required to file a consent to suits and services.
42. (d) Tiko will have to complete 30 hours of education within the first 12 months of being a licensee.
43. (c) Kim will have to complete 24 hours of continuing education.
44. (c) Neither John nor Mila can form a real estate firm with just salesperson licenses.

CHAPTER 11
Real Estate Financing Principles

1. (c) When borrowers sign a note and deed of trust, they agree to waive the hearing if they default.
2. (c) The lender has the responsibility for preparing the note and deed of trust involved in a closing.
3. (b) For a loan that is sold outside Virginia, the note must be notarized with a seal.
4. (b) The maximum late charge of five percent may be assessed on a mortgage loan payment.
5. (b) If M makes a payment on June 18, her lender can legally impose a late charge, but no more than $77.25 (5 percent of 1/12 of $18,540).
6. (d) A deed of trust that permits the borrower to receive advances from time to time up to a maximum amount secured by real property is referred to as a *credit line deed of trust* or a *HELOC* (Home Equity Line of Credit).
7. (a) On a first deed of trust, there is no maximum limit if the rate is stated in the loan agreement.
8. (b) The primary purpose of the Virginia Housing Development Authority is to make housing more affordable for low-income and moderate-income buyers.
9. (a) Assuming the sale of the property brings enough money, the order in which the various amounts will be paid is $15,000, $10,000, $12,000.
10. (b) The soonest that the broker may receive his or her commission check is June 15.
11. (c) They probably make too much income to qualify for a VHDA loan.
12. (a) A credit line deed of trust or a HELOC (Home Equity Line of Credit) allows the note holder to make advances from time to time secured by the real estate described in the deed.
13. (a) The expenses of executing the trust, including a commission to the trustee, must be paid first.
14. (b) Purchase-money financing offered by the seller is usually called a *seller take-back*.
15. (d) In writing a purchase contract a licensed real estate broker or agent should insure that if a first trust is to be obtained, the contract is made contingent on the purchaser's obtaining the loan, and there is a ceiling on the interest rate the borrower will accept, and the type of financing to be used by the borrower.

CHAPTER 12
Leasing

1. (d) The Secretary of the Commonwealth will receive these notices.
2. (b) 60 days' notice is required to terminate the tenants' month-to-month leases.
3. (d) No, because the tenant is not at fault. He or she is entitled to release from the lease or a reduction in rent until his or her use of the land is restored.
4. (a) The landlord's lien attaches to the tenant's property on April 1, 2007.
5. (c) If the landlord sells the apartment's contents at a "garage sale," *V* may be entitled to damages for the landlord's unlawful seizure, but because the seizure was for rent due, *V* is not relieved of the obligation to pay the outstanding rent.
6. (d) If the tenant decides not to sign a lease, all sums in excess of the landlord's actual expenses must be returned to the prospective tenant.
7. (c) The maximum amount the landlord can require as a security deposit is $1,500 (two months' security).
8. (d) Fifteen months' interest will accrue on *B*'s one-month rent security deposit.
9. (c) The tenant needs to inform the landlord, and the tenant must also give the landlord instructions and passwords.
10. (d) Nothing because he is in the military.
11. (d) Within five days of occupancy the landlord must disclose in writing the existence of any visible evidence of mold in the dwelling.
12. (b) Virginia law requires a one-month notice (30 days) to terminate a month-to-month lease.
13. (c) The tenant has seven days to give written notice to the landlord.
14. (d) The landlord can require that a tenant pay damage and renter's insurance premiums.
15. (b) Kendra's properties are *not* subject to the VRLTA because only two of Kendra's properties will be subject to a lease.

CHAPTER 13
Fair Housing and Ethical Practices

1. (b) Familial status is protected by the Virginia Fair Housing Law.
2. (b) A 62-year-old cocaine user is *not* protected by the Virginia Fair Housing Law's provisions.
3. (d) An owner may discriminate on the basis of religion in selling or renting his or her own property *only* when the owner is a religious organization or institution.
4. (c) The ad is legal because M is sharing her own home.
5. (b) The building manager cannot lawfully refuse to rent an apartment to *T* because *T*'s criminal conviction did not involve harm to persons or property.
6. (c) The rental company was guilty of the unlawful discriminatory housing practice of false representation.
7. (a) A "no pets" policy would *not* have to be waived for M, who is not handicapped and whose cats are not service animals.
8. (b) Based on these facts alone, if both *R* and *S* are turned down, Mighty Mortgage has most likely committed unlawful discrimination against *S* only.
9. (d) Investigations of fair housing complaints must be completed within one year after a complaint is filed.
10. (c) A civil action brought by the attorney general for a first violation of the Virginia Fair Housing Law could subject a guilty party to a monetary civil penalty of up to $50,000 for a first offense.
11. (a) Lei's case will be heard before the Real Estate Board because she is a licensee.
12. (b) The Fair Housing Board consists of 11 members. Of the 11 members, three citizen members are appointed to the board.

13. (d) According to the Virginia Fair Housing Law, a family care home, a foster home, and a group home in which no more than eight persons who are mentally ill, retarded, or developmentally disabled, live together with resident counselors, could exist in a community zoned for single-family homes.
14. (d) Under the Fair Housing Law, a religious cross or symbol would be deemed discriminatory if printed on a licensee's business card.
15. (a) Kirsten's ad may specify SF House to share, $650 per month, male nonsmoker only. She can specify sex; smokers are not protected.

Answer Key: Practice Examination

1. (d) In this situation, S is known as a *designated agent*.
2. (c) An officer of a limited liability company who specializes in listing commercial property *must* hold a real estate license in Virginia.
3. (a) The duties that an agent owes to his or her client are established by Virginia's agency statute.
4. (b) The death of the salesperson is *not* a way to terminate a brokerage relationship.
5. (a) The Residential Property Disclosure Statement must contain notice to purchasers regarding Megan's Law and advising them of the source for information on registered sex offenders.
6. (c) If the seller gives the buyer the required Residential Property Disclosure Statement three days after the contract is signed, the buyer can terminate the contract within five days of postmark, if mailed.
7. (b) If a married woman with three children dies intestate, her property will be distributed one-third to her husband, the remaining two-thirds to her children equally.
8. (b) *J* is an unmarried homeowner of a $475,000 mansion. The value of *J*'s homestead exemption is $5,000.
9. (c) If *D*'s wife renounces the will to claim her elective share, she will now be entitled to one-third of his estate.
10. (d) *H*, *M*, and *R* are joint tenants. M sells his tenancy to *T*. *H* and *R* are joint tenants with a tenancy in common with *T*.
11. (a) S and *J* are tenants in common, and *J* dies intestate. *J*'s interest passes to *J*'s heirs.
12. (c) *K* must show a copy of the current bylaws and rules and regulations to prospective buyers before *K* can sell the unit.
13. (c) They will be able to cancel this contract if they cancel within three days of receiving the POA disclosure packet.
14. (d) The following is a lot-and-block kind of legal description:
    All those certain lots, pieces or parcels of land, situated in the city of Roanoke, Virginia, known, numbered, and designated on the Plat of Hampton Square and recorded in the clerk's office of the Circuit Court of the City of Roanoke, Virginia, in Map Book 26, page 7, as Lots No. 9 and 10.
15. (b) A combination of the metes-and-bounds and lot-and-block methods is the most common description of real estate in Virginia.
16. (c) If a contractor records a mechanic's memorandum of lien on September 15, 2007, he or she will have six months to file a suit to enforce it.
17. (a) The real estate tax lien will be paid first.
18. (d) His broker tells him that his wife, *N*, will need to sign the contract even though she does not own the property because *N* is required to release any future interest in the property she might hold.
19. (b) An implied warranty against structural defects on new construction continues for one year after the date of transfer of title or the buyer's taking possession.
20. (a) The signature of the grantee is *not* a requirement for a valid deed.
21. (c) *F* buys *T*'s home for $250,000. *F* will pay $825.00; *T* will pay $1,250.
    $250,000 × 0.0033 = $825.00; $250,000 × 0.5 percent = $1,250.
22. (a) *S* will receive title to the property after the will has gone through probate court.
23. (d) Under the Wet Settlement Act, Virginia requires that a deed of trust be recorded and all settlement proceeds be distributed within two days of the date of settlement.
24. (b) The buyer's full legal name is *not* found on a title report.
25. (d) The sale of a property to a relative for $1 with a recorded deed could cause a gap in the chain of title.

26. (c) Under Virginia Real Estate License Law an "independent contractor" is a licensee representing a client other than as a standard agent.
27. (c) The Real Estate Board members are appointed by the governor.
28. (d) *H* has to apply for his license within one year of passing the Virginia licensing exam before being required to retake the exam again.
29. (a) The Real Estate Board may *not* impose a prison sentence on a licensee.
30. (b) The activities of the Real Estate Board include the issuance of real estate licenses.
31. (d) *K* will *not* have met her renewal education requirements because she has failed to take a course on fair housing laws and meet the new requirement for a total of 16 continuing education hours.
32. (b) *J* will need to send to the Real Estate Board the current annual fee for reinstatement for his renewal fee.
33. (a) If salesperson *R* is getting married and will be changing her last name, she *must* notify the REB within 30 days of the wedding.
34. (c) Salesperson *R* decides to leave Broker *K*'s firm and work at Broker *M*'s firm. *R* should fill out the application, obtain *M*'s signature, and send with fee to the REB.
35. (a) C should disclose her license status because disclosure is required regardless of an inactive license status.
36. (d) *W* should immediately give the check to his broker.
37. (d) A salesperson selling as For Sale By Owner with disclosure that owner is licensed is *not* required to include the name of the broker in all advertising.
38. (c) If the Real Estate Transaction Recovery Fund falls below $400,000, the Real Estate Board can assess $20 from each salesperson and broker, inactive or active.
39. (b) Failing to maintain all signed documents for a period of three years is *not* considered improper delivery of instruments. It is, however, a violation of the REB regarding the retention of records.
40. (b) In Virginia, VA and FHA notes require notarization to be valid.
41. (c) One of the primary functions of the Virginia Housing Development Authority (VHDA) is to provide housing financing for residents of Virginia.
42. (b) A foreclosure of a deed of trust could be achieved without court action or sale of the property through a deed in lieu of foreclosure.
43. (a) G has just purchased a rental property that has four months to go on the current lease. The present tenants now have the right to continue their lease under current terms.
44. (c) Twelve months' interest will accrue on *F*'s security deposit.
45. (c) The Virginia Residential Landlord and Tenant Act protects the rights of both landlords and tenants and applies to all apartment building rentals.
46. (a) If a tenant leaves one couch and two chairs in his apartment after the lease has ended, the landlord is allowed to sell them if the tenant is given ten days' written notice.
47. (a) A 58-year-old AIDS victim is protected by Virginia's Fair Housing Law. While age per se is not protected, disability and elderliness (55 years or older) are.
48. (d) *T* will *not* be in violation of the Virginia Fair Housing Law if he refuses to rent his two-bedroom apartment to applicants who do not have adequate income.
49. (c) Removing walls along a corridor of a common area to make the hallway wide enough for wheelchair access in an apartment building is *not* considered a reasonable request.
50. (d) An injured party has one year to file a complaint with the REB if an alleged fair housing discriminatory act has taken place.
51. (c) *J* is now an undisclosed dual agent.
52. (b) Vika may disclose, represent the seller only, and treat the purchaser as a customer.
53. (b) Q's new license will cost him $210.
54. (b) Jake and Mary should take title as tenants in common.
55. (a) If Cato is found guilty of discrimination, the maximum amount he could be fined is $100,000 for two violations ($50,000 each). Familial status and the elderly are protected.
56. (d) VHDA funding comes from bonds sold through the private sector.

57. (d) Because Giles is now a nonresident landlord with properties subject to the VRLTA, Giles must appoint a resident agent.
58. (d) After 13 months a landlord must pay interest on a security deposit.
59. (d) In no case may the landlord receive more than two months' rent as a security deposit. All units rent for $995 per month. The maximum the landlord can receive as a security deposit is $1,990; $995 × 2 = $1,990. Insurance is not part of the security deposit.
60. (b) A landlord could safely decline to rent to a handicapped person who requires major modifications for living and accessibility.
61. (d) Colonel Jackson could require a bond secured by not more than two months' security or require that the tenant secure and pay the premiums for damage insurance.
62. (d) George will probably work for Jennifer as an independent contractor according to a written contract between George and Jennifer.
63. (d) Corliss will be able to design and mail brochures for Artimus; all of the other answers will require that Corliss be licensed.
64. (d) Peter may sell his house himself; a license is not required.
65. (a) K must disclose that she is licensed.
66. (a) Bob's hearing will be held before the Real Estate Board because Bob is a licensee.
67. (d) A multidenominationally owned religious home for the elderly may exclude an avowed atheist.
68. (a) If tax liens do not have priority over the deed of trust at foreclosure, the payment of such liens can become subordinate.
69. (d) Zoë's landlord may not charge a pet deposit because Misha is a service animal and not a pet.
70. (d) If the applicant is in a wheelchair on making the application or if the applicant is applying for housing designated or designed for people with a disability, the landlord may ask questions related to a disability.

APPENDIX C

Code of Virginia—Selected Sections

§54.1-2131. Licensees engaged by sellers.

A. A licensee engaged by a seller shall:

1. Perform in accordance with the terms of the brokerage relationship;
2. Promote the interests of the seller by:
   a. Seeking a sale at the price and terms agreed upon in the brokerage relationship or at a price and terms acceptable to the seller; however, the licensee shall not be obligated to seek additional offers to purchase the property while the property is subject to a contract of sale, unless agreed to as part of the brokerage relationship or as the contract of sale so provides;
   b. Presenting in a timely manner all written offers or counteroffers to and from the seller, even when the property is already subject to a contract of sale;
   c. Disclosing to the seller material facts related to the property or concerning the transaction of which the licensee has actual knowledge; and
   d. Accounting for in a timely manner all money and property received in which the seller has or may have an interest;
3. Maintain confidentiality of all personal and financial information received from the client during the brokerage relationship and any other information that the client requests during the brokerage relationship be maintained confidential, unless otherwise provided by law or the seller consents in writing to the release of such information;
4. Exercise ordinary care; and
5. Comply with all requirements of this article, all applicable fair housing statutes and regulations, and all other applicable statutes and regulations which are not in conflict with this article.

B. Licensees shall treat all prospective buyers honestly and shall not knowingly give them false information. A licensee engaged by a seller shall disclose to prospective buyers all material adverse facts pertaining to the physical condition of the property which are actually known by the licensee. A licensee shall not be liable to a buyer for providing false information to the buyer if the false information was provided to the licensee by the seller and the licensee did not (i) have actual knowledge that the information was false or (ii) act in reckless disregard of the truth. No cause of action shall arise against any licensee for revealing information as required by this article or applicable law. Nothing in this article shall limit in any way the provisions of the Virginia Residential Property Disclosure Act. [§55-517 et seq.]

C. A licensee engaged by a seller in a real estate transaction may, unless prohibited by law or the brokerage relationship, provide assistance to a buyer or potential buyer by performing ministerial acts. Performing such ministerial acts that are not inconsistent with subsection A shall not be construed to violate the licensee's brokerage relationship with the seller unless expressly prohibited by the terms of the brokerage relationship, nor shall performing such ministerial acts be construed to form a brokerage relationship with such buyer or potential buyer.

D. A licensee engaged by a seller does not breach any duty or obligation owed to the seller by showing alternative properties to prospective buyers, whether as clients or customers, or by representing other sellers who have other properties for sale.

E. Licensees shall disclose brokerage relationships pursuant to the provisions of this article. (1995, cc. 741, 813)

§54.1-2132. Licensees engaged by buyers.

A. A licensee engaged by a buyer shall:

1. Perform in accordance with the terms of the brokerage relationship;
2. Promote the interests of the buyer by:
    a. Seeking a property at a price and with terms acceptable to the buyer; however, the licensee shall not be obligated to seek other properties for the buyer while the buyer is a party to a contract to purchase property unless agreed to as part of the brokerage relationship;
    b. Presenting in a timely manner all written offers or counteroffers to and from the buyer, even when the buyer is already a party to a contract to purchase property;
    c. Disclosing to the buyer material facts related to the property or concerning the transaction of which the licensee has actual knowledge; and
    d. Accounting for in a timely manner all money and property received in which the buyer has or may have an interest;
3. Maintain confidentiality of all personal and financial information received from the client during the brokerage relationship and any other information that the client requests during the brokerage relationship be maintained confidential unless otherwise provided by law or the buyer consents in writing to the release of such information;
4. Exercise ordinary care; and
5. Comply with all requirements of this article, all applicable fair housing statutes and regulations, and all other applicable statutes and regulations which are not in conflict with this article.

B. Licensees shall treat all prospective sellers honestly and shall not knowingly give them false information. No cause of action shall arise against any licensee for revealing information as required by this article or applicable law. In the case of a residential transaction, a licensee engaged by a buyer shall disclose to a seller the buyer's intent to occupy the property as a principal residence.

C. A licensee engaged by a buyer in a real estate transaction may, unless prohibited by law or the brokerage relationship, provide assistance to the seller, or prospective seller, by performing ministerial acts. Performing such ministerial acts that are not inconsistent with subsection A shall not be construed to violate the licensee's brokerage relationship with the buyer unless expressly prohibited by the terms of the brokerage relationship, nor shall performing such ministerial acts be construed to form a brokerage relationship with such seller.

D. A licensee engaged by a buyer does not breach any duty or obligation to the buyer by showing properties in which the buyer is interested to other prospective buyers, whether as clients or customers, by representing other buyers looking at the same or other properties, or by representing sellers relative to other properties.

E. Licensees shall disclose brokerage relationships pursuant to the provisions of this article. (1995, cc. 741, 813)

CRESPA–SPECIFIC LANGUAGE

All contracts involving the purchase of real estate containing not more than four residential dwelling units shall include in boldface, ten-point type the following language:

> *Choice of Settlement Agent: You have the right to select a settlement agent to handle the closing of this transaction. The settlement agent's role in closing your transaction involves the coordination of numerous administrative and clerical functions relating to the collection of documents and the collection and disbursement of funds required to carry out the terms of the contract between the parties. If part of the purchase price is financed, your lender will instruct the settlement agent as to the signing and recording of loan documents and the disbursement of loan proceeds. No settlement agent can provide legal advice to any party to the transaction except a settlement agent who is engaged in the private practice of law in Virginia and who has been retained or engaged by a party to the transaction for the purpose of providing legal services to that party.*
>
> *Escrow, closing and settlement service guidelines: The Virginia State Bar issues guidelines to help settlement agents avoid and prevent the unauthorized practice of law in connection with furnishing escrow, settlement or closing services. As a party to a real estate transaction, you are entitled to receive a copy of these guidelines from your settlement agent, upon request, in accordance with the provisions of the Consumer Real Estate Settlement Protection Act. (1997, c. 716.)*

APPENDIX D

Information Sources

Department of Professional and Occupational Regulations (DPOR)
9960 Mayland Drive, Suite 400
Richmond, VA 23233
(804) 367-8500
http://www.state.va.us/dpor

The Virginia Association of REALTORS®
10231 Telegraph Road
Glen Allen, VA 23059-4578
(804) 264-5033 or toll-free (800) 755-8271
http://www.varealtor.com/

The Virginia Fair Housing Office
9960 Mayland Drive, Suite 400
Richmond, VA 23233
(804) 367-8530
http://www.fairhousing.vipnet.org/

Virginia Housing Development Authority (VHDA)
601 S. Belvidere Street
Richmond, VA 23220-56004
(800) 227-VHDA (8432) or 800-968-7837
http://www.vhda.com/

The Virginia Real Estate Board (VREB)
9960 Mayland Drive, Suite 400
Richmond, VA 23233
(804) 367-8526
http://www.dpor.virginia.gov/

Virginia State Bar
707 E. Main Street, Ste. 1500
Richmond, VA 23219-2800
(804) 775-0570
http://www.vsb.org/

Virginia State Corporation Commission
http://www.scc.virginia.gov/

Virginia State Taxation
http://www.tax.virginia.gov/

Lead-Based Paint Information
http://www.epa.gov/lead

Sex Offender Information
http://www.vsp.state.va.us/

SAMPLE RESEARCH PROBLEM

What happens to a brokerage firm when a principal broker dies or is disabled?

1. Go to *www.virginia.gov* and search for "death of a broker" in the search bar.

   This search will yield the link to the Real Estate Board Regulations: *www.dpor.virginia.gov/dporweb/reb_reg.pdf*.

   (A Google search will yield the same result as above.)

2. Select the link to the PDF document listed above. Using the PDF search function, search for "death." This search will yield:

   "See §54.1-2109 of the Code of Virginia for termination relating to the death or disability of the principal broker."

3. Go to *www.virginia.gov* and search for "Code of Virginia" (in the search bar). *www.virginia.gov/cmsportal2/government_4096/codes_and_laws.html.*

4. Scroll down and click on "The Code of Virginia" link

5. Enter "54.1-2109" in the search bar at the Code of Virginia.

   The information will appear as follows:

   §54.1-2109. Death or disability of a broker.

   Upon the death or disability of a licensed real estate broker who was engaged in a proprietorship or who was the only licensed broker in a corporation or partnership, the estate, an adult family member, or an employee of the licensee may be granted approval by the Real Estate Board to carry on the business of the deceased or disabled broker for 180 days following the death or disability of the broker solely for the purpose of concluding the business of the deceased or disabled broker. In the event no such person is available or suitable, the board may appoint any other suitable person to terminate the business within 180 days.

   (1984, c. 283, §54-731.3; 1988, c. 765.)

APPENDIX E

Regional Sales Contract

FIGURE E.1

Regional Sales Contract

REALTOR® EQUAL HOUSING OPPORTUNITY

REGIONAL SALES CONTRACT

This SALES CONTRACT ("Contract") is made on ______________________ ("Contract Date") between ______________________ ("Purchaser") and ______________________ ("Seller") who, among other things, hereby confirm and acknowledge by their initials and signatures herein that by prior disclosure in this real estate transaction ______________________ ("Listing Company") represents Seller, and ______________________ ("Selling Company") represents ☐ **Purchaser** or ☐ **Seller**. The Listing Company and Selling Company are collectively referred to as ("Broker"). (If the brokerage firm is acting as a dual representative for both Seller and Purchaser, then the appropriate disclosure form is attached to and made a part of this Contract.) In consideration of the mutual promises and covenants set forth below, and other good and valuable consideration the receipt and sufficiency of which is acknowledged, the parties agree as follows:

1. **REAL PROPERTY** Purchaser will buy and Seller will sell for the sales price ("Sales Price"), Seller's entire interest in the real property (with all improvements, rights and appurtenances) described as follows ("Property"):
TAX Map/ID # ______________________ Legal Description: Lot(s) __________
Block/Square __________ Section _____ Subdivision or Condominium ______________________
Parking Space(s) # __________ County/Municipality ______________________
Deed Book/Liber #______________________Page/Folio # ______________________
Street Address ______________________
Unit # __________City ______________________State __________Zip Code __________

2. **PRICE AND FINANCING**

A. Down Payment $ __________

B. Financing 1. First Trust (if applicable) $ __________

2. Second Trust (if applicable) $ __________

3. Seller Held Trust $ __________
Addendum attached (if applicable)

TOTAL FINANCING $ __________

SALES PRICE $ __________

3. **DEED(S) OF TRUST**

A. **First Deed of Trust** Purchaser will ☐ **Obtain** or ☐ **Assume** a ☐ **Conventional** ☐ **FHA** ☐ **VA** ☐ **Other** __________ First Deed of Trust loan amortized over _____ years at a ☐ **Fixed or** an ☐ **Adjustable** rate bearing (initial) interest of _____ % per year or market rate available. Special Terms (if any): ______________________

B. **Second Deed of Trust** Purchaser will ☐ **Obtain** or ☐ **Assume** a Second Deed of Trust loan amortized over __________ years at a ☐ **Fixed** or an ☐ **Adjustable** rate bearing (initial) interest of __________% per year or market rate available. Special Terms (if any): ______________________

Please Initial: Seller _____/_____Purchaser _____/_____

FIGURE E.1 (CONTINUED)

Regional Sales Contract

C. **Assumption Only** Assumption fee, if any, and all charges related to the assumption will be paid by the Purchaser. If Purchaser assumes Seller's loan(s): (i) Purchaser and Seller ❒ **will**, or ❒ **will not** obtain a release of Seller's liability to the U.S. Government for the repayment of the loan by Settlement, (ii) Purchaser and Seller ❒ **will**, or ❒**will not** obtain substitution of Seller's VA entitlement by Settlement. Balances of any assumed loans, secondary financing and cash down payments are approximate.

4. **DEPOSIT**

A. Purchaser has delivered a deposit ("Deposit") to ____("Escrow Agent") of ❒ $__________________ by check and/or ❒ $ ____________________________by note due and payable on ____.

B. The Deposit will be placed in an escrow account of the Escrow Agent after Date of Ratification in conformance with the laws and regulations of the appropriate jurisdiction and/or, if VA financing applies, as required by Title 38 of the U.S. Code. This account may be interest bearing and all parties waive any claim to interest resulting from the Deposit. The Deposit will be held in escrow until: (i) Credited toward the Sales Price at Settlement; (ii) All parties have agreed in writing as to its disposition; (iii) A court of competent jurisdiction orders disbursement and all appeal periods have expired; or, (iv) Disposed of in any other manner authorized by the laws and regulations of the appropriate jurisdiction. Seller and Purchaser agree that Escrow Agent will have no liability to any party on account of disbursement of the Deposit or on account of failure to disburse the Deposit, except in the event of the Escrow Agent's gross negligence or willful misconduct.

5. **DOWN PAYMENT** The balance of the down payment will be paid on or before the Settlement Date by certified or cashier's check or by bank-wired funds. An assignment of funds shall not be used without prior written consent of Seller.

6. **SETTLEMENT** Seller and Purchaser will make full settlement in accordance with the terms of this Contract ("Settlement") on, or with mutual consent before, ____, ("Settlement Date") except as otherwise provided in this Contract. Purchaser selects: ____________________ ____("Settlement Agent") to conduct the Settlement. (For transactions in Virginia, use the Virginia Jurisdictional Addendum to select the Settlement Agent.) Either party may retain their own legal counsel. Purchaser agrees to contact the Settlement Agent within 10 Days after the Date of Ratification to schedule Settlement and to arrange for ordering the title exam and, if required, a survey.

7. **EQUIPMENT, MAINTENANCE AND CONDITION** Purchaser accepts the Property in the condition as of the Contract Date except as otherwise provided herein. Seller warrants that, except as otherwise provided, the existing appliances, heating, cooling, plumbing, electrical systems and equipment, and smoke and heat detectors (as required), will be in normal working order as of the Possession Date. Seller will deliver the Property in substantially the same condition as on the Contract Date and broom clean with all trash and debris removed. Purchaser and Seller will not hold the Broker liable for any breach of this paragraph. Seller will have all utilities in service through Settlement or as otherwise agreed.

8. **UTILITIES - WATER, SEWAGE, HEATING AND CENTRAL AIR CONDITIONING** (Check all that apply)

Water Supply:	❒ Public	❒ Private Well		❒Community Well		
Sewage Disposal:	❒ Public	❒ Septic for # BR ____		❒Community Septic	❒ Alternative Septic for # BR: ____	
Hot Water:	❒ Oil	❒ Gas	❒ Elec.	❒Other ______________		
Air Conditioning:	❒ Oil	❒ Gas	❒ Elec.	❒Heat Pump	❒Other ____	❒ Zones ________
Heating:	❒ Oil	❒ Gas	❒ Elec.	❒Heat Pump	❒Other ___	❒ Zones ________

Please Initial: Seller ______/______Purchaser ______/______

FIGURE E.1 (CONTIUED)

Regional Sales Contract

9. **PERSONAL PROPERTY AND FIXTURES** The Property includes the following existing personal property and fixtures: built-in heating and central air conditioning equipment, plumbing and lighting fixtures, sump pump, attic and exhaust fans, storm windows, storm doors, screens, installed wall-to-wall carpeting, window shades, blinds, window treatment hardware, smoke and heat detectors, TV antennas, exterior trees and shrubs. Unless otherwise agreed to in writing, all surface or wall mounted electronic components/devices **DO NOT** convey. If more than one of an item convey, the number of items is noted.

The items marked YES below are currently installed or offered.

Yes	No	#	Items	Yes	No	#	Items	Yes	No	#	Items
❒	❒	___	Alarm System	❒	❒	___	Freezer	❒	❒	___	Satellite Dish
❒	❒	___	Built-in Microwave	❒	❒	___	Furnace Humidifier	❒	❒	___	Storage Shed
❒	❒	___	Ceiling Fan	❒	❒	___	Garage Opener	❒	❒	___	Stove or Range
❒	❒	___	Central Vacuum	❒	❒	___	w/ remote	❒	❒	___	Trash Compactor
❒	❒	___	Clothes Dryer	❒	❒	___	Gas Log	❒	❒	___	Wall Oven
❒	❒	___	Clothes Washer	❒	❒	___	Hot Tub, Equip,& Cover	❒	❒	___	Water Treatment System
❒	❒	___	Cooktop	❒	❒	___	Intercom	❒	❒	___	Window A/C Unit
❒	❒	___	Dishwasher	❒	❒	___	Playground Equipment	❒	❒	___	Window Fan
❒	❒	___	Disposer	❒	❒	___	Pool, Equip, & Cover	❒	❒	___	Window Treatments
❒	❒	___	Electronic Air Filter	❒	❒	___	Refrigerator	❒	❒	___	Wood Stove
❒	❒	___	Fireplace Screen/Door	❒	❒	___	w/ ice maker				

OTHER ____

____

____

____

____

AS IS ITEMS
Seller does not warrant the condition or working order of the following items and/or systems:

____

____

____

____

If entire Property is sold "As Is", appropriate addendum must be attached.

LEASED ITEMS
Any leased items, systems or service contracts (including, but not limited to, fuel tanks, water treatment systems, lawn contracts, security system monitoring, and satellite contracts) DO NOT CONVEY absent an express written agreement by Purchaser and Seller. The following is a list of the leased items within the Property:

____

____

____

10. **CONVENTIONAL FINANCING TERMS**

A. **SELLER SUBSIDY** Based on the financing terms specified in this Contract, Seller will pay at Settlement $________________________ toward Purchaser's charges, (including but not limited to loan origination fees, discount fees, buy down or subsidy fees, prepaids or other charges as allowed by the lender). Purchaser will pay all remaining Purchaser's charges. If applicable, Purchaser will pay at Settlement or finance any initial private mortgage insurance required by lender. It is Purchaser's responsibility to confirm with his lender, if applicable, that the entire credit provided herein may be utilized. If lender prohibits Seller from the payment of any portion of this credit, then said credit shall be reduced to the amount allowed by the lender.

FIGURE E.1 (CONTINUED)

Regional Sales Contract

B. APPRAISAL **(Must Select Option 1 or 2)**

❐ **Option (1)** This Contract **is contingent** on Purchaser obtaining an Appraisal certifying the value of the Property to be no less than the Sales Price. See Attached Addendum. **If the appropriate Appraisal Contingency Addendum is not attached, this Contract is not contingent on an Appraisal and Option (2) below will apply.**

OR

❐ **Option (2)** This Contract **is not contingent** on an Appraisal. Purchaser shall complete Settlement without regard to the value of the Property set forth in any Appraisal and acknowledges that this may reduce the amount of financing available from lender and may require Purchaser to tender additional funds at Settlement. If Purchaser fails to settle except due to any Default by Seller, then the provisions of paragraph #26 (Default) shall apply.

C. FINANCING **(Must Select Option 1 or 2) Not to be used with Seller Financing**

❐ **Option (1)** This Contract **is contingent** on Purchaser obtaining approval for loan(s) to purchase the Property (The "Financing Contingency").

This Contract is contingent until 9 p.m. _______ Days after Date of Ratification ("Financing Deadline") upon Purchaser Delivering Notice to Seller on the Regional Form #100 removing this Financing Contingency. Such Notice
❐ **shall** or
❐ **shall not** be accompanied by a letter from the lender ("Lender's Letter"). Such Lender's Letter shall include the following statements or statements substantially similar thereto:

1) Purchaser is approved for the Specified Financing,
2) a ratified Contract has been received,
3) a written application for the financing has been made,
4) income, asset, and liability documentation on Purchaser have been received,
5) Purchaser's credit has been reviewed, and
6) the application has been reviewed and meets underwriter and investor guidelines.

If Purchaser fails to Deliver Regional Form #100 and Lender's Letter (if required) by the Financing Deadline, this contingency will continue, unless Seller at Seller's option gives Notice to Purchaser that this Contract will become void. If Seller Delivers such Notice this Contract will become void at 9 p.m. on the third day following Delivery of Seller's Notice unless prior to that date and time:

a) Purchaser Delivers to Seller Regional Form #100 and Lender's Letter (if required); or

b) Purchaser Delivers to Seller Regional Form #100 and provides Seller with evidence of sufficient funds available to complete Settlement without obtaining financing.

Upon Delivery to Seller of either (a) or (b) above, this Contract will no longer be contingent on Purchaser being approved for the Specified Financing and this Contract will remain in full force and effect.

Prior to satisfaction or removal of the Financing Contingency, if Purchaser receives a written rejection for the Specified Financing and Delivers a copy of the written rejection to Seller, this Contract will become void.

OR

❐ **Option (2)** This Contract is **not contingent** upon Purchaser obtaining approval for loan(s) to purchase the Property. Purchaser acknowledges that there is not a Financing Contingency. Purchaser has provided sufficient documentation to satisfy Seller that Purchaser has been approved for the Specified Financing or has sufficient funds available to complete Settlement without obtaining financing. If Purchaser fails to settle except due to any Default by Seller, then the provisions of paragraph #26 (DEFAULT) shall apply.

Please Initial: Seller _______/_______Purchaser ______/______

FIGURE E.1 (CONTINUED)

Regional Sales Contract

11. ☐ VA or ☐ FHA FINANCING AND APPRAISAL
Purchaser will ☐ **pay at Settlement**, or ☐ **finance** any VA Funding Fee or FHA initial Mortgage Insurance Premium. Based on the Specified Financing in this Contract, the Seller will pay ____________________toward Purchaser's charges (including but not limited to loan origination fees, discount fees, buydown or subsidy fees, prepaids or other charges as allowed by the lender) except that the total amount of any lender charges which cannot by law or regulation be charged to Purchaser will be paid by the Seller. These charges, if any, will first be deducted from any Seller credit, and the remaining balance, if any, will then be applied to Purchaser's other charges. Purchaser will pay all remaining Purchaser's charges. If VA or FHA financing applies, it is expressly agreed that, notwithstanding any other provisions of this Contract, Purchaser will not be obligated to complete the purchase of the Property described herein or to incur any penalty by forfeiture of earnest money deposits or otherwise unless Purchaser has been given in accordance with HUD/FHA or VA requirements a written statement by the Federal Housing Commissioner or Direct Endorsement Lender/Department of Veterans Affairs or the Lender Approval Processing Program (LAPP) underwriter setting forth the appraised value of the Property (excluding closing costs) of not less than $ ____________________________. Purchaser will have the privilege and option of proceeding with consummation of this Contract without regard to the amount of the appraised valuation. THE APPRAISED VALUATION IS ARRIVED AT TO DETERMINE THE MAXIMUM MORTGAGE THE DEPARTMENT OF HOUSING AND URBAN DEVELOPMENT/DEPARTMENT OF VETERANS AFFAIRS WILL INSURE/GUARANTEE. HUD/DEPARTMENT OF VETERANS AFFAIRS AND THE MORTGAGEE DOES NOT WARRANT THE VALUE NOR THE CONDITION OF THE PROPERTY. PURCHASER SHOULD SATISFY HIMSELF/HERSELF THAT THE PRICE AND CONDITION OF THE PROPERTY ARE ACCEPTABLE. If VA Financing applies, Purchaser agrees that should Purchaser elect to complete the purchase at an amount in excess of the reasonable value established by the Department of Veterans Affairs, Purchaser shall pay such excess amount in cash from a source which Purchaser agrees to disclose to the Department of Veterans Affairs, and which Purchaser represents will not be borrowed funds except as approved by the Department of Veterans Affairs. Purchaser's exercise of the option shall be made in writing within 3 Days of the notification to Purchaser of the appraised value, or this Contract shall become void. If FHA financing applies, Purchaser's exercise of the option of proceeding with consummation of this Contract without regard to the amount of the appraised valuation shall be made in writing within 3 Days of the notification to Purchaser of the appraised value, or this Contract shall become void.

12. FINANCING APPLICATION If this Contract is contingent on financing, Purchaser will make written application for the Specified Financing and any lender required property insurance no later than 7 days after the Date of Ratification. Purchaser grants permission for the Selling Company and the lender to disclose to the Listing Company and the Seller general information available about the progress of the loan application and loan approval process. If Purchaser fails to settle except due to any Default by Seller, then the provisions of paragraph #26 (DEFAULT) shall apply.

13. ALTERNATE FINANCING Purchaser may substitute alternative financing and/or an alternative lender for Specified Financing provided:

(a) Purchaser is qualified for alternative financing;
(b) There is no additional expense to Seller;
(c) The Settlement Date is not delayed; and
(d) If Purchaser fails to settle except due to any Default by Seller, then the provisions of paragraph #26 (DEFAULT) shall apply.

14. PURCHASER'S REPRESENTATIONS Purchaser ☐ **will**, or ☐ **will not** occupy the Property as Purchaser's principal residence. **Unless specified in a written contingency, neither this Contract nor the financing is dependent or contingent on the sale and settlement or lease of other real property.** The Selling Company ☐ **is**, or ☐ **is not** authorized to disclose to the Listing Company and Seller the appropriate financial or credit information statement provided to the Selling Company by Purchaser. Purchaser acknowledges that Seller is relying upon all of Purchaser's representations, including without limitation, the accuracy of financial or credit information given to Seller, Broker or the lender by Purchaser.

15. ACCESS TO PROPERTY Seller will provide the Broker, Purchaser, inspectors representing Purchaser and representatives of lending institutions for Appraisal purposes, reasonable access to the Property to comply with this Contract. In addition, Purchaser and/or Purchaser's representative will have the right to make a final inspection within **5** days prior to Settlement and/or occupancy, unless otherwise agreed to by Purchaser and Seller.

FIGURE E.1 (CONTINUED)

Regional Sales Contract

16. <u>TERMITE INSPECTION</u> The ❒**Purchaser at Purchaser's expense** or ❒ **Seller at Seller's expense**, will furnish a written report from a pest control firm dated not more than 30 days prior to Settlement showing that all dwelling(s) and/or garage(s) within the Property (excluding fences or shrubs not abutting garage(s) or dwelling(s)) are free of visible evidence of active termites and other wood-destroying insects, and free from visible structural insect damage. Any extermination and structural repairs identified in the inspection report will be made at Seller's expense.

17. <u>REPAIRS</u> If, as a condition of providing financing under this Contract, the lender requires repairs to be made to the Property, then Purchaser will give Notice to Seller of the lender's required repairs. Within 5 Days after such Notice, Seller will give Notice to Purchaser as to whether Seller will make the repairs. If Seller will not make the repairs, Purchaser will give Notice to Seller within 5 Days after Seller's Notice as to whether Purchaser will make the repairs. If neither Seller nor Purchaser will make the repairs, then this Contract will become void. This clause will not release Seller from any responsibilities set forth in the paragraphs titled UTILITIES; PERSONAL PROPERTY AND FIXTURES; EQUIPMENT, MAINTENANCE AND CONDITION; WELL AND SEPTIC; TERMITE INSPECTION; or OTHER TERMS, or any terms specifically set forth in this Contract and any addenda. If the Property is sold "as is", Purchaser will be responsible for all repairs.

18. <u>DAMAGE OR LOSS</u> The risk of damage or loss to the Property by fire, act of God, or other casualty remains with Seller until the execution and delivery of the deed of conveyance to Purchaser at Settlement.

19. <u>TITLE</u> The title report and survey, if required, will be ordered promptly and, if not available on the Settlement Date, then Settlement may be delayed for up to 10 business days to obtain the title report and survey after which this Contract, at the option of Seller, may be terminated and the Deposit will be refunded in full to Purchaser according to the terms of the DEPOSIT paragraph. Fee simple title to the Property, and everything that conveys with it, will be sold free of liens except for any loans assumed by Purchaser. Title is to be good and marketable, and insurable by a licensed title insurance company with no additional risk premium. Title may be subject to commonly acceptable easements, covenants, conditions and restrictions of record, if any; otherwise, Purchaser may declare this Contract void, unless the defects are of such character that they may be remedied within 30 Days beyond the Settlement Date. In case action is required to perfect the title, such action must be taken promptly by Seller at Seller's expense. The Broker is hereby expressly released from all liability for damages by reason of any defect in the title. Seller will convey the Property by general warranty deed with English covenants of title (Virginia); general warranty deed (West Virginia); special warranty deed (D.C. and Maryland) ("Deed"). Seller will sign such affidavits, lien waivers, tax certifications, and other documents as may be required by the lender, title insurance company, Settlement Agent, or government authority, and authorizes the Settlement Agent to obtain pay-off or assumption information from any existing lenders. The manner of taking title may have significant legal and tax consequences. Purchaser is advised to seek the appropriate professional advice concerning the manner of taking title. Unless otherwise agreed to in writing, Seller will pay any special assessments and will comply with all orders, requirements, or notices of violations of any county or local authority, condominium unit owners' association, homeowners' or property owners' association or actions in any court on account thereof, against or affecting the Property on the Settlement Date.

20. <u>POSSESSION DATE</u> Unless otherwise agreed to in writing between Seller and Purchaser, Seller will give possession of the Property at Settlement, including delivery of keys, if any. If Seller fails to do so and occupies the Property beyond Settlement, Seller will be a tenant at sufferance of Purchaser and hereby expressly waives all notice to quit as provided by law. Purchaser will have the right to proceed by any legal means available to obtain possession of the Property. Seller will pay any damages and costs incurred by Purchaser including reasonable attorney fees.

21. <u>FEES</u> Fees for the preparation of the Deed, that portion of the Settlement Agent's fee billed to Seller, costs of releasing existing encumbrances, Seller's legal fees and any other proper charges assessed to Seller will be paid by Seller. Fees for the title exam (except as otherwise provided) survey, recording (including those for any purchase money trusts) and that portion of the Settlement Agent's fee billed to Purchaser, Purchaser's legal fees and any other proper charges assessed to Purchaser will be paid by Purchaser. Fees to be charged will be reasonable and customary for the jurisdiction in which the Property is located. (Recording, Transfer and Grantor's Taxes are covered in the appropriate jurisdictional addenda).

22. <u>BROKER'S FEE</u> Seller irrevocably instructs the Settlement Agent to pay the Broker compensation ("Broker's Fee") at Settlement as set forth in the listing agreement and to disburse the compensation offered by the Listing Company to the Selling Company in writing as of the Contract Date, and the remaining amount of Broker's compensation to the Listing Company.

Please Initial: Seller _______/______Purchaser ______/______

FIGURE E.1 (CONTINUED)

Regional Sales Contract

23. **ADJUSTMENTS** Rents, taxes, water and sewer charges, front foot benefit and house connection charges, condominium unit owners' association, homeowners' and/or property owners' association regular periodic assessments (if any) and any other operating charges, are to be adjusted to the day of Settlement. Any heating or cooking fuels remaining in supply tank(s) at Settlement will become the property of Purchaser, unless leased. Taxes, general and special, are to be adjusted according to the certificate of taxes issued by the collector of taxes, if any, except that recorded assessments for improvements completed prior to Settlement, whether assessments have been levied or not, will be paid by Seller or allowance made at Settlement. If a loan is assumed, interest will be adjusted to the Settlement Date and Purchaser will reimburse Seller for existing escrow accounts, if any.

24. **ATTORNEY'S FEES** In any action or proceeding involving a dispute between Purchaser and Seller arising out of this Contract, the prevailing party will be entitled to receive from the other party reasonable attorney's fees to be determined by the court or arbitrator(s). In the event a dispute arises resulting in the Broker being made a party to any litigation or if the Broker is required to bring litigation to collect the Broker's Fee, Purchaser and Seller agree to indemnify the Broker, it's employees, and/or licensees for all attorney fees and costs of litigation against the responsible party, unless the litigation results in a judgment against the Broker, it's employees and/or licensees.

25. **PERFORMANCE** Delivery of the required funds and executed documents to the Settlement Agent will constitute sufficient tender of performance. Funds from this transaction at Settlement may be used to pay off any existing liens and encumbrances, including interest, as required by lender(s) or lienholders.

26. **DEFAULT** Purchaser will be in Default even if the Financing Contingency has not been removed if Settlement does not occur on the Settlement Date for any reason other than Default by Seller, including without limitation the following:

A. Failure to lock-in the interest rate(s) and the rate(s) increase so that Purchaser does not qualify for such financing; OR
B. Failure to comply with the lender's reasonable requirements in a timely and diligent manner; OR
C. Application is made with an alternative lender (one other than the lender who provided Lender's Letter) and the alternative lender fails to meet the Settlement Date; OR
D. Does not have the down payment, closing fees and any other required funds, including without limitation, any additional funds required to be tendered by Purchaser if the Appraisal is lower than the Sales Price; OR
E. Makes any deliberate misrepresentations, material omissions or inaccuracies in financial information that results in the Purchaser's inability to secure the financing; OR
F. Failure to make application for property insurance, if required, by lender within 7 days of Date of Ratification; OR
G. Does or fails to do any act following the Date of Ratification that prevents Purchaser from completing Settlement.

If Purchaser fails to complete Settlement for any reason other than Default by Seller, at the option of Seller, the Deposit may be forfeited as liquidated damages (not as a penalty) in which event Purchaser will be relieved from further liability to Seller. If Seller does not elect to accept the Deposit as liquidated damages, the Deposit may not be the limit of Purchaser's liability in the event of a Default. If the Deposit is forfeited, or if there is an award of damages by a court or a compromise agreement between Seller and Purchaser, the Broker may accept and Seller agrees to pay the Broker one-half of the Deposit in lieu of the Broker's Fee, (provided Broker's share of any forfeited Deposit will not exceed the amount due under the listing agreement). If Seller fails to perform or comply with any of the terms and conditions of this Contract or fails to complete Settlement for any reason other than Default by Purchaser, Purchaser will have the right to pursue all legal or equitable remedies, including specific performance and/or damages. If either Seller or Purchaser refuses to execute a release of Deposit ("Release") when requested to do so in writing and a court finds that such party should have executed the Release, the party who so refused to execute the Release will pay the expenses, including, without limitation, reasonable attorney's fees, incurred by the other party in the litigation. Seller and Purchaser agree that no Escrow Agent will have any liability to any party on account of disbursement of the Deposit or on account of failure to disburse the Deposit, except only in the event of the Escrow Agent's gross negligence or willful misconduct. The parties further agree that the Escrow Agent will not be liable for the failure of any depository in which the Deposit is placed and that Seller and Purchaser each will indemnify, defend and save harmless the Escrow Agent from any loss or expense arising out of the holding, disbursement or failure to disburse the Deposit, except in the case of the Escrow Agent's gross negligence or willful misconduct. If either Purchaser or Seller is in default, then in addition to all other damages, the defaulting party will immediately pay the costs incurred for the title examination, Appraisal, survey and the Broker's Fee in full.

FIGURE E.1 (CONTINUED)

Regional Sales Contract

27. <u>OTHER DISCLOSURES</u> **Purchaser and Seller should carefully read this Contract to be sure that the terms accurately express their respective understanding as to their intentions and agreements. The Broker can counsel on real estate matters, but if legal advice is desired by either party, such party is advised to seek legal counsel. Purchaser and Seller are further advised to seek appropriate professional advice concerning the condition of the Property or tax and insurance matters.** The following provisions of this paragraph disclose some matters which the parties may investigate further. These disclosures are not intended to create a contingency. Any contingency must be specified by adding appropriate terms to this Contract. The parties acknowledge the following disclosures:

A. PROPERTY CONDITION See paragraph #7 (EQUIPMENT, MAINTENANCE AND CONDITION) Various inspection services and home warranty insurance programs are available. The Broker is not advising the parties as to certain other issues, including without limitation: water quality and quantity (including but not limited to, lead and other contaminants;) sewer or septic; soil condition; flood hazard areas; possible restrictions of the use of the Property due to restrictive covenants, zoning, subdivision, or environmental laws, easements or other documents; airport or aircraft noise; planned land use, roads or highways; and construction materials and/or hazardous materials, including without limitation flame retardant treated plywood (FRT), radon, urea formaldehyde foam insulation (UFFI), mold, polybutylene pipes, synthetic stucco (EIFS), underground storage tanks, asbestos and lead-based paint. Information relating to these issues may be available from appropriate government authorities.

B. LEGAL REQUIREMENTS All contracts for the sale of real property must be in writing to be enforceable. Upon ratification and Delivery, this Contract becomes a legally binding agreement. Any changes to this Contract must be made in writing for such changes to be enforceable.

C. FINANCING Mortgage rates and associated charges vary with financial institutions and the marketplace. Purchaser has the opportunity to select the lender and the right to negotiate terms and conditions of the financing subject to the terms of this Contract. The financing may require substantial lump sum (balloon) payments on the due dates. Purchaser has not relied upon any representations regarding the future availability of mortgage money or interest rates for the refinancing of any such lump sum payments.

D. BROKER Purchaser and Seller acknowledge that the Broker is being retained solely as a real estate agent and not as an attorney, tax advisor, lender, appraiser, surveyor, structural engineer, mold or air quality expert, home inspector or other professional service provider. The Broker may from time to time engage in the general insurance, title insurance, mortgage loan, real estate settlement, home warranty and other real estate-related businesses and services. Therefore, in addition to the Broker's Fee specified herein, the Broker may receive compensation related to other services provided in the course of this transaction pursuant to the terms of a separate agreement/disclosure.

E. PROPERTY TAXES Your property tax bill could substantially increase following settlement. For more information on property taxes contact the appropriate taxing authority in the jurisdiction where the Property is located.

F. PROPERTY INSURANCE Obtaining property insurance is typically a requirement of the lender in order to secure financing. Insurance rates and availability are determined in part by the number and nature of claims and inquiries made on a property's policy as well as the number and nature of claims made by a prospective Purchaser. Property insurance has become difficult to secure in some cases. Seller should consult an insurance professional regarding maintaining and/or terminating insurance coverage.

28. ASSIGNABILITY This Contract may not be assigned without the written consent of Purchaser and Seller. If Purchaser and Seller agree in writing to an assignment of this Contract, the original parties to this Contract remain obligated hereunder until Settlement.

Please Initial: Seller _______/_____Purchaser _____/______

FIGURE E.1 (CONTINUED)

Regional Sales Contract

29. **DEFINITIONS**
   - **A.** "Appraisal" means a written appraised valuation of the Property.
   - **B.** "Day(s)" or "day(s)" means calendar day(s) unless otherwise specified in this Contract. For the purpose of computing time periods, the first Day will be the Day following Delivery and the time period will end at 9 p.m. on the Day specified. If the Settlement Date falls on a Saturday, Sunday, or legal holiday, then the Settlement will be on the prior business day.
   - **C.** "Date of Ratification" means the date of final acceptance in writing of all the terms of this Contract (not the date of expiration or removal of any contingencies).
   - **D.** For "Delivery" and "Notices" definitions, see appropriate Jurisdictional Addendum.
   - **E.** "Specified Financing" means the loan type(s) and amount(s), if any, specified in both paragraph #2 (PRICE AND FINANCING) and paragraph #3 (DEEDS OF TRUST).
   - **F.** The masculine includes the feminine and the singular includes the plural.
   - **G.** "Possession Date" - See paragraph #20 (POSSESSION DATE).

30. **MISCELLANEOUS** This Contract may be signed in one or more counterparts, each of which is deemed to be an original, and all of which together constitute one and the same instrument. Documents obtained via facsimile machines will also be considered as originals. Typewritten or handwritten provisions included in this Contract will control all pre-printed provisions that are in conflict.

31. **VOID CONTRACT** If this Contract becomes void and of no further force and effect, without Default by either party, both parties will immediately execute a release directing that the Deposit be refunded in full to Purchaser according to the terms of the paragraph # 4(DEPOSIT).

32. **ADDITIONS** The following forms, if ratified and attached, are made a part of this Contract. (This list is not all inclusive of addenda that may need to be attached).

☐Yes Jurisdictional Addendum for: ☐DC ☐ VA ☐MD/County ________ ☐WVA ☐Other________

FIGURE E.1 (CONTINUED)

Regional Sales Contract

☐ Yes	☐ No	Addendum of Clauses (DC/MD)
☐ Yes	☐ No	Contingency Clauses (NVAR)
☐ Yes	☐ No	Condo/Coop Addendum
☐ Yes	☐ No	Dual Agency Form
☐ Yes	☐ No	Designated Agency Form
☐ Yes	☐ No	FHA Home Inspection Notice
☐ Yes	☐ No	Home Inspection Contingency
☐ Yes	☐ No	Lead Paint Disclosure
☐ Yes	☐ No	Lead Paint Inspection Contingency
☐ Yes	☐ No	Pre Settlement Occupancy
☐ Yes	☐ No	Post Settlement Occupancy
☐ Yes	☐ No	Property Disclosure or Disclaimer
☐ Yes	☐ No	Radon Testing Contingency
☐ Yes	☐ No	Sale of Home Contingency
☐ Yes	☐ No	Seller Held Trust
☐ Yes	☐ No	Well and Septic Contingency

FIGURE E.1 (CONTINUED)

Regional Sales Contract

☐ Yes ☐ No Other (specify): ______________________________

33. **HOME WARRANTY** ☐ Yes ☐ No
Home Warranty Policy paid for and provided at Settlement by: ☐ Purchaser or ☐ Seller.

Cost not to exceed $______________. Warranty provider to be ______________________________.

34. **OTHER TERMS** ______________________________

35. **ENTIRE AGREEMENT** This Contract will be binding upon the parties, and each of their respective heirs, executors, administrators, successors and permitted assigns. The provisions not satisfied at Settlement will survive the delivery of the deed and will not be merged therein. This Contract, unless amended in writing, contains the final and entire agreement of the parties and the parties will not be bound by any terms, conditions, oral statements, warranties or representations not herein contained. The interpretation of this Contract will be governed by the laws of the jurisdiction where the Property is located.

SELLER:

_____/ ______________________ (SEAL)
Date Signature

_____/ ______________________ (SEAL)
Date Signature

PURCHASER:

_____/ ______________________ (SEAL)
Date Signature

_____/ ______________________ (SEAL)
Date Signature

Date of Ratification see paragraph #29 (DEFINITIONS) ______________

****

For information purposes only:

Listing Company's Name and Address:

____

____

Office # ______________ FAX # ______________

MRIS Broker Code and Office ID______________

Agent Name ______________________________

____
Real Estate License Number & Jurisdiction

Agent MRIS ID# ______________________________

Selling Company's Name and Address:

____

____

Office # ______________ FAX # ______________

MRIS Broker Code and Office ID______________

Agent Name ______________________________

____
Real Estate License Number & Jurisdiction

Agent MRIS ID# ______________________________

Please Initial: Seller _____/_____ Purchaser _____/_____

FIGURE E.1 (CONTINUED)

Regional Sales Contract

Team Leader/Agent ______________________________ Team Leader/Agent ______________________________

Agent Email Address ______________________________ Agent Email Address ______________________________

Please Initial: Seller _______/______Purchaser ______/______

FIGURE E.2

Virginia Jurisdictional Addendum

VIRGINIA JURISDICTIONAL ADDENDUM

This Addendum is made on ______________________________, to a Sales Contract ("Contract") dated ______________________________ between ______________________________("Purchaser") and ______________________________ ("Seller") for the purchase and sale of the Property: ______________________________
______________________________.

1. DELIVERY. Delivery ("Delivery", "delivery", or "delivered") methods may include hand-carried, sent by professional courier service, by United States mail, or by facsimile or email transmission. The parties agree that Delivery will be deemed to have occurred: on the day delivered by hand, on the day delivered by a professional courier service (including overnight delivery service), or by United States mail, return receipt requested, or on the day sent by facsimile or email transmission either of which produces a tangible record of the transmission.

Deliveries will be sent to the following:
1) Addressed to the Seller at: ______________________________ **OR**
☐ [check if applies] transmitted by facsimile to the Seller at (____) ______________ **OR**
☐ [check if applies] transmitted by email to the Seller at______________________________.
2) Addressed to the Purchaser at: ______________________________ **OR**
☐ [check if applies] transmitted by facsimile to the Purchaser at (____) ______________ **OR**
☐ [check if applies] transmitted by email to the Purchaser at______________________________.

Copies of any addenda, amendments, and Notices required by the Contract will also be provided as a courtesy to the Brokers at the following fax/mailing address/email address:

Listing Company: ______________________________
____

Selling Company: ______________________________
____

The parties agree that any documents sent to the Broker will NOT constitute Delivery.

The requirements for delivery of property or condominium owner's association documents are specified in the Virginia Property Owners' Association Act and/or Virginia Condominium Act paragraphs of this addendum.

No party to this Contract will refuse Delivery in order to delay or extend any deadline established in the contract.

2. NOTICES. Notice ("Notice", "notice", or "notify") means a unilateral communication from one party to another. All Notices required under this Contract will be in writing and will be effective as of Delivery. For the purposes of computing time periods, the first Day will be the Day following Delivery and the time period will end at 9 p.m. on the Day specified. Written acknowledgement of receipt of notice is a courtesy but is not a requirement.

FIGURE E.2 (CONTINUED)

Virginia Jurisdictional Addendum

3. FHA/VA Financing. If FHA or VA Financing is selected in paragraph 3 A of the Regional Sales Contract as the Specified Financing, then the FHA/VA Financing Addendum must be attached.

4. APPRAISAL CONTINGENCY FOR CONVENTIONAL FINANCING (ONLY). If Option 1 is selected and initialed in Paragraph 10 B in the Regional Sales Contract, this Contract IS CONTINGENT upon an Appraisal pursuant to this paragraph. Purchaser shall have until 9:00 p.m. __________Days (minimum of 14 days recommended) following the Date of Ratification to obtain an Appraisal ("Appraisal Deadline"). **Purchaser shall provide Notice to Seller by the Appraisal Deadline, as follows:**

A: The Appraisal is equal to or greater than the Sales Price. This contingency has been satisfied and removed. The parties shall proceed to Settlement;

OR

B: The Appraisal is equal to or greater than the Sales Price. However, the Purchaser elects not to proceed with consummation of this Contract because the subject Property does not satisfy the lender requirements, the Property appraisal does not allow for the specified financing or the Property is inadequate collateral. Such Notice must be accompanied by a written denial of the financing showing written evidence of the lender's decision concerning the Property. The Purchaser must provide such written evidence concurrently with the Purchaser's Notice of election not to proceed.

OR

C: The Appraisal is not equal to or greater than the Sales Price and the Purchaser elects not to proceed with consummation of this Contract, unless the Seller elects to lower the Sales Price to the appraised value. It will be the Seller's option to lower the Sales Price to the appraised value and the parties shall proceed to Settlement at the lower Sales Price. If the Seller does not make this election, the parties may agree to mutually acceptable terms. Each election must be made by Notice within 3 Days after Notice from the other party. The parties will immediately sign any appropriate amendments. If the parties fail to agree, this Contract will become void.

D: The Purchaser elects to proceed with consummation of this Contract without regard to the Appraisal. The parties shall proceed to Settlement;

If Purchaser fails to give Seller Notice by the Appraisal Deadline, this contingency will continue, unless Seller at Seller's option gives Notice to Purchaser that this Contract will become void. If the Seller delivers such Notice, this Contract will become void at 9 p.m. on the third day following Delivery of the Seller's Notice, unless prior to such date and time the Purchaser delivers the required Notice.

5. VIRGINIA RESIDENTIAL PROPERTY DISCLOSURE ACT. The Virginia Residential Property Disclosure Act requires the Seller to deliver a disclosure statement prior to the acceptance of this Contract unless the transfer of the Property is exempt. The law requires the Seller, on a disclosure statement provided by the Real Estate Board, to state that Seller makes no representations or warranties concerning the physical condition of the Property and to sell the Property "as is", except as otherwise provided in this Contract. The law further requires the Seller to make certain statutory disclosures concerning the Property. If the disclosure required by law is delivered to the Purchaser after the acceptance of this Contract, the Purchaser may terminate this Contract by giving written notice to the Seller either by hand delivery or by United States mail, postage prepaid, at or prior to the earliest of (1) 3 Days after delivery of the disclosure in person, (2) 5 Days after the postmark if the disclosure is properly mailed, (3) Settlement on the Property, (4) occupancy of the Property by the Purchaser, (5) written waiver by the Purchaser in a separate document, or (6) the Purchaser's application for a mortgage loan where such application contains

FIGURE E.2 (CONTINUED)

Virginia Jurisdictional Addendum

a disclosure that the right to terminate ends upon applying for the mortgage loan.

6. TARGET LEAD-BASED PAINT HOUSING. The Seller represents that any residential dwellings at the Property ❐ were **OR** ❐ were not constructed before 1978. If the dwellings were constructed before 1978, then, unless exempt under 42 U.S.C. 4852d, the property is considered "target housing" under the statute and a copy of the "Sale: Disclosure and Acknowledgment of Information on Lead-Based Paint and/or Lead-Based Paint Hazards" has been attached and made a part of the Contract as required by law. The Purchaser ❐ Yes **OR** ❐ No waives the right to a risk assessment or inspection of the Property for the presence of lead-based paint and/or lead-based paint hazards. If No, a copy of the "Sales Contract Addendum for Lead-Based Paint Testing" is attached to establish the conditions for a lead-based paint risk assessment or inspections.

7. PRIVATE WELL AND/OR PRIVATE SEWAGE SYSTEM.

A. Well. If the Property is on private well, the ❐ Purchaser, at Purchaser's expense **OR** ❐ Seller, at Seller's expense, will furnish the Purchaser on or before Settlement with a certified test results dated not more than 120 days prior to Settlement from the appropriate local government authority and/or a private company licensed to perform such tests.

B. Sewage. If the Property is on private Septic or private Alternate Septic Sewage Disposal System as indicated in Contract paragraph 8 (Utilities) then the Purchaser, at the Purchaser's expense **OR** Seller, at Seller's expense, will furnish the Purchaser on or before Settlement with certified test results dated not more than 120 days prior to Settlement from the appropriate local government authority and/or private company licensed to perform such inspections. An Alternative system may require regular maintenance in order to prevent failure. Seller ❐ does **OR** ❐ does not have a maintenance contract. If the Seller does have a maintenance contract Seller will provide a copy to the Purchaser, and that maintenance contract ❐ shall **OR** ❐ shall not convey.

C. Remediation. If either system is found defective or substandard according to the current governmental standards, the Seller will take appropriate remedial action at the Seller's expense. Nothing in this paragraph relieves the Seller of the obligations under the Title paragraph of the Contract.

8. VIRGINIA PROPERTY OWNERS' ASSOCIATION ACT. The Seller represents that the Property ❐ is, **OR** ❐ is not located within a development that is subject to the Virginia Property Owner's Association Act ("POA Act"). The POA Act requires the Seller of a property within such a development to obtain an Association Disclosure Packet from the property owners' association and provide it to the Purchaser. The information in the Association Disclosure Packet shall be current as of a date-specified on the Association Disclosure Packet. For delivery of the Packet or the Notice of non-availability of the Packet, the Purchaser chooses this address: ____
____.

The Purchaser may cancel the contract (a) within 3 days of the Date of Ratification if the Purchaser receives the Association Disclosure Packet on or before the Date of Ratification, (b) within 3 days after receiving the Association Disclosure Packet by hand delivery, (c) within 3 days after receiving the Association Disclosure Packet electronically with a receipt to sender, or (d) within 6 days after the postmark date if the Association Disclosure Packet is mailed to the Purchaser.

If the Association Disclosure Packet is not available, the Purchaser may cancel the contract (a) within 3 days of the Date of Ratification if the Purchaser receives notification that the Association Disclosure Packet will not be available on or before the Date of Ratification, (b) within 3 days after receiving notification that the Association Disclosure Packet will not be available by hand-delivery or electronic means, or (c) within 6 days after the postmark date of the mailed notification.

FIGURE E.2 (CONTINUED)

Virginia Jurisdictional Addendum

The Purchaser may also cancel this Contract at any time prior to Settlement if the Purchaser has not been notified that the Association Disclosure Packet will not be available and the Association Disclosure Packet is not delivered to the Purchaser.

Written Notice of cancellation may be (i) hand delivered; (ii) sent by United States mail, postage prepaid, provided that the Purchaser retains sufficient proof of mailing, which may be either a United States postal certificate of mailing or a certificate of service confirming that such mailing was prepared by the Purchaser; (iii) sent by electronic means to the facsimile number or electronic mailing address provided by the Seller in the "Delivery paragraph of this Addendum, provided that the Purchaser retains sufficient proof of the electronic delivery, which may be an electronic receipt of delivery, a confirmation that the notice was sent by facsimile, or a certificate of service confirming that such electronic delivery was prepared by the Purchaser, or (iv) by overnight delivery using a commercial service or the United States Postal Service.

Purchaser's failure to send Notice of cancellation within the allotted time frames shall extinguish Purchaser's rights to cancel the contract under the Virginia Property Owners' Association Act. Such cancellation shall be without penalty; this Contract shall become void, both parties shall promptly execute a release and the Deposit shall be refunded in full to the Purchaser.

The Purchaser, at the Purchaser's expense, shall have the right to request that the association provide an update of the Association Disclosure Packet previously furnished, along with the assurance that there have been no material change, or if there have been material changes, a statement specifying such changes.

The right to receive the Association Disclosure Packet and to cancel this Contract terminates at Settlement.

9. VIRGINIA CONDOMINIUM ACT. The Seller represents that the Property ☐ is, **OR** ☐ is not a condominium unit. If the Property is a condominium unit, this Contract is subject to the Virginia Condominium Act which requires the Seller to obtain from the condominium unit owners' association ("Unit Owners' Association") certain financial and other disclosures ("Resale Certificate") and provide it to the Purchaser. If the required disclosures are not available on the Date of Ratification, the Seller shall promptly request them from the Unit Owners' Association and provide them to the Purchaser who shall acknowledge receipt in writing upon Delivery. The information contained in the Resale Certificate shall be current as of a date specified on the Resale Certificate. For delivery of the Certificate, the Purchaser chooses this address: ____

____.

The Purchaser may cancel this Contract: (a) within 3 Days after the Contract Date, if the Purchaser receives the Resale Certificate on or before the date that the Purchaser signs the contract; (b) within 3 Days after receiving the Resale Certificate if the Resale Certificate is delivered by hand or electronically with a receipt to sender; or (c) within 6 Days after the postmark date if the Resale Certificate is sent to the Purchaser by United States mail, return receipt requested

After receiving the Resale Certificate from the Seller, the Purchaser, at the Purchaser's expense, may submit a copy of the Contract to the Unit Owners' Association along with a request for assurance from the Association that the information submitted in the Resale Certificate remains materially unchanged, or if there have been material changes, a statement specifying such changes. The Purchaser may cancel the Contract within three days of (a) receipt of a statement that there have been one or more material changes to the Resale Certificate, or (b) the date upon which the Unit Owners' Association was required to have furnished such statement, but only if the Unit Owners' Association failed to provide the required statement within the time permitted by law.

FIGURE E.2 (CONTINUED)

Virginia Jurisdictional Addendum

Written Notice of cancellation may be (i) hand delivered; (ii) sent by United States mail, postage prepaid, provided that the Purchaser retains sufficient proof of mailing, which may be either a United States postal certificate of mailing or a certificate of service confirming that such mailing was prepared by the Purchaser; (iii) sent by electronic means to the facsimile number or electronic mailing address provided by the Seller in the "Delivery paragraph of this Addendum, provided that the Purchaser retains sufficient proof of the electronic delivery, which may be an electronic receipt of delivery, a confirmation that the notice was sent by facsimile, or a certificate of service confirming that such electronic delivery was prepared by the Purchaser, or (iv) by overnight delivery using a commercial service or the United States Postal Service. Purchaser's failure to send Notice of cancellation within the allotted time frames shall extinguish Purchaser's rights to cancel the contract under the Virginia Condominium Owners' Association Act. Such cancellation shall be without penalty; this Contract shall become void, both parties shall promptly execute a release and the Deposit shall be refunded in full to the Purchaser.

The right to receive the Resale Certificate and to cancel this Contract terminates at Settlement.

10. NOTICE TO PURCHASER REGARDING THE CONSUMER REAL ESTATE SETTLEMENT PROTECTION ACT.
Choice of Settlement Agent: You have the right to select a Settlement agent to handle the closing of this transaction. The Settlement agent's role in closing your transaction involves the coordination of numerous administrative and clerical functions relating to the collection of documents and the collection and disbursement of funds required to carry out the terms of the contract between the parties. If part of the purchase price is financed, your lender will instruct the Settlement agent as to the signing and recording of loan documents and the disbursement of loan proceeds. No Settlement agent can provide legal advice to any party to the transaction except a Settlement agent who is engaged in the private practice of law in Virginia and who has been retained or engaged by a party to the transaction for the purpose of providing legal services to that party.

Escrow, closing and Settlement service guidelines: The Virginia State Bar issues guidelines to help Settlement agents avoid and prevent the unauthorized practice of law in connection with furnishing escrow, Settlement or closing services. As a party to a real estate transaction, you are entitled to receive a copy of these guidelines from your Settlement agent, upon request, in accordance with the provisions of the Consumer Real Estate Settlement Protection Act.

The Purchaser wishes to employ ____
("Settlement Agent") to represent the Contract. The Purchaser agrees to contact the Settlement Agent within 10 Days of the Date of Contract Ratification to schedule Settlement, which Settlement Agent shall order the title exam and survey if required.

11. NOTICE OF POSSIBLE FILING OF MECHANICS' LIEN.
Virginia law (Section 43-1 et seq.) permits persons who have performed labor or furnished materials for the construction, removal, repair or improvement of any building or structure to file a lien against the property. This lien may be filed at any time after the work is commenced or the material is furnished, but not later than the earlier of (i) 90 Days from the last day of the month in which the lien or last performed work or furnished materials or (ii) 90 Days from the time the construction, removal, repair or improvement is terminated. AN EFFECTIVE LIEN FOR WORK PERFORMED PRIOR TO THE DATE OF SETTLEMENT MAY BE FILED AFTER SETTLEMENT. LEGAL COUNSEL SHOULD BE CONSULTED.

12. ADDITIONAL FEES. Grantors tax shall be paid by the Seller. The Purchaser shall pay recording charges for the Deed and any purchase money trusts.

FIGURE E.2 (CONTINUED)

Virginia Jurisdictional Addendum

13. ARBITRATION. Nothing in this Contract shall preclude arbitration under the Code of Ethics and Standards of Practice of the National Association of REALTORS®.

14. TIME IS OF THE ESSENCE AS TO ALL TERMS OF THIS CONTRACT.

PURCHASER:	**SELLER:**
______/ ________________________(SEAL) Date Signature	______/ ________________________(SEAL) Date Signature
______/ ________________________(SEAL) Date Signature	______/ ________________________(SEAL) Date Signature

FIGURE E.3

NVAR Contingencies/Clauses Addendum to Sales Contract

NVAR CONTINGENCIES/CLAUSES ADDENDUM TO SALES CONTRACT

This Addendum is made on ____________, to a Sales Contract ("Contract") dated ______________, _________ between ____("Purchaser") and ____ ("Seller") for the purchase and sale of the Property: ____.

The following provisions if initialed by the parties are incorporated into and made a part of this Contract:

1. **CONTINGENCIES.**

A. SALE OF THE PURCHASER'S PROPERTY AND KICK-OUT. This Contract is contingent until 9 p.m. _________ Days after the Date of Ratification ("Deadline") upon the sale of the Purchaser's property located at ____("Purchaser's Property"). If the Purchaser does not satisfy, amend or remove this contingency by the Deadline pursuant to sub-paragraph (iii) below, this Contract will become void.

(i) The Seller may continue to offer the Property for sale and accept bona fide back-up offers to this Contract until this contingency is satisfied or removed. If a back-up offer is accepted, the Seller will Deliver Notice to the Purchaser requiring that this contingency be removed or satisfied pursuant to subparagraph (iii) below not later than 9 p.m. _________ days after the Delivery of the Notice or this Contract will become void. If the Purchaser fails to satisfy or remove the contingency by the Deadline this Contract will become void.

(ii) The Purchaser's Property will be listed exclusively and actively marketed by a licensed real estate broker and entered into a multiple listing service within ______ Days after the Date of Ratification at a price not to exceed $ ______________.

(iii) The Purchaser may:

(a) Satisfy this contingency by Delivering to the Seller a copy of the ratified contract for the sale of the Purchaser's Property with evidence that all contingencies, other than financing and appraisal, have been removed or waived by the contingency Deadline.

-OR-

(b) Remove this contingency by Delivering to the Seller (1) Form #100 along with a letter from the lender stating that the financing is not contingent in any manner upon the sale and settlement of any real estate or obtaining a lease of any real estate and that the Purchaser has sufficient funds available for the down payment and closing costs necessary to complete Settlement; OR (2) Evidence of sufficient funds available to complete Settlement without obtaining financing.

(iv) If the Purchaser satisfies the requirements of subparagraph (iii) (a) above, this Contract will remain contingent upon the settlement of the sale of the Purchaser's Property. This paragraph will survive the satisfaction of the contingency for the sale of the Purchaser's Property. Settlement (under this Contract) may not be delayed more than __________ Days after the Settlement Date (specified in this Contract) without the parties' written consent. If a further delay is required to obtain coinciding settlements and the parties do not agree, then this Contract will become void. If at any time after the Date of Ratification the contract for the sale of the Purchaser's Property becomes void, the Purchaser will immediately Deliver Notice to the Seller together with evidence of such voiding, at which time either the Seller or the Purchaser may declare this Contract void by Delivering Notice to the other party.

B. SETTLEMENT OF PURCHASER'S PROPERTY. Settlement of this Contract is contingent upon the settlement of the contract for the sale of the Purchaser's property located at ____ ("Purchaser's Property"). Settlement (under this Contract) may not be delayed more than ______ Days after the Settlement Date (specified in this Contract) without the parties' written consent. Seller ❒ will or ❒ will not accept an assignment of funds. If a further delay is required to obtain coinciding settlements and the parties do not agree, then this Contract will become void. If at any time after the Date of Ratification the contract for the sale of the Purchaser's Property becomes void, the Purchaser will immediately Deliver Notice to the Seller together with evidence of such voiding, at which time either the Seller or the Purchaser may declare this Contract void by Delivering Notice to the other party.

C. CONTINGENT ON THE SELLER PURCHASING ANOTHER HOME. This Contract is contingent until 9 p.m. __________ Days after the Date of Ratification to allow the Seller to obtain a ratified contract to purchase another home. This contingency will terminate at the Deadline and this Contract will remain in full force and effect unless the Seller delivers Notice, prior to the Deadline, to the Purchaser that this Contract is void.

NVAR Form K1344 Page 1 of 3 01/08

FIGURE E.3 (CONTINUED)

NVAR Contingencies/Clauses Addendum to Sales Contract

D. GENERAL. This Contract is contingent until 9 p.m. ____________ Days after the Date of Ratification ("Deadline") upon:
____
____
____
____
____
____

2. **CLAUSES.**

A. BACK-UP CONTRACT. This Contract is first back-up to another contract dated ______________ between the Seller and ____ as the Purchaser. This Contract becomes the primary Contract immediately upon Notice from the Seller that the other contract is void. All Deadlines contained in this Contract shall be measured from ❒ the Date of Ratification **OR** ❒ the date this Contract becomes primary. Additionally, the date of Settlement will be ________ Days after the date this Contract becomes primary. The Purchaser may void this back-up Contract at any time by Delivering Notice to the Seller prior to Delivery of Notice from the Seller that this Contract has become the primary Contract. If the other contract settles, this Contract will become void. The rights and obligations of the parties under the primary contract are superior to the rights and obligations of the parties to this back-up Contract.

B. "AS IS" PROPERTY CONDITION. The Property is sold in its "As Is" physical condition, to be determined as of the ❒ Contract Date, ❒ date of the home inspection ❒ Settlement Date **OR** other ❒ ______________________. The Seller makes no representation or warranty, express or implied, as to the condition of the Property or any equipment or system contained therein. The Seller will have no obligation to make repairs to the electrical, plumbing, heating, air conditioning, or any other mechanical system, equipment or fixture. Smoke detectors will be installed and functioning as required by the laws or regulations of the appropriate jurisdiction.

The Property ❒ shall or ❒ shall not be delivered free and clear of trash and debris and broom clean.

The following clauses in this Contract are also hereby deleted (check all that apply):
❒ All clauses pertaining to termites and wood-destroying insects
❒ All clauses pertaining to Private Well and/or Private Sewage Systems
❒ All clauses pertaining to compliance with city, state or county regulations
❒ All clauses pertaining to compliance with Property Owner's or Condominium Owner's Associations

C. REAL ESTATE LICENSED PARTIES. The parties acknowledge that ______________________ is an ❒ active or ❒ inactive licensed real estate agent in ❒ DC ❒ MD ❒ VA ❒ WV ❒ Other and is either the ❒ Buyer ❒ Seller or ❒ is related to one of the parties in this transaction.

D. POST-SETTLEMENT OCCUPANCY OPTION. Purchaser will allow the Seller to occupy the Property for up to ________Days after Settlement. Seller must provide to the Purchaser a completed Post-Settlement Occupancy Agreement with dates and terms _______ Days before the Settlement Date or this option expires.

The Seller shall be responsible for:
❒ the carrying costs of Purchaser (defined as Principal, Interest, Taxes and any Mortgage Insurance of the Specified Financing and the Hazard Insurance, HOA or Condo fees, if applicable, pro-rated accordingly) as calculated by the Settlement Agent at Settlement; **OR**
❒ $__________________ per day.
❒ a flat fee in the amount of $______________.

The Security Deposit of $______________ will be held by ______________________.

E. UNREPRESENTED SELLER OR BUILDER AND PURCHASER'S BROKER. Upon Seller's irrevocable instruction, it is understood and agreed by all Parties that ______________________ (Selling Agent's name) of ______________________ (Selling Agent's firm) is acting as an agent solely representing the Purchaser in this transaction ("Purchaser's Broker"). The Seller agrees to pay the Purchaser's Broker a payment of ❒ $__________________ in cash or ❒ ________ % of the total sales price. The Settlement Agent is hereby irrevocably directed to deduct Purchaser's Broker fee from the Seller's proceeds of the sale at Settlement. The Parties acknowledge that the Purchaser's Broker relationship was disclosed to the Seller and/or Seller's agent prior to showing the Property to the Purchaser.

FIGURE E.3 (CONTINUED)

NVAR Contingencies/Clauses Addendum to Sales Contract

F. 1031 EXCHANGE (BUYER). This Property is being acquired to complete an IRC Section 1031 tax-deferred exchange pursuant to an exchange agreement. This Settlement will be coordinated with ____________________________________ ____________________________________, Intermediary, who shall instruct Seller as to the manner Property shall be conveyed to Purchaser. There shall be no additional expense to Seller as a result of the exchange and Seller shall cooperate with Purchaser and Intermediary in the completion of the exchange.

G. 1031 EXCHANGE (SELLER). Seller and Purchaser agree to transfer the Property by utilizing an IRC Section 1031 tax-deferred exchange. Purchaser agrees to cooperate with Seller, at no expense or liability to Purchaser, in the completion of the exchange, including execution of all necessary documents, the intention of the parties being that the Seller utilizes Section 1031 to defer taxes by acquiring like-kind real estate through an exchange agreement established at Settlement. The parties will execute all necessary documents as determined by Intermediary at Settlement, which documents are prepared at Seller's expense.

Copies of any addenda, amendments, and Notices required by the Contract will be provided to the Brokers at the Brokers' addresses provided in the Contract. The parties agree that any such copies sent to the Broker will NOT constitute Delivery and will be for informational purposes only.

Except as modified by this Addendum, all of the terms and provisions of this Contract are hereby expressly ratified and confirmed and will remain in full force and effect.

SELLER:	**PURCHASER:**
____/________________	____/________________
Date Signature	Date Signature
____/________________	____/________________
Date Signature	Date Signature

Index

M

N

O

P

R